Olive Thomas

ALSO BY MICHELLE VOGEL
AND FROM McFARLAND

*Marjorie Main: The Life and Films of
Hollywood's "Ma Kettle"* (2006)

*Children of Hollywood: Accounts of Growing Up
as the Sons and Daughters of Stars* (2005)

Gene Tierney: A Biography (2005)

OLIVE THOMAS

The Life and Death of a Silent Film Beauty

Michelle Vogel

McFarland & Company, Inc., Publishers
Jefferson, North Carolina, and London

LIBRARY OF CONGRESS CATALOGUING-IN-PUBLICATION DATA

Vogel, Michelle, 1972–
Olive Thomas : the life and death of a silent
film beauty / Michelle Vogel.
p.   cm.
Includes bibliographical references and index.

ISBN-13: 978-0-7864-2908-0
softcover : 50# alkaline paper ∞

1. Thomas, Olive, 1898 [*sic*; 1894]–1920.
2. Thomas, Olive, 1898 [*sic*; 1894]–1920—Death and burial.
3. Motion picture actors and actresses—United States—Biography.
I. Title.
PN2287.T39V64   2007
791.4302'8092—dc22   [B]   2007001155

British Library cataloguing data are available

©2007 Michelle Vogel. All rights reserved

*No part of this book may be reproduced or transmitted in any form
or by any means, electronic or mechanical, including photocopying
or recording, or by any information storage and retrieval system,
without permission in writing from the publisher.*

On the cover: "Everybody's Sweetheart" Olive Thomas

Manufactured in the United States of America

*McFarland & Company, Inc., Publishers
Box 611, Jefferson, North Carolina 28640
www.mcfarlandpub.com*

Acknowledgments

In no particular order of importance, I'd like to thank the following individuals and foundations for their contributions and expert opinions:

Robert Simonson, Susan Olsen, Keith Lawrence, Hugh Munro, Ben Model, Robert Arkus, Patricia Duffy Erhardt, the late Rick Hasley, Jonathan Pettit, Laurie Jacobson, Robert Viagas, Brenda Tenny, Daniel Selznick, Sarah Baker, Andi Hicks, William M. Drew, Eve Golden, Greta de Groat, Leslie DeLassus at the Harry Ransom Humanities Research Center, Olive E. Thomas, Liz Nocera, E.J. Fleming, Charlie Abad, Helen Demeestere, Kathy Anderson, Neil Maciejewski, Terry Harbin, The Mary Pickford Foundation, Woodlawn Cemetery, Timeline Films, Getty Images and the loyal members of "The New Coven of Olive Thomas" Yahoo group.

My husband, Matt, for introducing me to the wonderful world of silent cinema. Our adorable son, Ryan, who unknowingly helped me write this book for the nine months that he took to grow inside me. My stepsons, Josh and Reeve, for asking what dead person I'm writing about now and looking interested when I replied. My parents and late mother-in-law for their constant love and support.

And, a very special thank you to Joe Yranski and Suzanne Dwyer. Your generosity and willingness to share your invaluable collections of Olive Thomas memorabilia made this book possible.

Contents

Acknowledgments v
Introduction 1
Prologue 5

1—Rags to Riches	13
2—Follies and Frolics and Film... Oh My!	24
3—Jack and Ollie	35
4—Selznick Pictures	48
5—Paris	75
6—The Investigation	91
7—What Jack Told Mary...	115
8—A Broken Man and His Women	120
9—Memories of a Lost Love	128
10—Ghostly Encounters	132

Epilogue 139
Stage and Film Appearances 145
Bibliography 195
Index 199

Introduction

Olive Thomas, affectionately known as "Ollie," was the first of the Hollywood scandals that sent the movie industry reeling in the early 1920s. Just one month shy of her 26th birthday, Olive died an agonizing death after ingesting mercury bichloride in a Paris hotel room during a second honeymoon with her film star husband, Jack Pickford.

The months of speculation surrounding her sudden and shocking death created a media circus the world over:

> OLIVE THOMAS, MOTION PICTURE ACTRESS—DEAD!

Newspapers and fan magazines splashed that shocking headline across their front pages and for months following her death they ran in-depth articles with theories and opinions on why the tragedy happened. Paris was instantly blamed for its carefree, drug- and alcohol-laden nightlife and her troubled husband Jack was blamed for a number of reasons, all of which will be examined later.

There were (and still are) a lot of unanswered questions surrounding the death of Olive Thomas. But, rest assured, every conceivable piece of information and/or evidence is presented within these pages. With that said, some eighty-six years after her passing, the ultimate question still remains unanswered: Was it suicide, accident or ... murder?

Olive Thomas had come a long way since leaving Charleroi, the small Pennsylvania coal-mining town she loathed. After a hasty marriage at sixteen (and eventual divorce) Olive ventured to New York City where she eventually realized her dream of appearing on Broadway as one of Ziegfeld's famous Follies girls. Her ethereal beauty caught Hollywood's eye and she became one of filmdom's most popular stars (in the prime of her acting career she was earning $200,000 a year—approximately 2.5 million today). She married into Hollywood royalty, snaring Jack Pickford, to the dismay of his family.

Her long brown curls and flashing smile, combined with delicate features reminiscent of a porcelain doll, made Olive the perfect muse for a number of artists' portraits. The most famous, "Memories of Olive," was a tribute painted by Alberto Vargas and some say commissioned by Florenz Ziegfeld, Jr., in honor of his most prized Ziegfeld lovely. Vargas denied this claim.

Shortly before the death of Vargas (1896–1982), *Playboy* magazine published a book with comments on some of the models he immortalized on canvas. Vargas had this to say about Olive:

> She was one of the most beautiful brunettes that Ziegfeld ever glorified. Luckily, as was my habit, I made ["Memories of Olive"] for my own collection after doing two or three others of her for the master. I say "luckily" I made this portrait because there was to be no opportunity to do so ever again, for me or any other artist. She journeyed to Paris with her husband, and tragically, died there a short time later.

"Memories of Olive" depicts her nude from the waist up. Her left hand clasps her bare breast, her right hand holds a flame-red rose. Her head is tilted back in order to capture the full fragrance of the flower and her scarlet lips are slightly parted. It is a timeless image depicting feminine perfection. Olive posed for the portrait three days prior to her voyage for Paris. She never saw the finished work.

It is difficult to accept the fact that this image of flawlessness, so full of life, was now lifeless and gone forever. The San Francisco Art Exchange sold the original "Memories of Olive" painting (measuring 18" × 24") for $250,000. Limited edition prints of the erotic pose are highly sought after by collectors to this day.

Whether it was commissioned by him or not, Ziegfeld proudly hung "Memories of Olive" in his office at the New Amsterdam Theatre in New York City; his wife, actress Billie Burke, despised the portrait because it was a constant reminder of the heartbreaking affair between her philandering husband and the Ziegfeld beauty.

Still, Billie admitted in her autobiography (*With a Feather on My Nose*, 1948) that she knew what she was getting herself into on the very first night she met Flo Ziegfeld, saying, "I felt the impact of his threat and charm at once. But even if I had known then precisely what tortures and frustrations were in store for me during the next eighteen years because of this man, I should have kept right on falling in love."

The only positive that can be taken from Olive's passing is that she obtained eternal fame as the light that was snuffed out way too early. She is mostly remembered today because of her death but it is important to remember her life too. Ironically, her life carries just as many mysteries as her death. That's what makes her story so intriguing.

A portrait of Billie Burke and her furry friend, circa 1917.

Introduction

Even after sifting through piles of newspaper reports, medical records and library special collections, and after speaking with countless experts (both in the U.S. and France) relating to the case, there's plenty of conjecture but still no conclusive answer on whether Olive's death was accidental (as it was eventually ruled), suicide ... or murder.

There are an equal number of conflicting reports and contradictions and all of them are noted within this book. It's impossible and ignorant to rule out "most" of the theories surrounding Olive's story. Some theories are unlikely while others are entirely probable. You will get a sense of my opinion and you will read the opinions of others but the final conclusion will be yours, based on what you read here.

Olive's life (and death) is akin to Marilyn Monroe's tragic story. The mystery, the unanswered questions, the continuing speculation piques an interest, morbid or otherwise, that would not be there had the case been all black and white.

"Memories of Olive" by Alberto Vargas was so titled because Olive did not live to see the finished work.

Almost a century after her death and with all the hearsay and uncertainty about what actually happened before, on and after that fateful night (September 5, 1920) in a Paris hotel room, one fact remains indisputable: Olive Thomas' death at the tender age of twenty-five has ensured that she eternally remain "The Most Beautiful Girl in the World."

PROLOGUE

Hollywood—the motion picture capital; a community of dissolute actors and actresses and others of the movie industry; the worst of them unspeakably vile, the best suspicionable; a colony of unregenerates and narcotic addicts; given to wild night parties commonly known as "orgies"; heroes of the screen by day and vicious roisterers by night; a section of civilization gone rottenly to smash.

That was the way the *New York Herald* (March 19–April 2, 1922) described the state of the movie capital in the early twenties. Hollywood in its heyday is repeatedly referred to as being the "Golden Years." The term implies the best of the best, a magical time that we're never likely to see again. In reference to the number of films made, the amount of money generated as a result of the manic production schedules and the countless nobodies who became somebodies overnight ... yes, it really was a groundbreaking time. But, there's a tarnished, dark side to those "Golden Years."

Time may have now tempered the impact of the earliest Hollywood scandals but back when they occurred some of the biggest names in the business would become both accused criminals and innocent victims. Hollywood quickly became known as "sin city."

Suicide, rape and murder were not the sinister plots of pre–Code Hollywood films; they were real-life situations surrounding many of the biggest names in the industry. The roaring 20s, Hollywood's infancy, was a time when movies were made in a few short days and young hopefuls wanting to get into the business would simply walk through the studio gates and ask to star in a moving picture. The ongoing scandals and the stigma of being in the movies did little to discourage the thousands of wannabes who flocked to Hollywood in pursuit of their dream. In the decade between 1920 and 1930 alone, Hollywood's population increased by over 120,000.

Back then there really was such a thing as overnight success. Unfortunately, the swiftness of the celebrity lifestyle and the money that went along with it made for a melting pot of bohemians who supported each other's promiscuous boozing, drugging and self-destructive lifestyles. The results were often fatal. A *New York Times* article (February 26, 1922) attempted to explain why:

Hollywood's residents are certainly no worse than would be any similar number of attractive, uneducated young people who had suddenly come into great wealth and a peculiarly heady sort of fame. Most of us, in their situation, would do as they do; since we are not in their situation, but one materially far less prosperous, we make the best of our comparative moral grandeur. Because the temptations of wealth and luxury have never assailed us we fall on those who have succumbed. We may have done as badly with less excuse, but we haven't been caught; and if we were caught, we should never gain the unhappy notoriety of the rich and famous. So what we take out on Hollywood is our resentment, not at its wickedness, but at its wealth.

We go forth joyfully to indulge in the national, perhaps the universally human sport, of kicking a man who is down. On vague, confusing and perhaps wholly unfounded suspicion we are willing to lynch a town and an industry en masse; and, as in most lynching mobs, righteous wrath is perhaps less potent than a sort of envy.

As a result of the numerous scandals that rocked Hollywood in its infancy, the "morality clause" was included in all future film contracts. The studios could now release contractees based on their embarrassing or immoral behavior, thus avoiding bad press. At the time, Hollywood, the studios and the business in general were being blamed for all of society's problems. This February 10, 1922, article from the *Gary–Post Tribune* calls for the government to step in and regain control of the runaway industry:

> Hollywood must be purified by the government, Canon William Sheafe Chase, veteran movie reformer, declared today in an interview. He demanded passage by Congress of a resolution to investigate the film colony and prevent its scandals from debauching the mind of America.
>
> "Actors and actresses of the screen," he charged, "are teaching the public free love, adultery, murder, infidelity and lust. And," he added, "too many of them naturally are practicing what they teach."

Two more victims of Hollywood scandals. *Left:* **Mary Miles Minter.** *Above:* **Comedian Mabel Normand.**

PROLOGUE

A February 9, 1922, article in the *Detroit Free Press* was harsher still, saying:

> There seem to be two ways in which the Hollywood situation may be handled by the producers. One is by cleansing the colony so effectively that the world will believe it is purified. The other is by uprooting it from the face of the earth. On the whole, the latter course seems much the simpler.

Protesting the scandalous actions of certain movie stars, on February 26, 1922, the Motion Picture Theater Owners' Association of America released the following statement:

> There should be some effective way to remove the garbage element from the producing end of the motion picture business. The elimination of the dirty birds who have befouled the high positions into which the theater owners and public boosted them must be accomplished in some way.
>
> The odium of their malodorous conduct falls on the theater owner and this polluting group must no longer be permitted to hang their smeared linen on this exhibitors' line. It must be made plain to the public that the theater owners are not responsible for the conduct of these human filth gushers in the industry, that we utterly repudiate them and demand their removal from every place where their foul presence tends to contaminate our business.
>
> The belief in some quarters that the motion picture business is on the one side festering with crass immorality and on the other distended with bulgy and bulky money bags makes it very essential that theater owners become alive to the situation confronting them. It must be emphasized that theater owners are not responsible for these conditions and that they will keep faith with the public, that no person tainted with scandal shall appear in actor guise or otherwise on our screens.

That face, that smile—Olive looks the picture of happiness here.

Olive Thomas' death was looked upon differently. In the eyes of the public she was a sympathetic figure, a victim of circumstance. But it must be remembered that her death was the first of a succession of scandals that rocked Hollywood. No major movie star had died before her. As time went on, as Hollywood literally unraveled, the public became jaded and ashamed of the sinful lifestyles of the stars. Innocent victim or not, they were far less forgiving of the tragedies that followed.

After Olive's death, audiences flocked to see her innocent face on the screen one last time. Theaters ran her pictures, both old and new, to packed movie houses for weeks after her death. In a morbid attempt to cash in on her death, a *Wid's* theater manual suggested that theater managers decorate their lobbies with paper coffins to promote the re-release of her films. Theatergoers cried at the sight of Olive on the screen. Some theaters even called for police protection to control the out-of-control crowds who were overcome with grief. Many of Olive's films were re-released immediately upon the announcement of her death, before her lifeless body was back in the United States.

It became increasingly apparent that movies not only reflected society, they influenced it as well. So, in a desperate attempt to maintain a moralistic reputation, "Hollywood" (the press agents and screenwriters hired to whitewash the controversies) quickly blamed Paris for Olive's demise. With the naïve thought that her death would be an incident not likely to befall another star, Hollywood's self-preservation plan was certainly understandable. However, when a succession of scandals hit closer to home, there were no more excuses to be made. The film industry was now in serious trouble and Paris had nothing to do with any of it.

Thanks to a consistent stream of harshly written articles about Hollywood and the filth that inhabited it, the media had ensured the public now looked upon *all* actors and actresses as lowly individuals of questionable morals. Even those few stars that remained clear of controversy were unfairly targeted. An April 1, 1922, article in *Movie Weekly* quoted Dorothy Gish as saying, "When I walk down the street nowadays and someone recognizes me, I feel like turning my head so that I won't hear them say: 'Oh, there's another one of *those* picture actresses.'"

To this day, the infamous Arbuckle rape and murder scandal is still wrongly thought to be the beginning of Hollywood's unraveling. But, it was exactly a year to the day *after* Olive's death, on September 10, 1921, that a starlet of questionable morals, Virginia Rappe, died (from a possible botched abortion) after a Labor Day weekend party hosted by lovable comedian Roscoe "Fatty" Arbuckle. He was later charged with manslaughter and it would take three long trials to acquit him of any wrongdoing.

Ironically, Arbuckle was notified of the shocking murder of his friend and director, William Desmond Taylor, as he awaited the verdict in his second trial. Incidentally, it was Taylor who delivered the eulogy at Olive Thomas' funeral.

On February 1, 1922, Taylor was

Starlet Virginia Rappe died after a party thrown by comedian Roscoe "Fatty" Arbuckle. Charged with manslaughter, Arbuckle was eventually acquitted after three long trials. Despite his proven innocence, the scandal essentially ruined him.

found shot to death in his bungalow. The list of suspects consisted of many of Hollywood's A-list stars. Arbuckle's friend and regular co-star, Mabel Normand, was the last person to see him alive. As Mabel got into her car to head home, Taylor confessed, "I have the strangest and most ghastly feeling that something is going to happen to me" (*Movie Weekly*, February 1922). Had he already been threatened? Mabel thought nothing of the comment. She went home, ate dinner, read for a while and went to bed. Early the next day, a friend called to tell her that Taylor had been murdered.

It was later confirmed that Taylor was shot shortly *after* Mabel left his home at 7:45 P.M. Several witnesses testified that Mabel had left Taylor very much alive. Despite the facts, the public refused to be swayed by the truth and Mabel's career soon hit rock bottom. Crushed, not only by the sudden loss of her dear friend but also by the decline of her once booming career because she was his friend, Mabel turned to drugs and alcohol for comfort. The trial of her other friend and co-star Roscoe "Fatty" Arbuckle also took its toll, as did the womanizing ways of her fiancé, director Mack Sennett. Not willing to play second fiddle to the bevy of starlets he chased and often caught, Mabel called off their July 4, 1915, wedding. Despite Sennett's profuse apologies and hearts-and-flowers promises, Mabel refused to take him back. Still in love with Sennett but too heartbroken to attempt a reconciliation, on September 17, 1926, Mabel married a childhood friend, fellow actor, Lew Cody. But it was too little too late. After spending six months in a sanitarium, Mabel Normand died or February 22, 1930, of tuberculosis. She was 37 years of age.

Taylor was the first victim, but not the only one. Ironically, many of the suspects eventually became victims themselves. The discovery of young starlet Mary Miles Minter's nightgown in Taylor's dresser, along with a bundle of love letters penned by her (found stuffed into the toe of one of his shoes), made her a possible but not likely suspect. Her over-protective stage mother, Charlotte Shelby, seemed like the number one suspect. An irate mother out to avenge her daughter's reputation after learning of the affair with a man more than twice her age; now *that* was a motive. She had been openly antagonistic toward the director for months. It was later reported that Shelby owned a pistol and bullets matching the kind that killed Taylor, but as this became known, she reportedly threw the "evidence" into a bayou in Louisiana. Despite her dubious actions making her the prime suspect, her "friendly" association with the Los Angeles district attorney was a safety net that held many advantages.

The laundry list of theories for Taylor's murder include:

Taylor's jealous and bitter first wife returning to kill him.

His current valet killing him to hide evidence of sexual crimes.

A former valet returning to rob him or exact revenge.

A portrait shot of slain director William Desmond Taylor. His murder is still unsolved.

Left: **Charlotte Shelby, the prime suspect in the Taylor murder case, pictured with her famous daughter, Mary Miles Minter, circa 1921.** *Right:* **Olive Thomas, "The Most Beautiful Girl in the World."**

Murder by a disgruntled young man who had offered sexual favors to Taylor only to be rejected.

An associate from the Canadian Army killing him because of a grudge.

Mabel Normand committing a drug-related murder.

Mack Sennett in a crime of passion over the director's perfectly innocent relationship with Mabel.

Mary Miles Minter killing him in a fit of jealousy.

Or, her mother, Charlotte Shelby killing him out of either maternal sentiment or jealousy over her daughter's relationship with Taylor, a man she herself loved.

Whatever the case, Taylor's assassination is unsolved to this day and many a Hollywood career was destroyed by the innuendo and involvement in the director's bloody murder, including Minter's.

Distraught over Taylor's death, Minter locked herself in her room and didn't emerge for a month. By the following year she moved out of her mother's home and voluntarily dropped out of pictures forever. At 22 years of age, she was heartbroken and washed up. She still had six more decades to mourn her lover, eventually dying of heart failure in Santa Monica, California, on August 4, 1984. She was 82 years old.

Throughout the Taylor mystery, Arbuckle's woes continued and his second trial once again resulted in a hung jury. On April 22, 1922, the third Arbuckle jury acquitted the comedian in just six minutes. It was finally over ... or was it?

The jury issued the following statement:

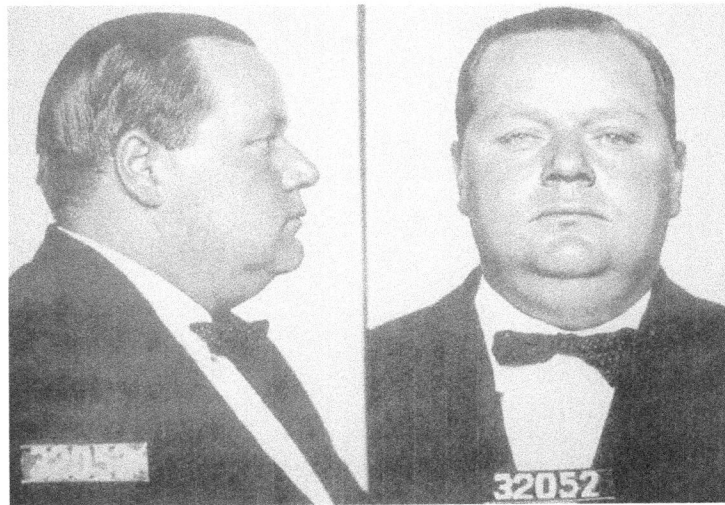

The other victim. Roscoe "Fatty" Arbuckle's official mug shot taken by San Francisco police shortly after his arrest in connection with the death of Virginia Rappe.

> Acquittal is not enough for Roscoe Arbuckle. We feel a grave injustice has been done him. We feel also that it was only our plain duty to give him this exoneration, under the evidence, for there was not the slightest proof adduced to connect him in any way with the commission of a crime. He was manly throughout the case, and told a straightforward story on the witness stand, which we all believed. The happening at the hotel was an unfortunate affair for which Arbuckle, so the evidence shows, was in no way responsible. We wish him success and hope that the American people will take the judgment of fourteen men and women who have sat listening for thirty-one days to the evidence, that Roscoe Arbuckle is entirely innocent and free of all blame.

Arbuckle may have been a free man but his career was finished. He was banned from the screen and theaters everywhere destroyed his movies. People spat on him and cruelly shouted, "I'm coming, Virginia!" when they recognized him on the street. His once booming career and innocent reputation was forever tarnished because of an evil woman by the name of Maude Delmont.

Nicknamed "Madame Black," Delmont would provide girls for parties and set up a prominent producer, director or actor by prompting one of the girls to cry rape. The innocent victim would pay whatever amount Delmont asked in order to prevent the "scandal" from making the papers and subsequently destroying their career. After Rappe died, Delmont plucked Arbuckle's guilt out of thin air and the rest, as they say, is history. It was a malicious lie that destroyed an innocent man's career, and ultimately his life too.

Understandably, the stresses and strains of the scandal and the drawn-out trials took their toll on the rotund comedian. He succumbed to a fatal heart attack in New York City on June 29, 1933. He was 46 years old. Sadly, the night before his death he had signed a long-term contract with Warner Brothers to return to the screen (after an eleven-year absence) in a series of features. His third wife, Addie McPhail, told the media that he died a happy man, with a smile on his face.

To this day, Roscoe "Fatty" Arbuckle is mostly known for "the scandal" rather than for the millions he made laugh at the height of his career. His rightful place as one of history's founding fathers of comedic film has been hampered by a malevolent tale motivated by nothing more than spite and the desire to make a quick buck.

A portrait shot of screen heartthrob Wallace Reid.

One of the first matinee idols, Wallace Reid, can certainly be included in the spate of 1920s Hollywood scandals that followed Olive's death. After all, he needlessly died on January 18, 1923, due to nothing more than studio greed.

While starring in *The Valley of the Giants* (1919), Reid was involved in a train crash and his extensive injuries prevented him from finishing the film. Thinking only of the money they were losing on their current production (Reid had single-handedly made Paramount millions throughout his career), they swiftly sent the studio doctor to Reid with a supply of morphine that would numb his pain so that he could continue to work. He soon became addicted and the studio was more than happy to keep him supplied so long as he continued to make movies and money for them. Short-term the arrangement worked; he was able to make at least another two dozen films for the studio. Long-term the studio's "quick fix" would be the cause of his death.

By 1922, Reid was a full-blown drug addict. He was frequently in and out of sanitariums in order to try and beat his demons, alcohol included. On January 18, 1923, he died in his wife's arms. He was 31 years old.

Yet another early suspect in the Taylor murder was eccentric movie producer/director Mack Sennett. He claimed he spent the night in question at the home of movie producer Thomas Ince; ironically Ince would become the center of yet another major Hollywood scandal just a few years later, in 1924. Incidentally, it was Ince who signed Olive Thomas to Triangle Pictures Corporation. *Follies Girl with Ince* was the blazing headline featured in *Motography*, April 14, 1917. The article reported, "Ince will cast her in roles that will give full play to her sunny and whimsical personality."

After "falling ill" at a party on board a yacht owned by newspaper man William Randolph Hearst, Ince was rushed to the hospital, dying soon after. He was 42 years old. The morning papers (rivals to Hearst's publications) ran the shocking headline, *Movie Producer Shot on Hearst Yacht!* A carefully thought-out counter-headline was generated by the powerful Hearst publicity machine by that evening. As ridiculous as it now sounds, the Hearst headline emphatically stated that Ince died of acute indigestion.

It's been long suspected that the bullet that Ince took (at the hand of Hearst) was meant for Charles Chaplin, who was also a guest at the party and was supposedly having an affair with Hearst's much younger mistress, Marion Davies. It was a case of mistaken identity but Hearst was never implicated. He had enough money and enough power to ensure that all the messy loose ends were very well tied. Crucial evidence that would shed new light on many of Hollywood's biggest scandals was bought with the almighty dollar. Hollywood hush money rewrote history—and Olive's death, the first movie star tragedy, was no exception.

✯ *Chapter 1* ✯

RAGS TO RICHES

It gripped me as it had gripped its other millions.
—Olive Thomas on her first impressions of New York City

Oliveretta Elaine Duffy was born in Charleroi, Pennsylvania, on October 20, 1894. There are various versions of her name on record and her official birth certificate reads Oliva R. Duffy (the R. for her mother, Rena). She was known as Olive for most of her life, "Ollie" to her closest friends and family.

After the untimely work-related death of her father, James Duffy, a structural steel worker, in 1906, Olive and her brothers James (born in 1896) and William (born in 1899) moved to McKees Rocks (a suburb of Pittsburgh) and were taken in by their grandparents while their mother worked long hours in a local factory to make ends meet. Rena's financial burdens eased when she met and married Harry M. Van Kirk, an employee of the Pittsburgh & Lake Erie Railroad. Together, Rena and Harry had a daughter, Harriet, whom Olive adored. She was five years old when Olive died but tragedy would strike a second time (in 1931) when Rena would lose her second daughter in a fatal automobile accident. Harriet was just seventeen years old.

Olive was educated in the public schools of Pittsburgh, leaving at age fifteen to work as a stock girl in Horne's department store. *Motion Picture,* June 1919, reported that she wore short dresses with her hair down her back when she was promoted to salesgirl in ginghams and went around bragging how lucky she was to be "the youngest saleslady at Horne's." It would take just a couple of years for Olive to make the drastic switch from Horne's to Hollywood but she always remembered back to her days as a modest shop girl with fondness. "My ideal of those days," said Olive, "was Miss Milligan, the head of ginghams. She was small and cute and to be like her some day was the top hope of my childhood!"

Despite Olive's apparent talent as a gingham sales girl, the daily grind (and stench) of the smoky Pennsylvania industrial town depressed her. It was a far cry from the bright lights of New York City and the only thing that kept her going was the dream that she would one day get there and be famous. Olive would often stop by the drugstore window on her way to work and compare her reflection to the Ziegfeld girls on the elaborate chocolate boxes on display. She'd sweep up her mane of golden curls, pile them on top of her head, strike a model pose and imagine *her* face on one of those boxes. Olive concluded she was just as pretty, if not prettier, than the Ziegfeld girls in the window and one day it would be her.

Olive wasn't just pretty, she was stunning. In her book, *A Darling of the Twenties* (1989), Madge Bellamy, who later became a star herself, remembered the time when she and her mother saw Olive Thomas, the famous showgirl, emerging from her car. "She wore a black satin dress and a purple picture hat. Mama thought that she was the most beautiful person she had ever seen. As we stared at her, Mama heard her say about me, 'What a lovely girl!' But I missed that."

By 1911, Olive had fallen in love and married Bernard Krug Thomas. For most of their years together he worked as a clerk at a local train car manufacturer. At the time of their marriage it was widely reported that he was working as a timekeeper in a steel mill but he was not employed in this field until much later. Olive was a sixteen-year-old bride but despite her young age it wasn't long before she realized the marriage was a horrible mistake. It was the impetus that Olive needed to flee Pittsburgh for New York City.

Once there she took refuge in a relative's home in Harlem. She wandered the streets of uptown New York looking for work and soon found it behind the basement counter of a department store. She had managed to escape the poverty of Pittsburgh and, although she was still selling gingham, she was now one step closer to her dream of making something of herself. That's what kept her going. Olive's radiant, doll-like beauty improved the chance of that dream coming true. Her spontaneous decision to enter a competition for the title of "The Most Beautiful Girl in New York City" was the beginning of one of the most inspirational show-biz-rags to-riches stories ever lived.

A newspaper bidding for shop girl circulation announced that commercial artist, Howard Chandler Christy, was holding a competition for a perfect model, the supreme New York beauty. There were prizes to be awarded, and the glory of having one's picture published in the paper.

Olive had recovered from the depression of Pittsburgh, and there was a glowing Irish beauty just back of her eyes, ready to bloom. She took a chance, reported sick at the store and in her pathetic best clothes went downtown to the Christy studio to sit

Olive loved animals. Here she is with her Pekinese friend, circa 1916.

Left: **A promotional shot of Olive advertising her appearance in Ziegfeld's Follies revue show.** *Right:* **Olive in costume for Ziegfeld's Midnight Frolic.**

waiting with a throng of ambitious girls. It was a convention of the piquant beauties of the New York shop girl. Every race of the metropolitan melting pot was represented in that array. Olive won. The prize, the picture in the paper, the publicity, everything (*Photoplay*, January 1925).

The competition was held in New York and Olive happily took the winning title of "The Most Beautiful Girl in New York City." Famed artist Harrison Fisher took things one step further, claiming that Olive Thomas was without doubt "The Most Beautiful Girl in the World!"

It was no exaggeration. Fellow artists and photographers agreed and Olive quickly became a sought-after model. At fifty cents an hour (approximately $6 today) she posed for the likes of Penryhn Stanlaws, William Haskell Coffin, and Alberto Vargas.

According to writer Lenore Coffee (*Storyline: Recollections of a Hollywood Screenwriter*, 1973), Olive's modeling career had started when she was much younger, "When Olive was barely fourteen, her two sailor brothers, when on shore leave, used to take her to a studio where the photographer specialized in nude studies. I don't think, at this stage, [she knew] what many of her poses represented. She only knew that after her brothers had pocketed the money there was usually enough left over for her to buy a new pair of shoes or a new dress, and, on especially successful days, sometimes both."

Times were tough after the death of Olive's father and such promiscuous work would have paid well; however, the dates of that story just don't add up. Olive was the eldest in the family. When she was fourteen her brothers were twelve (James) and nine (William). The boys certainly weren't old enough to be sailors and they weren't mature enough to persuade their sister to become a nude model either. But, it's entirely possible that Olive took the job on herself, without persuasion. The payoff of being able to afford a new dress or shoes (and handing over the rest of the money to help her struggling family) is not uncharacteristic of Olive's personality. Her family meant everything to her.

It's been long reported that one of her later employers and rumored lover, Harrison Fisher, wrote a letter of recommendation to famed showman Florenz Ziegfeld, Jr., on her behalf (*New York Clipper*, September 15, 1920). However, Olive disputes this story (*Motion Picture*, June 1919): "I just went up [to Ziegfeld] and asked for a job and got it. I didn't do much of anything at first—just posed around, standing in boxes and frames while someone sang songs at me."

Fisher did comment on Olive's much anticipated Follies debut, saying, "Beauty is not one feature or quality but the sum of them all. Olive Thomas has that sum in an amazingly high degree" (Marjorie Farnsworth, *The Ziegfeld Follies*, 1956).

The 1915 Follies were the most visually stunning to date. Despite Ziegfeld's efforts to make each year's show bigger and better than ever, Joseph Urban's art deco sets of 1915 were never topped. The opening scenes had the showgirls swimming in waves of blue light, and massive golden elephants spouted water from their upturned trunks.

Left: **With a little bird on her shoulder, Olive is the picture of innocence.** *Right:* **A sorrowful look.**

1. Rags to Riches

Lower row—Odette Myrtil, Allyn King, Oscar Shaw, Dolly Sisters, Paul Frawley, Marion Harris and Sybil Carmen.
Top row—Olive Thomas, Will Rogers, Genevieve Warner, and Ziegfeld Trio.
THE PRINCIPAL FROLICERS IN THE "ZIEGFELD MIDNIGHT FROLIC."

The principal "frolickers" in Ziegfeld's Midnight Frolic. Olive is second from the left in the top row.

Leon Errol, W.C. Fields, Ann Pennington, Ed Wynn, Bert Williams, George White, Ina Claire, Justine Johnstone, Mae Murray and of course Olive were all billed as stars of the history-making show. Fields was given lines for the very first time and, to the shock of the audience, out of nowhere he unexpectedly smacked Ed Wynn over the head with a billiard cue because he was stealing his laughs. The crowd went wild. They naturally thought that it was part of the act.

Olive's newfound success as a Ziegfeld girl (and Ziegfeld mistress) gave her enough confidence to divorce her small-town husband (February 25, 1915) of four years on the grounds of cruelty and neglect; the only reminder of the ill-fated union was her married name (Thomas) which she decided to keep. Aside from returning to Pittsburgh to finalize her divorce proceedings, Olive would revisit her roots on few occasions in the coming years. This is not to say she neglected her family; far from it. Olive would send a sizable weekly check home to her mother along with such luxuries as silk stockings and assorted trinkets to make life easier. Now that she was a Ziegfeld showgirl, Olive was earning $75 per week (approximately $1400 today) and despite her humble beginnings as a shop girl with a weekly wage of $3 (approximately $55 today), she was never afraid of spending money when she had it, especially on those she loved most. Her generosity often got her into financial trouble. Despite her newfound wealth, her bank account was frequently overdrawn.

As a Ziegfeld girl, Olive was a sudden sensation, the toast of Broadway. Florenz Ziegfeld, Jr., was engaged in his business of "glorifying the American girl" per the Follies. His merchandise was solely based on feminine beauty, preferably famous beauty. Olive was youth and beauty, with a brand new fame in the papers. Men grew dizzy under her eyes. She was overwhelmed with admiration and gifts of treasure, diamond necklaces, pendants, rings, parties, orchids, everything that the dreaming little shop girl might fancy on the screen of her imagination. It was even whispered that the great Bernstorff, the German ambassador, had sent Olive a $10,000 (approximately $100,000 today) string of pearls (*Photoplay*, January 1925).

Men were captivated by her beauty, charm and wit. As an example, Philip Mindil, dramatic editor of the *New York Tribune*, was quoted as saying, "To know Olive Thomas personally, is like being on friendly terms with an angel." Sunday supplement editors would vie for the job of visiting the theater in order to photograph Olive for their papers. She was *that* popular.

Flo Ziegfeld had affairs with many of his Broadway beauties, and Olive was no exception. According to Randolph Carter's 1974 book *The World of Ziegfeld*, Billie Burke was on location making a film called *Peggy* (1916) for Thomas H. Ince when disturbing rumors reached her about her husband's involvement with Olive. There were comments in the newspapers and friends contributed interesting anecdotes concerning yachting parties, even going so far as to send telegrams asking point blank when she intended to divorce Flo. Billie was particularly incensed, having just turned down a five-year contract with Ince. Realizing she couldn't hope to stay in Hollywood and remain Mrs. Florenz Ziegfeld, Jr., she fled to San Francisco where Flo joined her and they argued for two days; that is to say, Billie argued while Flo sat quietly puffing cigars, imperturbable even when she tore down draperies and threw china. *The World of Ziegfeld* reported Ziegfeld's arrogant response:

"The trouble with you, Billie," he finally announced, "is that when you accuse me, you always pick the wrong girl." That comment did nothing to curtail Billie's anger. Indeed there were many girls and Olive was most certainly one of them. But their affair ended with the appearance of Jack Pickford; Ziegfeld moved on to the next willing showgirl.

The 1915 season of the Follies had Olive appearing as "Miss January" in the "A Girl for Every Month of the Year" parade. She then moved on to become the shining star of the more risqué Midnight Frolics. The 680-seat rooftop of the New Amsterdam Theatre in New York City was home to the most beautiful showgirls the world had ever seen.

A bit of background on Ziegfeld and the Follies: Ziegfeld opened the *Follies of 1907* in that very year. It was a never-before-seen

Florenz Ziegfeld, Jr., at age 40.

An ad for Ziegfeld's Midnight Frolic revue show.

live revue in the style of the Paris revues he had seen while overseas in 1905. Emphasizing glamour and beauty, the Follies became a mainstay of Broadway and ran in annual installments until Ziegfeld's death in 1932.

In 1911 Ziegfeld renamed the Follies "The Ziegfeld Follies." Four years later he instigated the Ziegfeld Midnight Frolic, a revue which served as a training ground for the Follies, commencing at midnight and featuring dance music between the acts. The first Ziegfeld Nine O'Clock Frolic (later called the Ziegfeld Nine O'Clock Revue) opened in 1918. (By 1922, Prohibition killed the Frolics, which, for their success, had depended on the refreshments as much as the entertainment. The Frolic enjoyed a brief reprisal in 1928 and 1929.)

When it was built, the New Amsterdam was the largest theater in New York, and could seat 1800 people. In 1913, the New Amsterdam became the home of the Ziegfeld Follies. In 1914, the rooftop theater was renamed Danse de Follies and Ziegfeld added a dance floor on the rooftop. Later, in 1923, the rooftop would be renamed again, becoming the Frolic Theatre (www.nyc-architecture.com).

While it was not unusual to have a small stage on the roof of a theater, most rooftop stages contained no more than a platform that served as a simple stage and were only usable in warm weather. They were more like gardens than theaters. The

New Amsterdam had a complete miniature theater that could be used all year, although it was only used in the summer months. On the rooftop, it was primarily variety shows that were presented.

The Frolics shows were just as spectacular as the Follies revues but the girls wore less (some of them were nude) and the audience members were openly encouraged to be involved in the show. The prettiest, sexiest, most appealing girls would perform for the world's richest men. Some of the luckier girls married them!

Showgirls scantily dressed and with balloons discreetly in place would get close enough to the ogling men in the audience to playfully permit them to pop the balloons with their cigars. Many of the girls would fling their garters into the audience. It was not unusual for the girls to place bets amongst themselves on who could hit the most bald men with their lacy leg pieces; it helped keep the nightly shows (running from midnight to 3 A.M.) spontaneous. Legendary set designer, Joseph Urban, even created a glass walkway so the girls could dance over the customer's heads. The $5.00 (approximately $60 today) cover charge ensured only the most elite, well-behaved crowd attended the shows. Ziegfeld wouldn't stand for an audience made up of riffraff. As risqué as his shows were, they were never vulgar.

In 1916, Olive progressed to the point of singing a solo in one of the Frolics scenes. Ziegfeld was so impressed with her voice that he was prepared to offer her a more prominent position on a regular basis. To his dismay, Thomas Ince lured her to Hollywood before he could make his proposal. It was the beginning of a nerve-wracking time for Ziegfeld. While he was at first flattered at the prospect of his girls being handpicked to go into the new and exciting business of motion pictures, he began to realize that Hollywood was the biggest threat ever to rival the great Ziegfeld shows. He started a campaign with paid advertisements that read: *Ziegfeld Follies—Glorifying the American Girl in the flesh ... not canned.*

Ziegfeld continued to expand the Follies shows. The shows became more and more grandiose and Ziegfeld's extravagance for lavish sets and production in the most expansive fashion became legendary. In one case, he paid an actress $600 (approximately $5000 today) and dressed her in a $1200 (approximately $10,000 today) gown just to elegantly walk across the stage in a single scene.

Olive and Catharine Daly in costume for one of Ziegfeld's Midnight Frolics shows.

In another case he ordered a set for $25,000 (approximately $250,000 today) and when it was finished, he discarded it for being too garish. Each production became more expensive and ambitious than the last and as a result Ziegfeld tottered on the line between being financially flush or broke (www.parlorsongs.com).

There was still a place for the Ziegfeld Follies and Frolics, for now, but Olive wasn't the only one to jump ship, Ziegfeld would eventually lose some of his most prized beauties to the movie industry (Billie Dove, Paulette Goddard, Irene Dunne, Mae Murray, Marion Davies, Barbara Stanwyck, and Hedy Lamarr, just to name a few). Ironically, Hollywood made movie stars out of several girls who were passed on by Ziegfeld for not being pretty enough. As an example, Norma Shearer and Alice Faye were dismissed from auditions for not being up to "showgirl standard."

Comedians who got their start on Ziegfeld's stage included Will Rogers, Eddie Cantor, W.C. Fields, Fanny Brice, Leon Errol, Ray Bolger, Bert Lahr and countless others. Despite those prominent names, Ziegfeld always maintained that his showgirls were the main attraction.

He openly admitted to having no sense of humor, saying, "Half of the great comedians I've had in my shows and that I paid a lot of money to and who made my customers shriek were not only not funny to me, but I couldn't understand why they were funny to anybody. You'd be surprised how many of the expensive comics I've run out on and locked myself in my office when they were on stage" (Billie Burke, *With a Feather on My Nose*, 1948).

His personal feelings aside, Ziegfeld knew he had the right recipe for success and the combination of practical jokers and pretty girls was the basis for every Ziegfeld show. From a business standpoint the comedians were mere fillers to allow for set changes and to give the girls enough time to change into different costumes. From an audience standpoint the combination of comedy and beauty was the reason the Ziegfeld shows consistently played to full houses for over twenty years.

The onset of the film business saw an initial slump in audience numbers but eventually the prestige of seeing a Ziegfeld show brought audiences back to Broadway and allowed both forms of entertainment to comfortably co-exist. The last Follies produced by Ziegfeld was in 1931. Most of the show was rehashed from past successes and, unlike the years before it, there was nothing new to see. It was time to say goodbye ... in more ways than one.

Florenz Ziegfeld, Jr., the world's great showman of the musical stage, died of pleurisy on July 22, 1932. In his delirium he shouted stage directions from his deathbed; "Looks good! Looks good!" were his last words. He was 63 years old. Despite his years of success, his lavish lifestyle had left him bankrupt.

Ziegfeld's behavior grew increasingly bizarre in the few years leading up to his death. With his finances in a shambles, he would leave letters and bills unopened and unanswered for months at a time. The increased presence of creditors waiting for him at the main entrance of the theater would cause him to use the fire escape to leave his office. All clocks and watches were banned because the ticking hands reminded him of death.

In order to convince himself that death was far from knocking on his door, Ziegfeld experimented with hormone pills that promised to restore his virility. He tested the effectiveness of the medication in his office on willing chorus girls, and on weekends, while his wife Billie Burke was in Hollywood making a movie, he would invite groups of girls home for wild all-night orgies. It was a sad end to a man who was scared to death of death itself. He did all that he could to continually prove to himself and others that he was still young and full of life; yet the inevitable end came and Ziegfeld had no choice but to attend the very first funeral of his life—his own.

A private memorial service was arranged by Will Rogers and held in Hollywood, away from the garish arrangement that was being talked about in New York. Despite losing many important friends and colleagues over the years, Ziegfeld's morbid fear of death caused him to avoid funeral services his entire life. Incidentally, he arranged the service and paid for most of Olive's funeral expenses (he was known to send lavish floral arrangements to others who had passed on in the industry) but he dared not show his face. In hindsight, Jack Pickford was lucky that Ziegfeld didn't attend Olive's funeral. Ziegfeld blamed him for her death and he swore he'd kill Jack if he ever set eyes on him again.

Will Rogers paid tribute to his former employer and friend with a touching speech summing up what Florenz Ziegfeld, Jr., had meant to the world of entertainment:

> He picked us from all walks of life. He led us into what little fame we achieved. He remained our friend regardless of our usefulness as an entertainer. He brought beauty into the entertainment world. To have been the master amusement provider of your generation, surely a life's work has been accomplished. He left something on earth that hundreds of us will treasure till our final curtains fall, and that is a "badge," a badge of which we are proud and want to read the lettering, "I worked for Ziegfeld." So goodbye, Flo, save a spot for me, for you will put on a show up there some day that will knock their eyes out.

Left: An artistic pose. With Olive draped in satin with nothing underneath, this photograph was quite provocative for its time. *Right:* A 1916 Moriarty playing card bearing Olive's portrait.

Incidentally, Ziegfeld would not have to hold a place in Heaven for his good friend Will Rogers for long. He was killed in a plane crash (at fifty-five years of age) just three years after Ziegfeld's death. The plane was piloted by world record–breaking one-eyed pioneer aviator, Wiley Post; Post also perished in the crash.

Florenz Ziegfeld, Jr., may have been the perfect showman but he was far from being the perfect husband. His second wife Billie Burke (his first was Anna Held) learned to turn a blind eye to the countless chorus girls he had affairs with (including Olive) during their eighteen-year marriage and she worked tirelessly after his death to repay the mountainous debts he left behind. Billie and their daughter, Patricia, did all they could via books, media, stage and film to ensure the Ziegfeld name and all that it stood for was not lost to time.

Billie Burke allowed the name "Ziegfeld Follies" to be used for several revival shows in the years following her husband's death. However, without the "Ziegfeld touch" these shows ended up being miserable failures.

It's ironic, given the grief that the motion picture business initially gave him, that several films have commemorated the life of the great showman. William Powell played Ziegfeld in two of the most popular films based on his life and career, *The Great Ziegfeld* (1936) and *Ziegfeld Follies* (1946).

The Great Ziegfeld won the Best Picture Oscar and Luise Rainer won the Best Actress Oscar for her portrayal of Ziegfeld's first wife, Anna Held. Myrna Loy portrayed Billie Burke and Frank Morgan gave an outstanding performance as a rival showman. The extravagant $3 million (approximately $30 million today) *Ziegfeld Follies* had an all-star cast with Judy Garland, Fred Astaire, Gene Kelly, Fanny Brice, Red Skelton, Cyd Charisse, Esther Williams and Lucille Ball reviving many of Ziegfeld's most spectacular numbers. Other films showcasing the life and work of Flo Ziegfeld include *A Ziegfeld Midnight Frolic* (1929), *Ziegfeld Girl* (1941) and a television movie, *Ziegfeld: The Man and His Women* (1978) with Penny Ciarlo playing the part of Olive Thomas.

Ironically, the motion picture, the very nemesis that once threatened Flo Ziegfeld's livelihood and poached his girls from the "Follies" stage, repeatedly honored his life and paid homage to his work in the grandest of Hollywood ways.

✯ *Chapter 2* ✯

FOLLIES AND FROLICS AND FILM... OH MY!

People think that nothing is required of a Follies girl but beauty... Well, I worked harder in the Follies than I ever did in my life.

—Olive Thomas

It was inevitable that Olive's success in the Follies and Frolics would soon lead to a film career. Her first role was in the popular *Beatrice Fairfax* (1916) film series for Wharton Studios, shot in Ithaca, New York. She starred as Rita Malone in episode ten, "Play Ball."

By 1914, the Wharton Brothers leased the expansive piece of land known as Renwick Park and used it as an outdoor location site for their movie productions. Between 1914–1919 from their headquarters located in present-day Stewart Park, Wharton Studios produced numerous short film series, most notably the *Elaine* serials and the controversial *Patria* serial, which are now regarded as precious classics of the era. William Randolph Hearst financed numerous silent pictures made in Ithaca, most notably the *Beatrice Fairfax* series.

A March 18, 1914 edition of *The Cornell Daily Sun* ran the headline *Wharton Brothers to Use Natural Beauties of Ithaca for Scenes of Picture Plays*. The article boasted that Theodore Wharton "saw the exceptional scenic advantages in Ithaca which would be especially valuable for their use." They also announced that one play a week would be made there.

Ithaca's gorges, lake, trolleys and buildings made for natural settings that were not often seen in early filmmaking. The Whartons' moviemaking, with stars such as Irene Castle, Pearl White, Oliver Hardy and Warner Oland and stunts such as cars and trolleys falling into gorges, drew large crowds of fascinated locals and tourists alike.

On July 17, 1915, *The Sun* reported on one of the more spectacular movie stunts to be filmed in Ithaca in an article titled, "Whartons Send Car Over High Cliff." *The Sun* was very impressed by the special effects efforts of the day, saying: "The thorough-

Olive happily poses with some of the players on the 1916 New York Yankees baseball team.

going realism which the Wharton Company is striving to show on the screen was shown Wednesday when at Taughannock Falls an automobile was sent plunging from a high cliff down 300 feet to the rocks below."

Wharton Brothers graciously allowed people to continue to visit the Renwick Park site, provided they did not interfere with their work. The Whartons left by 1919 after finding the climate of California more conducive to year-round movie production.

Much of the park went into a state of decline after the Whartons' departure. However, Mayor Edwin C. Stewart's inauguration speech on January of 1920 showed his determination to renew the park for public use, saying, "It is a disgrace to our city that there is not a place where Ithacans and their guests may go to enjoy our lake without trespassing on private property."

Thanks to the mayor's determination, the lake swiftly became available for public enjoyment and by 1921 a full restoration plan was underway. Unfortunately, the dedicated mayor died before he could see the finished effect. Fittingly, Renwick Park is now Stewart Park, renamed for the mayor who donated $150,000 of his estate toward a preservation and maintenance program that continues to this day.

"Play Ball" was filmed at Renwick Park (aka Stewart Park) and the combination of Olive and baseball was a hit with audiences; Olive even became the official mascot of the 1916 New York Yankees baseball team. The ads for "Play Ball" stated, "Managers McGraw and Donovan and their teams of Giants and Yankees, together with 18,000 enthusiastic New York fans, are among the actors in this episode of *Beatrice Fairfax*.

A magazine ad for "Play Ball," the *Beatrice Fairfax* series episode in which Olive starred.

A scene from the *Beatrice Fairfax* series, "Play Ball." Photograph by Levi Bacon, September 1916.

Harry Fox and Grace Darling, as usual, are the stars. With them are featured Olive Thomas and Nigel Barrie."

After Olive appeared in the Paramount production, *A Girl Like That* (1917), Thomas Ince, of Triangle Pictures, offered her an exclusive contract. *Motography* (April 14, 1917) reported, "All the former members of her company (Follies and Frolics) have sent Olive telegrams of congratulations upon her affiliation with Ince, which is a mark of popularity few Broadway beauties can match."

Olive's first lead role was in *Madcap Madge*, released on June 24, 1917; she played, Betty. It was the second of six films that Olive appeared in that year. *Moving Picture Stories*, March 15, 1918, reported:

> Olive Thomas' training before the footlights was a splendid beginning, but she frankly admitted that she had everything to learn about the screen. When the history of the screen is written, she may be credited with setting a world's record. In twenty-four days she completed two five-reel comedy-dramas in order to make a visit to Pittsburgh and New York. Her latest vehicle, *Heiress for a Day* (1918) was a whirlwind. She worked almost continuously on this picture, night and day, eating her meals in her dressing room with her director in order to discuss scenes, even in the short time allowed for refreshments.

It seems Olive's dedication to her role in *Heiress for a Day* paid off. A *Motion Picture News* (March 9, 1918) review for the film was full of praise:

A *Photoplay* magazine ad for Ingram's Milkweed Cream featuring Olive and promoting her new film *Heiress for a Day* (1918).

The pretty and dainty Triangle star, Olive Thomas, comes to the screen in *Heiress for a Day*, a charming society drama. Miss Thomas is said to be prettier and daintier than ever in this, her latest production, in which she plays the role of a manicurist who suddenly inherits millions. An able cast supports the star, with Joe King appearing in the leading male role of Jack Standring. Helen Thurston, manicurist at a fashionable hotel, is in love with her wealthy patron, Jack Standring, the most sought after popular bachelor in society, but realizes that her station in life precludes her winning him. While she is brooding over it all she suddenly hears that she is heir to millions left by her grandfather who has just died. Before learning the extent of the bequest she plunges into society, where she is welcomed as the city's richest heiress, but she fails to impress Standring.

In the midst of her social preparations she discovers that her grandfather has left her only $1,000, the bulk of the fortune going to her cousin, Spindrift, under certain conditions. Recovering from her shock, she decides to use her $1,000 to be an heiress for a day. Society bows at her feet and her triumph seems complete except that Standring does not respond. Suddenly creditors clamor for the thousands due them and at a fashionable ball a detective threatens her with arrest. She is deserted by all except Standring, to whom the fact that she is only a poor girl after all, and not a member of the useless society set, appeals. However, the conditions of the will have been violated by Spindrift and Helen wins not only the fortune but a husband as well.

The applause of an audience and noise and excitement of the metropolis are necessary ingredients of a stage favorite's existence, "But," declared Miss Olive recently, "life as a Broadway favorite is tame compared to being a screen star. It would take me a week to tell you of the stunts they make you do, but never have I been so frightened as in a picture, when I had to race four stories down a swinging fire-escape, pursued by an intoxicated man and a flock of detectives. The director didn't have to tell me to register fright, for I was just plumb scared."

California has its compensations for her, enough to give her genuine pleasure in her film work. Plenty of dainty clothes, fun, and laughter keep Triangle's "joy of living" girl a happy person, whose sunny personality adds real worth to a delicate, perfect-featured beauty that delights the foremost artists and fans with its whimsical appeal. During the filming of her Triangle release, *Limousine Life* (1918), Olive was arrested for careless driving. It happened when Miss Thomas and Lee Phelps were playing a love scene while driving forty miles an hour on the highway passing the Culver City studios. The car was wobbling from one side of the road to the other. Giving chase, a cop picked them up for speeding and driving a car while intoxicated. An irresistible smile from Olive, accompanied with an explanation, and the scene was continued with the motorcycle officer as a spectator.

A demure pose. Olive was often portrayed as the wholesome good girl, but off-screen she was a party girl who loved to dance and kick up her heels.

In an aptly titled article, "Broadway Queen Gone West" (*Photoplay*, December 1917), Jack Lloyd reported:

> No one is more popular in the big lot at Culver City than Olive Thomas. In tailored suit and jaunty cap, she strolls about, with a pert offering or a ready reply for everyone. It is one of the legends of the studios that no one can "get ahead" of Olive in repartee, and no situation is too unusual for her to puncture it with a pungent comment....
>
> "You know," confided Olive naively, "I'd rather eat Boston beans and butter cakes in Childs than the most expensive mess the French chef can dope out on Broadway's most expensive lobster palace." Which is quite some confession. Also, it added proof of Olive's lack of upstaginess.
>
> "Life's too short and fate too funny to get upstage," philosophized Olive. "Today they may be showering us with roses on Broadway and tomorrow some fool director who used to be a waiter may be rejecting us as atmosphere in a five-reel five-cent feature."

Olive knew how fickle the film business was and she did all that she could to ensure that she wasn't just a pretty face in front of a camera. She wanted to know the ins and outs of making a moving picture. With an insatiable appetite for knowledge she observed others and asked questions constantly. Herbert Howe of *Motion Picture Classic* (February, 1918) wrote about Olive's need-to-know personality:

> A blithe young hurricane could not have created more disturbances than did Ollie that bright morning when she swept thru the gates of the Triangle studio in her shining motorcar. Question marks sparkled in both eyes! In two hours she knew the nicknames of every man, dog and "prop" on the lot. In two weeks she was ready to direct, turn the camera or design sets.
>
> "Madcap" some called her, by virtue of the appropriate title of her first play (*Madcap Madge*, 1917). "Pep" was another sobriquet. But the director who was given charge of the human dynamo preferred, "Miss Inquisitive." Every day during the course of production he was volleyed with such questions as:
>
> "What do you do that for? Why can't I weep real tears instead of glycerine ones? Why do some actresses smell an onion when they want to cry? Onions make me sneezy, not weepy."
>
> The eternal question mark that punctuated all her utterances became the terror of more than one expert. Soon it became the practice to explain to Miss Ollie all the intricacies of a production before she had a chance to commence her "third degree." In four weeks she was capable of turning her hand to anything, from taming a wild animal, or director, to building the sets.
>
> "Why the thirst for knowledge?" she was asked.

A promotional glass slide for *Heiress for a Day* (1918).

"Well, you see, I'm only a Follies girl, and may turn out a flivver star in pictures, so I'd better be prepared for a carpenter's job if necessary. Oh, by the way, why...."

But the other party to the colloquy fled as the question mark flashed thru the air, and Ollie was left to solve the problem that she had suddenly conjured up.

Her interrogative exuberance finally caused the scenario editor to lay down his arms and give her a place at his typewriter, where she proceeded to collaborate on a play. For several days her inquisitiveness was quelled. She wrote with two fingers, and soon wanted to know how she could write with all ten and at the same time be legible. When the play was ready for production and Olive, with her supporters, was removed to the mountains for filming the most important scenes, she inquired if she might direct. Of course that was out of the question. No actress has brains enough to direct. Why, some gentlemen who have never been on a lot say that regular directors haven't enough brains to do it, so how could an ex Follies girl?

"But why not?" retorted the irrepressible one. Finally, in sheer desperation, the company and director signed a petition asking that the Queen in Question be given a chance at the megaphone. Thereupon, the electric energies of the young star fairly shot sparks. She directed with a zeal that caused one of the players to moan, "Oh Lord! It's going to be a regular Keystone—speed—speed—speed! She's a demon for action. Does she ever rest long enough to do anything but ask 'why?' or 'how?'"

Olive's avocation came to a sudden and almost disastrous end. She was directing a scene with all the fierceness of a Simon Legree, when a snake ambled up and, as though bewitched by the charmer, curled up affectionately at her feet, with his neck up stretched. "Madcap" gave a wild scream, did a leap that would have made Doug Fairbanks look paralyzed, and shot down the mountainside like a forty centimeter shell, exploding as she went. When the director in charge took over, she was breathless, but soon recovered enough to say:

"Where did that infernal thing come from? Did he bite me? Was the scene spoiled? What kind of a snake was it? Do you think there are many more around here? Will you ... will you finish directing that scene?"

"YES!" shouted the director.

Olive returned meekly to her duties as star, and for several days had no questions to ask. Then she suddenly had a desire to pick the next location. By that time the question-riddled crowd offered no resistance. She went forth to explore. Hours passed and the fair Columbus returned not.

"We'd better hunt for her," suggested one of the men.

"If you do, she'll ask why you did it," shrieked one of the women.

Toward sundown Olive returned looking as though she had done an Annette Kellerman [Australian swim star portrayed by Esther Williams in *Million Dollar Mermaid,* 1952] without heeding the maternal advice anent hanging one's clothes on a hickory lamb.

"Where on earth have you been?!" chorused the company. "And where on earth did you gather so many wet clothes?"

"Why be so deuced inquisitive?" retorted the dripping young person.

"I was looking around, when a lake got under my foot and went up over my head, and I thought I'd found my last location."

That same night one of her pet Japanese poodles wandered forth, presumably in search of the location which Olive had failed to find ... due to the lake getting in her way. The mistress discovered her dog's absence, became worried, and finally insisted on organizing a search party for him. The tired associates, fearful of eternal "why," trailed forth, but the canine explorer could not be found. He turned in during the wee hours of the morning, stuck full of burs and looking as though he had enjoyed a rough and riotous night.

"Where do you suppose he has been?" asked one of the players.

"You reprimand me for asking questions," retorted Olive, "and yet you would ask a gentleman that. Chow-chow," she said, addressing the accused, "you need not answer.

The question is irrelevant, impertinent, no bearing on the case. Don't commit yourself. But you do look like you'd been sitting in a patch of burs."

Olive returned to the studio declaring that she had spent the most glorious time of her life up in the mountains, and that she had almost learnt to write poetry from gazing over the clouds that clustered around the mountain ridges.

Instead of being called Miss Inquisitive, she now has the title of Miss Encyclopedia at the studio. When a visitor, a very dignified and commanding woman called at the studio not long ago, she was escorted to the stage where the star was working. The lady made several inquiries that puzzled the guide, so he referred her to the director.

"Turn her over to Miss Encyclopedia. She knows," replied that gentleman.

Olive, who at that moment was draped over a chair watching a festive cabaret scene and propounding a question under her curl-frescoed head, obliged.

"What is that the players are drinking?" asked the visitor.

"Champagne," promptly replied Miss Encyclopedia.

"Do tell!" exclaimed the woman, raising her lorgnette to scrutinize the effervescent liquor. Then she hurried away. Shortly after Olive was summoned to appear in the manager's office.

"What did you tell this lady that the players were drinking?" she was asked sternly.

"Champagne."

"But you know they are not. This lady is a prohibitionist, and she accuses us of plying the actors with intoxicating liquor."

"Oh!" murmured the wide-eyed star. "Oh! Well, you see, I didn't want her to think we faked our scenes. Come on back and I'll give you a drink," she suddenly exclaimed, turning toward the accuser.

After considerable argument the woman returned and was presented with a glass of the sparking beverage. She sipped hesitatingly, then with more boldness.

"Why," said she, "it tastes like apple-cider."

"Yes, that's what it is. Sparkling apple juice," replied the chastened Olive. "Come back tomorrow and we'll give you some Burgundy strawberry pop or Cook's lemon phosphate."

The lady departed satisfied, and as she passed out she remarked, "I think your star, Miss Thomas, is charming, so entertaining and interesting. She took me around and explained everything in the place."

This ingratiating manner makes it possible for the young actress to accumulate her stock of information with arousing rebuke. No one star, director, scenario writer or property man is permitted to upset the discipline of the Triangle studio, where an efficient and smooth running system of production has been recently perfected. So only during waits or off-duty hours does Olive receive instruction in the various phases of work. The single directorial effort was made possible because of the weather, but she insists that she is always studying the methods of directors with the intention of becoming a regular producer some time.

A recent production required a dancing

A pretty portrait shot signed "Sincerely, Olive Thomas."

scene in which a large company of girls appeared. The director was on the point of calling in an instructor to drill the dancers, when the star volunteered her services. For several days she labored consistently with the coryphées until they had mastered the intricacies of the latest Broadway steps. In return for this assistance the director agreed to reveal some of the mysteries of his art, but only on condition that the star was willing to spend time at the studio after the work for the day had been completed. Was she willing? She certainly was.

Golf, tea and motoring were forgotten while she went over the script of her next play, studying the author's descriptions of scene, setting and character, and endeavoring to originate the little bits of business that give the touch of reality and human interest in a photoplay.

"That girl has a business woman's head," remarked the director after this course of study. "I believe she will be capable of directing some day, but tragedy will never be her line. She'd speed up Lady Macbeth and have her doing a fox trot and a handspring. Olive is a joy-of-living optimist ... but an intelligent one."

Soon it became known that Olive possessed brains ... that she had been actually caught using them in several instances. Such scandalous rumor about a film player had to be stopped. I discovered the Thomas tornado teaching a crowd of girls a new dance that called for considerable athletic agility. As I approached, primed to question her, she ceased her dervish whirl, brushed back her hair and gasped.

"Have you brains?" I asked her.

"Brains?" she puffed; and then, with a mischievous smile, "What are brains?"

"Brains. Brains are ... brains are..." I stuttered, and then reached for my pocket dictionary. With considerable gusto I declaimed the Webster:

"Brains" (a) in vertebrate animals the large mass of nerve tissue enclosed in the shell or

Above: **A response card sent to a fan who requested an autographed photograph.** *Below:* **A promotional photograph of Olive when she was with Triangle Pictures.**

cranium, regarded as the seat of consciousness. It includes the cerebrum in front and above and cerebellum below at the back. (b) In many invertebrates, a large ganglion more or less corresponding to the brain of the vertebrate."

I paused and regarded the lady before me.

"A vertebrate!" she muttered in awed manner, "You want to know if I am a vertebrate?"

I nodded solemnly.

"I don't know. I hope not," she replied. "But they call me most everything around here."

Then with a flash of inspiration and a smile, she exclaimed:

"The best way to find out whether I've got them is to ask somebody, isn't it? Do you think I ask too many questions? Do you think it pays to learn something about pictures? Are all film actresses boobs? Maybe I'm getting my celluloid diploma too fast, eh? Think I have brains?"

"I'm sure I don't know. You are almost too good looking, Miss Thomas, to be so afflicted."

"Is it an affliction? Don't good-looking people have them? Why don't they? Do just homely people have them? Have you..." I spun dizzily around on one heel, Chaplin fashion, and did a Keystone marathon through the studio gates. I have an awful hunch that the young lady with the interrogation points dancing in both eyes is a super vertebrate ... a beauty *with* brains! But where did she get 'em? Why, in the business without brains!

That lengthy article, personally observed and written by Herbert Howe (just three years before Olive's death), is a perfect study of how full of vim and vigor she was. With such an inquiring mind for her newly discovered work environment, had Olive lived beyond her twenty-five years, she may well have gone on to become one of the great female directors. Women weren't given the right to vote until 1920 (the year of Olive's death) so for a woman to have such high career aspirations above and beyond being "just an actress" was quite remarkable. The more Olive achieved, the more she wanted. Despite her success, and at such a young age, she rarely seemed satisfied or content. This would prove true in many areas of her life.

★ *Chapter 3* ★

JACK AND OLLIE

I didn't want people to say that I'm succeeding because of the Pickford name.
—Why Olive took a year to announce her marriage to Jack Pickford

It was no secret that Florenz Ziegfeld, Jr., had affairs with many of his Follies girls and Olive was no exception to the rule. Ziegfeld's long-suffering wife, Billie Burke, admitted in her autobiography, "Olive was one of the only Follies that he truly cared about." So, it is perhaps not surprising that Ziegfeld became resentful of Olive's whirlwind romance with Jack Pickford, actor-brother of "America's Sweetheart," Mary Pickford. Ziegfeld not only lost his mistress to Pickford, but he also lost one of his most popular showgirls to her new beau's industry—moving pictures.

Olive's first meeting with Jack was at a dance in a beach café founded by Nat Goodwin. "Jack," she said, "is a beautiful dancer. He danced his way into my heart. We knew each other for eight months before our marriage and most of that time we gave to dancing. We got along so well on the dance floor that we just naturally decided that we would be able to get along together for the remainder of our lives" (*Motion Picture*, June 1919).

On their third date, a besotted Jack gave Olive a $12,000 (approximately $125,000 today) platinum cigarette case with the inscription, "To Olive Thomas—the only sweetheart I will ever have."

Despite Jack's reputation as a boozing, drug-abusing womanizer, the pair seemed genuinely in love and were "said" to be secretly married in New Jersey (yet no marriage license can be located) on October 25, 1916. Fellow actor and friend, Thomas Meighan, acted as witness to the ceremony. Since no marriage license can be located, the question remains, were Jack and Olive legally married at all?

It was close to a year before they publicly declared they were husband and wife and suddenly a new Hollywood golden couple had emerged. The other Pickfords made no secret of their ill feelings for Olive, especially Jack's overbearing mother, Charlotte Pickford. Immensely proud of her children's achievements in the motion picture industry, she declared that Olive should not have married into her family. Among other reasons for objecting were that Olive was not a good enough actress to marry into the Pickford family, and that she would use her relationship to make herself a rival of Mary. So, the marriage began under rather unhappy conditions and Olive was determined that she would become a truly great star, *without* using the Pickford name, just to prove her mother-in-law wrong. She succeeded in doing just that but she was never fully accepted by the Pickfords. In their eyes, no woman would have been good enough for Jack. Of course, fan magazines of the day painted a rosy picture for the public. According to published reports, Charlotte and Mary were thrilled with Jack's choice of a wife. It could not have been further from the truth.

Jack was the wild child of the Pickford family, and his sister Mary would make countless excuses for her kid brother's outrageous behavior. Without a doubt, Mary's position of power in the business gave her less talented sibling the help that he needed to get his foot in the door. The Pickford name meant something on a theater marquee, it drew a crowd, and it certainly couldn't hurt to have another Pickford in the industry. Mary had hoped that a steady career would tame her brother and give him a sense of purpose, but Jack took nothing seriously and his movie career was no exception.

Ironically, Jack's onscreen persona was that of a winsome boy next door. In reality his wild ways, together with his alcoholism, drug addictions and complications relating to syphilis, would kill him at the tender age of thirty-six. It's interesting to note that Jack contracted syphilis in 1917, the year *after* he wed Olive. The marriage and countless claims that Olive was "the love of my life" did little to curb his womanizing ways because he reportedly passed the disease on to his wife. Some suicide theorists adamantly claim that syphilis was the primary motivation for Olive's overdose. The mercury bichloride that Olive ingested was prescribed to topically treat the disease in Jack.

In Mary's eyes, the union between Jack and Ollie was doomed from the very beginning. She stated in her autobiography that they were just "two children playing house." Olive was twenty-one and Jack was nineteen. Mary claimed their mother shouted, "You're too young to be married!" Mary also pleaded with Jack to build up his career before settling down. On the other hand, Jack and Mary's free-spirited sister Lottie was all for it, saying, "Go ahead. Love is all we can expect out of life" (*Photoplay*, January 1918).

It was a joint decision to keep their marriage a secret for at least a year until Olive could establish herself in the motion picture business. "I didn't want people to say that I'm succeeding because of the Pickford name," explained Olive in the December 1917 issue of *Photoplay*. By the time their marriage became public knowledge, Olive had become a star in her own right and her marriage into the Pickford clan, a family often

Thomas Meighan was witness to Olive and Jack's marriage.

referred to as Hollywood royalty, was the icing on the cake. Olive had always been a fantasist but her life was now beyond her wildest dreams. She was a movie star, she was rich, she was popular with the theatergoing public and her legal name was now Olive Thomas Pickford.

In her book, *Sunshine and Shadow* (1955), Mary Pickford's recollections of her former sister-in-law had obviously mellowed from times past. There was still a sense of snobbery in her writing yet she did praise Olive's stunning good looks, saying:

> I regret to say that none of us approved of the marriage at that time. Mother thought Jack was too young, and Lottie and I felt that Olive, being in musical comedy, belonged to an alien world. Ollie had all the rich, eligible men of the social world at her feet. She had been deluged with proposals from her own world of the theater as well. Which was not at all surprising. The beauty of Olive Thomas is legendary. The girl had the loveliest violet-blue eyes I have ever seen. They were fringed with long dark lashes that seemed darker because of the delicate translucent pallor of her skin.

Mary's comment about Olive coming from an "alien world" was a direct reference to her theater roots—the exact same place that Mary and the rest of the Pickford family had started their own careers. Furthermore, Mary stated that their sister Lottie wasn't happy with Jack and Olive's marriage either. Not true. From the very beginning Lottie was most encouraging to the pair and she was inconsolable at news of Olive's death. An *Oakland Tribune* obituary for Olive stated:

A pretty close-up.

> While no word of the reported death of Olive Thomas had been received by her relatives here (Los Angeles), the Pickfords, sisters of Jack Pickford, husband of Miss Thomas, clung to the hope that reports of Miss Thomas' death were untrue.
> "It isn't true, is it?," sobbed Miss Lottie Pickford. "Oh, it can't be true. Just yesterday afternoon I received a cable from Jack saying that he was hoping for a change for the better."

As their marriage became public knowledge, the inevitable comparisons between Olive and Mary began to appear in the media. Mary Pickford was (and still is) known as "America's Sweetheart." Not surprisingly, Olive quickly became known as "Everybody's Sweetheart." Despite mixed critical reviews for her films, Olive was the new darling of the silver screen. She was so successful with the public that several publications dared to write that she was beginning to rival the success of her sister-in-law, Mary. This competitive media hype did nothing to smooth the waters between the two women. Careers aside, on a personal note, both women were competing for the love and attention (on a different level) of one man—Jack Pickford.

On another personal level, Mary was exceedingly jealous about Olive's close relationship with her new niece, Lottie's daughter (also named Mary). Little Mary Rupp (her father was George Rupp) affectionately referred to Olive as Aunt Tottle and Olive adored her. Longing for children of her own, Olive would lavish "Little Mary" with motherly attention.

In hindsight, Mary may have been right about her brother's new relationship. Jack and Ollie were both like-minded personalities. They drove too fast, partied too hard and drank too much, too often. They supported each other's weaknesses and before too long their co-dependent relationship would suddenly come to a crashing end.

Because Olive's work kept her on the West Coast and Jack worked on the East Coast (except for the spring of 1919 when they happily worked side by side at the Robert Brunton Studios in California), the newlyweds endured long separations and ached to be back in each other's arms. When they were together they partied hard, fought even harder and proceeded to make up with extravagant gifts in the form of diamonds and new cars. They both helped to destroy the cars and Olive would often lose the expensive jewels that Jack bestowed upon her.

A September 21, 1917 edition of *Variety* reported:

> Jack Pickford returning from a party at four A.M., September 9th, Los Angeles, in his machine, with Olive Thomas, Catherine Walker, Mr. and Mrs. William Gordon and Jack Dillon, crashed into a light truck, demolishing the truck and upsetting the Pickford car and its occupants. Pickford was taken to University police station. The driver of the truck suffered lacerations about the face and body, a fractured hand and concussion of the brain. The occupants of the Pickford car escaped with cuts, scratches and bruises.

Although the article doesn't say it, alcohol and/or drugs combined with fatigue were the most likely causes of these accidents. Pickford biographer, Scott Eyman, confirms this: "Jack was known to his contemporaries as a ladies man who was always loaded. His drinking problem was widely documented."

The *New York Telegraph* (June 30, 1918) reported that Olive was driving around town in a brand new canary yellow sixteen-valve roadster. She had purchased the car for Jack but grew tired of waiting for him to arrive from New York on a furlough and started driving it herself. On September 5, 1918, two months after that article was written, the *Los Angeles Herald* reported two additional accidents:

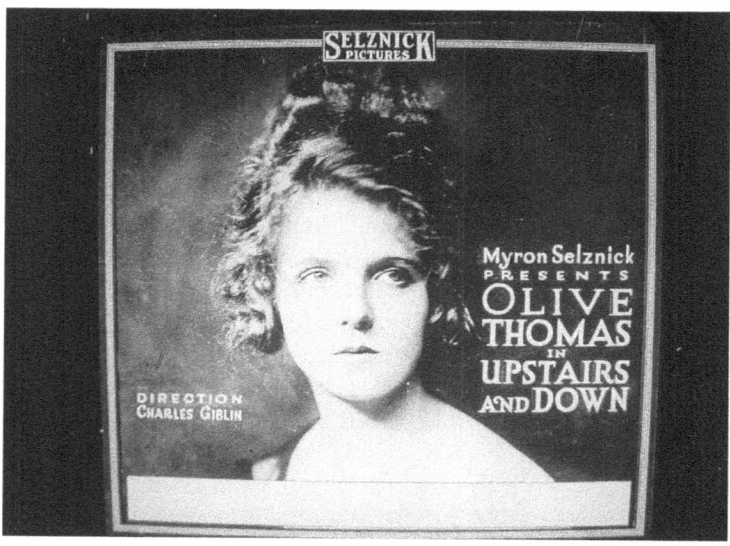

A promotional glass slide for *Upstairs and Down* (1919).

A jinx seems to hover over Olive Thomas, Triangle star, and her new automobiles. Just before leaving for her vacation in New York, her new roadster figured in a collision in which it came off second best, and, as her coupe was being overhauled, the dainty little screen favorite was forced to resort to the hard riding taxi. The other day, Miss Thomas and a friend were motoring to the home of Julian Eltinge for tea. Eltinge lives in a castle on top of one of the picturesque Hollywood hills and in making the steep climb the Triangle star lost control of her car, crashing into a stone wall. The machine is now in the "hospital," although Olive and her companion escaped injury.

Leaving her car woes behind her, Olive traveled to New York to vacation briefly with Jack. Arriving back in Los Angeles on August 6, she prepared herself for the live reading of an original piece ("My California") that she penned for a banquet given by Samuel Goldwyn, honoring Sid Grauman.

A little over six months after her last car accident, the March 21, 1919, *Variety* reported: "Olive Thomas' car struck a nine-year-old boy and seriously injured him. A week before the same auto driven by Jack Pickford also hit a boy."

A winsome portrait signed "Sincerely, Olive Thomas."

Several articles around the same time period speak of other less serious collisions the pair had in their automobiles. Hiring a chauffeur and bestowing alternate expressions of love on each other seemed like the sensible thing to do. It seems Jack's attempts at doing just that and adorning his wife with luxurious gems wasn't the answer either:

The New York Telegraph (January 3, 1920) even ran a story ("Olive Thomas Mourning Loss of $5,000 Bracelet") in the hope that it could recover Olive's Christmas gift from her husband:

> There is mourning in the house of Pickford-Thomas, the Pickford in the case being the ordinarily debonair Jack, and the Thomas being Olive Thomas, who, away from the screen, is Mrs. Jack, and neither of the parties will be comforted.
> That beautiful diamond and sapphire bracelet which Mrs. Jack so proudly displayed to her friends Christmas morning as a present from her spouse is gone, lost, strayed or stolen, and both declare they only wish it was a press agent loss.
> Instead of that, it is the real thing, and any one finding a little article of adornment, which cost $5,000 [approximately $45,000 today] in good cash, or giving information which may result in its recovery to the Val O'Farrel Detective Agency can draw down a very substantial reward for his or her services.
> Mr. and Mrs. Pickford attended the Sixty Club dinner and party at the Ritz-Carlton on New Year's Eve, and just naturally Mrs. Pickford wore the new present. She knows it was on her arm when she arrived; she believes it was in place after she had been there

for some time. After that all memory ceased, until, as the time came for her to go home, or when she was on her way home, she became conscious that it was gone.

She has not the remotest idea when it disappeared, and, therefore can only hope that somebody found it who will prefer the reward to the possession of an article which will be thoroughly described for all pawnshops, jewelers and policemen.

A July, 1920, issue of *Photoplay* reported even more extravagant spending when in honor of the pair working on the same coast they celebrated the rare occasion as only they could. Jack presented Olive with a new car and Olive spent a week's salary on a new dog for Jack. This lavish gift giving, for no special occasion in particular, was a pattern they kept up throughout their entire relationship.

A tinted fan postcard.

Despite the rare moments when Jack and Olive were working in the same part of the country, the lovebirds would soon be separated by something more distressing than their bi-coastal careers—World War I.

In early 1918, after the United States joined World War I, Canadian-born Jack faced a no-win ultimatum: Either volunteer to serve the United States, or be drafted into the Canadian military. Giving up a $2,500 per week (approximately $30,000 today) movie contract, Jack opted for the U.S. Navy.

Olive, once again left husbandless, continued to work (first for Triangle, then for the newly formed Selznick Pictures. A July 1918 issue of *Photoplay* reported just how difficult it was for her to keep her mind on the job at hand:

Olive Thomas complained the other day that she was simply all out of tears. Her director made the request that she shed a few saline drops over the prostrate form of William V. Mong and Olive sobbed and sniffled and thought of all the saddest things in the world, but nary a teardrop would come. "Most times," she said, "I can cry to order, but now I think I'm all cried out. First I was called East by my mother's illness (Spanish Influenza). I spent weeks with her at the hospital in Pittsburgh where she almost died and then Jack enlisted in the aviation corps and went to war, and I'm afraid that these bigger things have blotted up the tears that once I could give to the screen." Whereupon her director, hearing that remark about Jack, took her to one side and began talking to her about what might happen to Jack in the war zone. He was still bound to have those tears. But he failed, even though Olive did faint at the railway station when she bade Jack good-bye. "I'm not afraid. Whatever happens, Jack's doing the thing I would want him to do. And I can be brave, too," she said.

Olive needn't have worried herself. Jack was in no danger of getting killed or wounded. Once again trading on the famous Pickford name, he became involved in a scheme that allowed rich young men to pay bribes to avoid military service. He was also reportedly procuring young women (Hollywood starlets) for officers in order to

A provocative still from *Upstairs and Down* (1919).

avoid being assigned dangerous missions. For his involvement in the scheme, Jack came embarrassingly close to being dishonorably discharged but speculation has it that his sister, Mary, stepped in and "arranged" for him to give evidence to the authorities in exchange for a more respectful medical discharge (www.filmbug.com).

Jack Pickford made over one hundred films during his career, yet (despite his apparent Hollywood success) his lavish lifestyle, frivolous spending habits and addictive personality often had him running to his big sister for handouts and Mary bailed him out each and every time.

On the flip side to her husband's less than honorable stint in the service, Olive's youngest brother, William, loyally served in the U.S. Marines. He enlisted the day after the United States declared war against Germany and served in France with the men that held back the Huns in their rush toward Paris. After safely returning home and landing in New York, William was looking forward to catching up with his sister but upon arriving at her hotel he was told that she had been rushed to hospital with a chronic case of influenza-pneumonia. In a wild panic he hurried to her side. "I wanted to see you alive!" he said. "I knew they could never get you into hospital unless you were near dead!" (*Motion Picture*, June 1919).

It was an eerily prophetic statement to make. A little over a year into the future, Olive would be rushed to hospital again and this time the outcome would indeed be fatal.

Sue Roberts of *Motion Picture Classic* (April, 1919) interviewed Olive about her bout with the flu and found her to be a most frustrated patient:

> "I certainly do have the worst luck," Olive announced. "Here I come to New York on a two-week vacation, to get clothes and do the theaters before starting our new picture and, lo and behold! I have to get the flu. They trundled me off to a hospital, and there I spent my vacation being told if I didn't do this and didn't do that, they wouldn't be responsible and I'd probably get worse and maybe die.
>
> No theaters, no shops, nothing. Jack is out on the coast taking pictures, you know, and he wired frantically every day. I spent my Christmas in bed. Jack sent me a diamond necklace by a friend of his who had been in the navy. He showed it to me the day before Christmas, but we were afraid to leave it around, so he offered to put it in his safe-deposit box. Came Christmas, and I wanted my necklace, at least to look at. No way of getting it—wouldn't you know?—We had forgotten that he couldn't get it out on Christmas day. No theater, no necklace, nothing. Just bed and ice bags.
>
> "But, I fooled everybody New Year's. All the boys and girls had sent me flowers—pityingly, don't you know. But I made up my mind I was going out if it killed me. When I walked into the club, you'd have thought I was a ghost. Everyone was surprised. They greeted me with, 'Why Olive Duffy!' My real name was Duffy, you know.
>
> "For the last two days I have been staying with a friend of mine, and I can't see how she puts up with me. I have turned her apartment into a regular office. There have been insurance agents examining me for $300,000 worth of insurance to protect the company (Selznick Pictures) in case I should expire before my contract ran out; there were photographers, shoemakers, dressmakers, fitters, and people running in with this paper and that for me to sign. You see, the doctors didn't want me to go out. Today's the first day I've left the house for any length of time, and tonight I have to catch the train to Pittsburgh to visit my mother and then hurry to the coast and work."

Back then, contracting the flu was a serious, often life-threatening medical condition. Pneumonia quickly set in and many people died as a result. Olive was not being dramatic about the worse case scenario if she failed to obey doctor's orders. The deadly Spanish Influenza that almost claimed Olive's mother's life (she was hospitalized from March–May) had now swept the world. It was so serious, the National Association of the Motion Picture Industry went on a four-week hiatus during the 1919 pandemic, unanimously voting to forego the release of any new films until November 9; the deadly "flu" had already shut down over fifty percent of the nation's theaters. The Association asked that all actors and actresses give up their salary payments during this period. With an estimated 50 million deaths worldwide, Spanish Influenza (between 1918-19) claimed more lives than WWI. It has been cited as the most devastating pandemic in world history. More people

A rare lobby card for *Upstairs and Down* (1919).

died of the "flu" in a single year than in four years of the Black Death Bubonic Plague (1347–51). Those who survived were lucky (recovery took many months); those who died succumbed within hours. Nearly half of those who died were young adults.

In 1918, children would skip rope to the rhyme (Crawford):

> I had a little bird
> Its name was Enza
> I opened the window
> And in-flu-enza.

In May of 1919, one of the most influential show biz reporters of the day, Louella Parsons, interviewed Olive, who had just been released from the hospital due to her own bout with the flu. Olive was her usual exuberant self and her down-to-earth demeanor and happy-go-lucky nature impressed Parsons. Louella said:

> Olive Thomas came into town a few weeks ago with the Selznick Company. She has since I last saw her become the first Myron Selznick star and created for the screen the baby vamp role in *Upstairs and Down*. Broadway has been blazing with electric signs with her name, magazines have been filled with her pictures and the papers have told all about Jack Pickford's wife who, refusing to bank on the Pickford name, went out for herself and signed a contract in its weekly demands, only a motion picture story could bring to pass.
>
> And Olive Thomas might still be a little girl dancing on the Amsterdam roof in "Ziegfeld's Follies" every night for all the differences this contract makes to her. In the beginning I had to put her disposition to the acid test and she met the situation so splendidly. One broken engagement and another one an hour later, which I expected would bring an icicle reception, had no more effect on Miss Thomas than to say to my apologies:
>
> "Oh, that's all right; I am often later. I know you were busy."
>
> Later I commented on this and on how much I liked her way of being natural, without temperamental camouflage so many actresses feel a necessity.
>
> "I am only a little Irish girl," she said. "Why should I pretend to the world I am something wonderful—when everyone knows who I am and what I am?"
>
> The Pickfords have taken Olive Thomas to their hearts for just that quality. They are themselves wholesome real people, who dislike pretense of any sort. I remember Mrs. Pickford—Mother, as Olive calls her—talked at some length on the new daughter-in-law and gave me to understand she couldn't have done a better job if she had picked a wife for Jack herself. And they are in love with these two young people. The very first thing Olive told me was that she had talked to Jack the night before in Los Angeles and he would be in New York in about two weeks.
>
> "We have leased the Hitchcock place in Great Neck—the Raymond Hitchcock house for the summer, and Jack is coming on to make pictures here so we can be together. There is a tea garden, and a private bathing beach and we are going to have just lots of parties there this summer!"
>
> Jack and Olive slipped over into New Jersey and were married without any family. Thomas Meighan who acted as a chaperone and stood sponsor for the two youngsters was immediately dubbed "our illegitimate father" by Olive, who said she loves him for having helped her marry Jack.
>
> "One of these days," Olive told me, looking at me out of her big blue eyes, "we are going to have a family. I love children. You know I have a little sister five years old, the most beautiful child you ever saw. I have teased mother to give her to us, but of course she won't. Little Harriet is my half-sister, but I love her to death. Little Mary Rupp, Lottie Pickford's child, too, is a darling, unspoiled despite all the affection and gifts lavished on her by the whole family. She and I had some pictures taken together—she calls

me Aunt Tottle," explained Aunt Tottle, showing me with pride a photograph of herself and little Mary.

While Olive Thomas' screen beauty is one of the things which has helped her win stardom, she isn't half as lovely in pictures as she is off the screen. She has light brown hair, with a golden glint. It reaches to her shoulder and falls in soft waves; then her eyes are the blue black eyes which only an Irish heritage can give. She wore a pink negligee, all soft crepe and lace, which brought out the pink in her cheeks. A saucy little dimple in her chin completed a picture Howard Chandler Christy or James Montgomery Flagg might have been glad to have sketched for a magazine cover.

Usually when Dame Fortune comes a smiling and pours into the laps of one of her children everything which wealth can give, she creates dissatisfaction and horrid discontent. In the case of Olive Thomas, she has managed to avoid this error. Olive Thomas is as pleased over her blessings as a child. She makes no secret of her happiness, and her enthusiasm over the good things which have come her way.

"Mrs. Selznick gave me a gorgeous hat," she said, "with two paradise plumes on a lovely blue, so smart and good looking."

And then we talked of clothes, and of all the pretty things young Mrs. Pickford has purchased for her summer wardrobe, such adorable blue frocks, the color of her eyes, and such dainty white and lavender dresses to wear when the hot days come. While we were chatting, Blanche, who does Miss Thomas' nails and keeps her hair in good condition, came in to give a manicure. She had no more than started when a telephone call took her client into the next room. Thereupon Blanche, who is colored, launched into a description of Miss Thomas, her virtues, her beauty and why she would rather manicure and shampoo her than any other customer.

A bizarre publicity photograph of Olive riding an ostrich!

"She's so popular, too," said Blanche. "You ought to have been here Easter. This here room was a blooming garden. She had lilies, roses, orchids and that plant of azaleas was in bloom then—everybody likes her...."

Blanche would have probably been talking yet if the door hadn't opened and a young man burst in calling loudly for Olive. At that particular moment Olive emerged from the inner room and astonished me to the point of speechlessness by throwing herself in the youth's arms, kissing him and calling him darling.

"My brother," she said, "destined to be the world's greatest cameraman. He has been in the Marines and is out now and I am having him learn the motion picture business."

Miss Thomas has brought her chauffeur and a new Locomobile all the way from California. Just now she is sticking to the California license. That is, until the chauffeur learns New York, she said. It may be cheaper if he gets in any difficulties.

"Has he ever been in any difficulty?" I asked.

"Well, once," she said. "I bought Jack a Stutz for a present—a surprise. I asked the chauffeur to have it all ready for my husband and he promised. I was leaving town. He had it ready all right. He took some girls out and smashed the car into bits."

"Did you discharge him?" I asked.

"Oh, I couldn't do that. You see, he was sorry and the car was insured."

Which is like Olive Thomas, who is the most human young person it has been my pleasure to meet in many a day, and I forgot to say Miss Thomas is just out of the hospital where she went to get rid of an attack of the flu. She explained she was still a little wobbly and she thought she might die she felt so sick during the first days of the flu.

Brother and I watched Blanche manicure Miss Olive, and then I found I had stayed so long. I would have to hurry if I hoped to get my department written by night. That's the difficulty of conducting a column; it's always intruding when you are having a nice time.

And I do like chatting with this little star who calls herself "just a little Irish girl" and instead of ranting over a picture of herself which came out very badly, she smiles and says:

"Here you have the only cross-eyed motion picture star in the world. I told Mr. Selznick I dared him to advertise me that way" [*New York Telegraph*, Louella Parsons, May 11, 1919].

Olive fully recovered from her bout of influenza-pneumonia and enjoyed a long-awaited reunion with her brother, William. Always one to take care of her family, Olive promised to send him $1000 (approximately $12,000 today) when he got back to Pittsburgh so he could start his own business. It was sent via a bank transfer but there was an unexpected delay in transmission, which naturally caused him great concern. He wrote Olive a letter asking her to trace the funds, saying, "I'd hate to lose all that money!"

That incident in connection with her brother caused her to recall a fan letter she received soon after Jack entered the service. The newspapers had reported that Olive was going to New York to see her husband, and the letter came from a fan living in a little country town. Enclosed was $5 (approximately $60 today) sent, as the writer explained, "Because I know you must be under very heavy expenses, with so much traveling and your husband in the service, and I don't think it right that you should have to spend all the money you so laboriously earn."

"I appreciated that," Olive said, earnestly, "It reminded me of the time when $5 looked mighty big to me" (*Motion Picture*, June 1919).

There is nothing "upstage" about Olive Thomas, said an article in *Motion Picture*, June, 1919. "She'll kid backward and forward with all comers. She delights in startling people and especially shocking the dignified ones. Excess of dignity is as provocative to her as a red flag to the bull, and she loves to take its possessors down all the pegs she can. Underneath all the kidding, no matter what she might say, there is a bubbling humanity, a freedom from sarcasm that wins her way into the hearts of all."

A different view of Olive's personality came from Billy Bitzer, D.W. Griffith's cameraman who described his one fiery encounter with her in his 1973 autobiography, *Billy Bitzer: His Story*:

"Say, Billy," [Harry] Aitken suggested, "how'd you like to direct a flier for a change, until D.W. gets started again? He might be away a long time. I'll pay you one grand a week, with a bonus if you finish in less than the three weeks the schedule calls for."

The picture was to feature Olive Thomas, a Ziegfeld Follies girl, who later became the first wife of Mary Pickford's spoiled brother, Jack.... I took several test shots of Miss

Thomas to ascertain her photographic propensities. She had beauty, but she was a type new to me—arrogant, brassy, and curt to the point of being rude....

Even before Griffith warned me that Miss Thomas could not act, I was skeptical of her ability. From the very first rehearsal, she showed a lack of seriousness and any semblance of concentration....

Miss Thomas and I had to go to the costumers in Los Angeles and on the way we passed the Alexandria Hotel. She suddenly decided to stop and refresh herself with a champagne cocktail. I objected. She ordered the car stopped and made off without me. I followed, however, joined her at the bar, and had one cocktail. (She was well ahead of me.) Then I asked her to leave.

"Another drink wouldn't be bad, Billy," she replied.

"Listen, if you don't do as I say and come along, there'll be no picture. Either you come or we're through."

She knew I meant it. Her friend Miss Cassidy joined us at this point. "Don't let that big slob tell you what you can or can't do. Order your drink."

Turning to me, Miss Thomas said, "Go soak your head!"

With that said, it's hard to comprehend Olive getting desperate enough, about anything, to end it all with a deliberate suicide. She'd worked too hard. She was at the height of her film career. More importantly, she'd made it to the top *without* the help of the Pickford name. With or without Jack, she was still Olive Thomas—movie star.

By mid-1920, those closest to the couple were convinced a divorce announcement was imminent; instead the pair did the exact opposite and sailed to Paris, France on an impromptu second honeymoon. The photo (Olive's last) of a smiling, seemingly "in love" young couple ready to take a well-earned break from their busy careers was published in newspapers and magazines across the country. Was it one last attempt to save the marriage, maybe?

Without question, their relationship was a tumultuous one. Work and war had separated them for long periods of time, they constantly accused each other of infidelities and when they were together they fought about anything and everything. In the brief moments of peace they partied hard, supported each other's wild ways and spent money like it was water. Sailing to France and spending *that* much time together was the closest they'd ever come to being a real married couple. One way or another, disaster was in the cards.

Had Olive made the decision to leave Jack, she would surely have done it via divorce, just as she did with Bernard Krug Thomas years earlier. Leaving Jack in death meant leaving her family, leaving her career, leaving the world forever. Losing Jack was one thing, but losing everything, losing her life, *because* of Jack just doesn't add up.

Jack and Olive spent the Christmas of 1919 together in New York. They seemed happy. It was one of the rare moments of togetherness that they both looked forward to, and Christmas time was the perfect excuse for buying even more presents for each other.

"I call Jack my long distance lover," she told *Motion Picture Classic* in an interview given in December of 1919 (published March 20, 1920). She enthusiastically spoke of moving into (and decorating) their new apartment and awaiting the arrival of Jack for the festive season. The article continues with the reporter stating:

> The apartment, she told me, was to be well on its way to completion before the arrival of the "long distance lover" for Christmas. It was going to be, she said, with

anticipation, the best Christmas they have ever had. Their first was spent in Pittsburgh in the hospital with Olive's mother, who was very ill. Last Christmas Olive was here in the East in the hospital herself, with influenza and quite alone, and so this third Christmas must do a great deal of atoning.

All told, the young Jack Pickfords were going to make a high and festive occasion at Yuletide. That very morning Olive had been buying Jack's gift, consisting of a set of black pearls for evening wear, at Tiffany's, and there was also a resplendent lounging robe of sumptuous silk, and then it was only the first part of December.... Olive laughingly remarked that her mother says she and Jack spend all their salaries giving one another presents.

"He's always sending me something and then I send him something back," Olive said. "You see, we have to bridge the distance in some way. At first I just couldn't get used to the idea of living this way, but I suppose one gets used to anything, given time. When we were together we used to use up the time fighting over things. I'd say, 'You were out with this person or that person,' and he'd come back at me in the same way, and we'd have a lively time of it, but we're over that now. We know that we can't sit home by the fireside *all* the time just because we cannot be together."

The reporter concludes the article with:

As I was leaving, Olive showed me through the whole of the apartment and told me, with the pretty pride of possession, of what she was doing, intended to do, with every nook and corner. One feature of her boudoir is to be an antique desk, lined—she is having it relined with purple leather, and before which she will sit to write, Turk-wise, upon a mammoth cushion. All about there were pictures, framed in heavy silver, which "Jack gave me," of Jack himself, of Olive and various other screen luminaries. I came away with the impression of a child playing, very successfully, at being grown up, and having a thoroughly good time in the playing.

Life appeared to be going well for the pair. Despite Jack's "hush-hush" dishonorable discharge from the military, his career was starting to pick up again (thanks to a studio cover-up, the scandal received little media attention) and Olive was at the top of her game too. Professionally, they were one of Hollywood's power couples and Olive was now the star at the newly formed Selznick Pictures, a company formed especially for her. Personally, they continued to at least try to make their complicated long-distance relationship work. Christmas of 1919 was a happy one. Sadly, it would be their last Christmas together. Little did they (and the world) know that fate would soon step in and change everything ... forever.

A discovery on July 7, 2007, answered the longstanding question, Were Olive and Jack married at all? The Bride and Groom Index *(NYC) lists Oliveretta Duffy and John Charles Smith, married in Manhattan, January 8, 1918. The certificate number is 2075. Credit: Bill Cappello.*

✯ *Chapter 4* ✯

SELZNICK PICTURES

Selznick Pictures had arrived and Olive Thomas had helped them get there.
—Daniel Selznick, son of David O. Selznick

Many admirers have tried to describe the wonderful, radiant eyes of Olive Thomas. "Celtic blue rubbed in with a smudgy finger," was one picturesque way of putting it, while another enthusiast says they are, "round and innocent, and glistening, sparkling with a spirit similar to that which must have lighted the eyes of Columbus when he discovered America." The proud possessor of these much-discussed eyes is quite the little girl, not more than five feet four, with an abundance of hair which sometimes appears to be light brown and at others a luxurious gold.

That *Picture Show* article (August 2, 1919) attempted to verbally express Olive's innate beauty to its readers.

Aside from her obvious acting talent, it was undoubtedly Olive's striking good looks that helped make her a movie star. She had the complete package—the so-called "It" factor—and Selznick Pictures knew it. By 1919, Olive had become *the* star of Selznick Pictures. It's been long reported that Myron Selznick managed to convince his influential producer-father Lewis (known as L.J.) to give him $25,000 (approximately $350,000 today) for his own production company. But a Louella Parsons article in *The Morning Telegraph* (Saturday, November 30, 1918) suggests that his father had no idea that his son had caught the producing bug and goes on to say that his mother produced the cash to start the company. It reads:

Welcome to our midst—the Selznick Pictures Corporation, Myron Selznick, president and owner. This new company was formed yesterday, as an independent concern, to produce pictures. It came as a surprise to Lewis J. Selznick, who had no idea his young son had any producing bee in his youthful bonnet.

With the influenza playing havoc in the picture business and Myron Selznick setting out to prove to "dad" he can make pictures, Lewis J. Selznick thinks he has enough worry for one man.

Where did Myron get his wherewithal? Ah! That's another story. He stands pretty well with his mother, and there are those who say Mrs. Selznick produced the cash. L.J. is trying to pretend he is going to disinherit the boy, but he is so proud of him he cannot down the smile which will come when he talks about Myron's new company.

Eventually it will probably be father against son—Select versus Selznick—for Myron says he is going to prove he can make pictures, and good ones. There are some things he could have told Select, but since they refused his advice, he is out to make a million for himself.

Mr. Selznick Jr. will produce in East and will have two stars in his company. Their names and the name of the studio are not yet ready for publication. There is no reason why young Selznick won't succeed. He has had experience in the picture business and has ideas of his own.

As it happened, Olive's Triangle Pictures contract was up for renewal and Myron traveled to California to convince the already established star that she should sign with him. Section 7 of Olive's contract confirms the suspicions that it was Mrs. Selznick who helped her son form the company. It reads:

(7) Contract between Olive Thomas and Florence A. Selznick dated December 14, 1918, assigned to Selznick Pictures Corporation. Employment contract for a period of two years beginning January 13, 1919. The producer agrees to pay the artist for her services $1,000.00 per week during the first year and $1,250.00 per week during the second year. Producer has option of renewal of contract for a year commencing January 16, 1921, upon the same terms and conditions excepting that her salary during the last additional year shall be $2,250.00 per week, notice to be given in writing of the renewal on or before July 1, 1920.

Forming Selznick Pictures Corporation was Myron's way of celebrating his twenty-first birthday as well as getting back at the men he felt had betrayed his father. The senior Selznick had lost a power struggle with Adolph Zukor and been forced out of Select Pictures the year before. Myron had apprenticed with his father and then served as the studio manager for Norma Talmadge; he already had Olive Thomas and several other stars under exclusive contracts and was determined to put the name of Selznick back in lights. (Cari Beauchamp, *Without Lying Down: Frances Marion and the Powerful Women of Early Hollywood.*)

A 1920 edition of *Who's Who on the Screen* gives a brief account of Selznick Pictures and what the public should expect from the expanding company in the future:

Of all the outstanding successes in the motion picture industry none can point with greater pride to their achievements than the Selznick Enterprises, of which the astute executive, Lewis J. Selznick, is President. The Selznick history reads

Myron Selznick signed Olive to an exclusive contract for the newly formed Selznick Pictures.

like a tale from some modern Arabian Nights. Never, in all the remarkable history of the silent drama, has any single producing and distributing enterprise offered so comprehensive a program as the Selznick forces announce for the future.

The plans of the Selznick organization cover the production and distributing of film plays and features, ranging from super-spectacular specials, based on books and plays of known quality, by prominent authors and playwrights, to beautiful scenics, for which the world will be scoured for locations, and dare-devil serials, enacted not merely by stunt performers, but by stars of distinction. The total number of subjects to be offered the public through the vastness of the Selznick operations will be five hundred and thirty-seven, a figure never before approached by any one producing or releasing organization in the history of the industry.

The scope of the Selznick forces is so wide that there are at all times no less than twelve producing units at work in the various studios controlled by the makers of the pictures that "Create Happy Hours."

Their newest enterprise is the building of an immense studio in Long Island City (New York). Every modern device that will make for better and greater film productions will be incorporated in this new Selznick plant, and it will be at once the largest and most thoroughly equipped plant for the making of the motion pictures under one roof, in the world.

Always a leader in the field of motion pictures, the Selznick Enterprises has made every effort to make their organization truly representative of the best. With this thought in mind, they have secured for its stars such popular players as Olive Thomas, Elaine Hammerstein, Eugene O'Brien, Owen Moore, William Faversham, Louise Huff and Zeena Keefe, who is announced as the Selznick star for 1920.

Myron Selznick—though probably the youngest executive in the Motion Picture business—is recognized by all concerned as one of the most thorough and efficient men connected with the industry. Being in absolute charge of the purchasing of all stories and supervising productions for all the Selznick stars, young Mr. Selznick is indeed a busy executive.

When the wonderful new Selznick studio building is formally opened in Long Island City [the Selznick Pictures offices were located in the Astor Trust Building, Room 1503, 501 Fifth Avenue, NY, NY] Myron Selznick will assume command and Studio Managers, Casting, Directors, and Film Editors will work under the youthful executive's wing. He is still in his early twenties and from all indications will become one of the great leaders of the fourth industry in the United States.

In the same publication, a bio on Olive describes her as being five foot three (most accounts document her to have been five foot four), one hundred eighteen pounds, with brown hair and blue eyes. "Expert on a horse and as a golfer, she plays tennis and swims with equal effectiveness."

Olive's Selznick Pictures contract stipulated that she was to make a staggering eight films per year, with a new film being released to theaters every six weeks. The Brunton Studios in Los Angeles, California were used for shooting Olive's films on the West Coast.

In David Thomson's book, *Showman*, Myron's brother David O. Selznick elaborated on the arrangement between Olive and Selznick Pictures. "[Olive] was so intrigued with the kid producer that she told Myron that when she had received the highest offer she could get from the other companies, she would sign a contract with him for exactly half—which is exactly what she did."

In the Milestone documentary, *Olive Thomas: Everybody's Sweetheart*, Daniel Selznick, son of David O. Selznick, spoke about his uncle Myron's plan to convince his father Lewis to form an exclusive production company in order to make Olive Thomas productions. "If we're to believe the legends, other companies were offering her twice as much, but she told Myron she'd sign with Selznick Pictures for half the amount, reportedly $1,000 a week [the equivalent of approximately $10,000 today] to be increased to $1,250 a week in the second year [the equivalent of approx. $12,500 today]. I don't know what that was all about."

The truth is, Olive was getting desperate. Her studio, the Triangle Motion Picture Company, was founded in the summer of 1915, and envisioned as a prestige studio based on the producing abilities of filmmakers D.W. Griffith, Thomas Ince and Mack Sennett. It was founded by Harry and Roy Aitken, two brothers from the Wisconsin farmlands who pioneered the studio system of Hollywood's Golden Age. Combining production, distribution, and theater operations under their Triangle Film Corporation, the young upstarts created the most dynamic studio in Hollywood. They attracted the greatest directors and stars of the day, including Mary Pickford, Lillian Gish, Roscoe "Fatty" Arbuckle and Douglas Fairbanks Senior, and produced some of the most enduring films of the silent era, from the Keystone Cops to the defining cinematic epic *The Birth of a Nation* (1915). Eventually the studio suffered from bloat, and in 1917 lost all three of its principal producers. Triangle gradually dwindled, and was swallowed by the emerging Hollywood studios.

A Selznick Pictures ad promoting their new acquisition, Olive Thomas.

By late 1918, it was all but finished. Triangle was facing liquidation and Olive was facing the insecurity of not being connected to a studio at all. Her fellow Triangle star, Alma Rubens, had left the failing company and had signed with William Randolph Hearst's Cosmopolitan Pictures.

A Broadway show starring Olive had lost its backing and several film offers had fallen through. The Selznicks appeared to have come along at the right time. Olive needed the security of a contract and being the exclusive star at Selznick Pictures, even at a monetary loss, was the best offer on the table.

On December 14, 1918, Selznick Pictures had signed Olive Thomas as their exclusive star. Myron was president, his brother Howard was his assistant, his other brother David was secretary and L.J. was treasurer. Some publications around the time the company was formed also list Mrs. Selznick as treasurer and claim that L. J. had no business interest in the company at all.

A *Moving Picture World* article entitled "Selznick Pictures a Family Affair" (March 15, 1919) read in part:

> Lewis J. Selznick, accompanied by Mrs. Selznick and their son David, arrived in the city February 24. Mrs. Selznick and her son went on to Los Angeles for a stay of six months to join Myron and Howard Selznick, who are now engaged in making pictures, in which Olive Thomas is the star. Their organization is known as the Selznick Pictures Corporation, Myron Selznick being president and Howard his assistant. Mrs. Selznick, who is backing the enterprise, which is strictly a family concern, is treasurer of the company, and David, who will join his brothers in the production of pictures, is secretary.
>
> The organization is now contracting for electric signs in all the leading cities of the country, for the purpose of advertising Olive Thomas. Four of these signs have already been secured in New York, one in Buffalo (facing Lafayette Square), one in Pittsburgh and one in Chicago, all being stationed at points prominently located on busy thoroughfares....

Olive on the cover of the June 1919 issue of *Photoplay* magazine.

No expense was spared when it came to promoting Olive. Aside from the electric signs, one of which was the largest theatrical sign in the world, a national advertising campaign was in full swing via the fan magazines. Advertisements in two of the most prominent movie-related magazines of the day were printed to coincide with the electric signs in Times Square, New York. In addition to that, the usual publicity campaign consisting of news items and special articles and interviews were being arranged in the lead-up to the release of *Upstairs and Down*. If the public hadn't heard the name "Olive Thomas" before she got to Selznick, they certainly did now. She was everywhere!

In one interview, "Beautiful Olive Thomas Talks about Vamping and Also of the Baby Vampire," Olive speaks to E.V. Durling about her days with Ziegfeld as well as her new role in *Upstairs and Down*. It read:

> Once I knew a man who had a friend who shook the hand of a man who knew Olive Thomas

personally. There was a time in New York when to know Olive Thomas personally gave a man a better standing than to be seen at lunch with J. Pierpont Morgan. Bankers, brokers, senators, congressmen and even mayors fought for the honor of a smile from the Queen of the Midnight Frolic, and a reporter for "Who's Who," in New York, could have compiled his data for a new edition without ever stirring off the roof of the Amsterdam theatre. Broadway will never forgive the motion pictures for permanently luring Olive Thomas to a little Grey Home in the West. Beauties come and go, Ziegfeld sends to the four corners of the world to bring them to his exacting patrons at the Frolic and the Follies, but no matter what the degree of their pulchritude is or how sensational their debut, the professional Broadwayite will say, "Yes, yes, I know, you should have seen Olive Thomas."

I met Olive the other day. She is Irish, and interesting. She has beauty, brains, and a sense of humor. No wonder she captured Broadway. No more is necessary to conquer the world. Consider her views on the tired businessman.

"The tired businessman insofar as the Follies are concerned," says

Another full page ad for Selznick Pictures, promoting Olive as "The Most Beautiful Girl in the World."

Olive, "is a myth, a snare and a delusion. I should say the Follies and its people are supported by the retired businessmen. The men who patronize the Follies and entertain the feminine portion of the organization probably visit their offices for about one hour each day. Sometimes they drop in about once a month. The real tired businessman, the young fellows who are chained to the desk from nine to five, cannot afford the Follies, and they seek their recreation in the movies.

"I feel now that in the moving pictures I am really reaching the well known tired businessman, and reaching him all over the world. The moving pictures are a benefit to him. Of course, he has the same feeling, he would like to meet the girls after the show, but that is impossible, therefore he sits down and writes a letter. This is quickly done and by twelve o'clock at the latest he is in bed, gets a good night's sleep and is ready for work in the morning. Then as these boys rarely actually meet the girls of the films they have no disillusionments. I know I could never live up to what some of them think I am. But not knowing me, and thinking as they do, I really am in a way an inspiration to them. And the young tired businessman needs nothing more than inspiration. What the retired businessman needs is a little sense in his old age, and something useful to occupy his spare time.

"The greatest competitor the Follies has just now is golf. The patrons of the Follies who have taken this up are so tired by curtain time that they go to bed instead of going down to Mr. Ziegfeld's place."

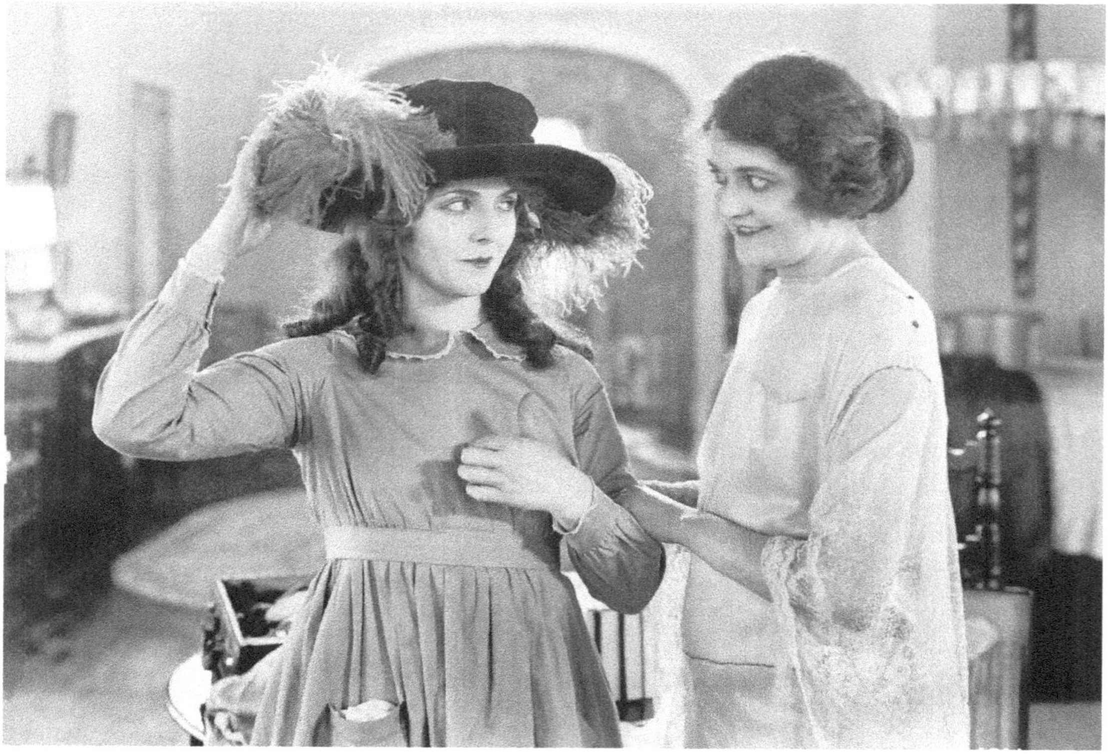

Just now Olive is playing a baby vampire (a sexually aggressive female) in the motion picture version of the stage play *Upstairs and Down*. Her views on vampires are also worth considering.

"The baby vampire," says Olive, "is a greater menace to the world just now than the Bolsheviki. Many a man who would think nothing of throwing a Bolsheviki out of his office, even if it were twenty stories high, would hesitate before being as much as impolite to an apparently sweet young thing. And everybody knows what happens to the man who hesitates.

"In the well-known and late war," continued Olive, "most of the women spies captured were of the ingénue type with the baby stare, and not the tall, tiger skin variety of magazine and screen fiction. When a man reaches the age of sixty, as most of the men who were big factors in the war have, he is very susceptible to youth, particularly feminine youth. Many a statesman on both sides undertook to offer protection to some sweet young thing only to find a little later she had the papers, plans and everything. One baby vampire actually 'vamped' the officer in charge of the firing squad into letting her escape.

An autographed promotional photograph for Selznick Pictures.

"It is a peculiar thing that while the old-fashioned vampires were all brunettes, the baby vampire is invariably blonde, and most of them have blue eyes. There should be a law against them, or at least a boycott. I ask you, with baby vampires allowed full rein, is any husband safe?"

Just now, Olive is being starred in a series of eight pictures with Myron Selznick, son of his famous father, Lewis J. Selznick. The first production will be *Upstairs and Down*, and the second, *The Spite Bride*, a story by Louise Winter. Cosmo Hamilton, author of *Scandal*, has been selected to write three original stories for Miss Thomas. Therefore, it seems, according to present arrangements, that Olive is lost to Broadway, and the Midnight Frolic for a long, long time.

Olive's personal relationships with her mentors, namely Florenz Ziegfeld and artist, Harrison Fisher, was no secret. The film industry was well known for its casting couch and it's not too far-fetched to believe that Myron, David and perhaps L.J. were all possibly intimate with their star player at some time. Myron seems to be the obvious

Opposite, top: **Olive and Rosemary Theby in *Upstairs and Down* (1919).** *Opposite, bottom:* **A scarce original lobby card promoting *Upstairs and Down*.**

A studio handout promoting Olive Thomas.

and most likely choice out of the three men; after all he "handpicked" Olive to be his first star at his new company and most of his telegrams were signed lovingly; not businesslike at all. David was most certainly infatuated with Olive but it isn't clear if their relationship went any further than that. L.J. it seems was more of a father figure to Olive. In one telegram to Myron she refers to him as "Daddy." A couple of the other Selznick Pictures house telegrams to Olive were signed "love" and "all my love, Myron."

Several letters and telegrams in the Selznick files at the Harry Ransom Center at the University of Texas prove that Olive was regularly advanced thousands of dollars at a time, sometimes in advance of her paycheck, yet at other times there were checks wired to her bank account at the Harriman National Bank and delivered personally to her at the studio. Close to $10,000 (approximately $100,000 today) was advanced to Olive in the few months prior to her departure abroad. Without a doubt, it was money the Selznicks were *not* contractually obligated to give her. Despite her hefty salary with bonus money thrown in, Olive was still having severe financial problems and her bank account was often overdrawn. An April 17, 1920, letter from Selznick Pictures, to Olive, read:

> Dear Miss Thomas:
>
> We have been notified by the Harriman National Bank that your account has been overdrawn, so we have had an additional check of $1,000 placed to the credit of your account.
>
> We are also going to send you a check for $250. This will pay you in full on account of salary up to and inclusive of May First.

A house telegram dated April 30, 1920, from Myron to Olive, read:

> CHECKS DEPOSITED FOR SALARY TO WEEK ENDING MAY EIGHTH. WIRE WHETHER YOU WANT ME TO DEPOSIT ANY MORE MONEY. LOVE MYRON.

Another Selznick Pictures house telegram dated May 13, 1920, read:

> GLAD YOU LIKE STORY WRITTEN FOR YOU BY LYNCH. HAVE NOT HEARD FROM YOU FOR SOME TIME. HAVE YOU FORGOTTEN ME OLLIE. MYRON.

The next Selznick Pictures house telegram dated May 23, 1920, read:

> ALL ARRANGEMENTS HAVE BEEN MADE TO DO YOUR NEXT PICTURE ON COAST STOP TO DO IT IN NEW YORK WOULD UPSET PRODUCTION SCHEDULE AND WILL CROWD ME FOR STUDIO SPACE AS BIOGRAPH LEASE EXPIRES NEXT

WEEK AND I DO NOT TAKE POSSESSION OF PARAGON FOR ANOTHER MONTH STOP AWFULLY SORRY OLLIE BUT IT WILL BE IMPOSSIBLE TO DO IT HERE. MYRON.

The telegram's reference to "Paragon" is the New Jersey Studio that Selznick Pictures would eventually take possession of. Jules Brulatour built the last of the great Fort Lee studios, the Paragon, just south of Universal in 1915. Maurice Tourneur was a partner in the Paragon, and it was here that he made *A Girl's Folly, Poor Little Rich Girl,* and *The Blue Bird.* Later it became the New Jersey headquarters of Famous Players–Lasky, and eventually of Selznick Pictures. In fact, the Selznicks would be the last traditional studio operation in Fort Lee. After a series of political, economic, and even environmental pressures forced out most other producers in 1918, only Selznick remained and prospered. By the early 1920s he controlled two-thirds of the studio space in Fort Lee, as well as the Biograph stages across the river in the Bronx. Unfortunately, Selznick himself was out of business by 1923, and the last silent films shot in the borough were independent productions featuring stars like Richard Barthelmess and Barbara La Marr.

The sheet music dedicated to Olive Thomas for the film *Upstairs and Down*.

Another Selznick Pictures house telegram skips forward to June 1, 1920, and communication from Olive now seems to have ceased. The telegram reads:

HAVE NOT HEARD FROM YOU ALMOST TWO WEEKS. IS ANYTHING WRONG OLLIE. LOVE MYRON.

The last Selznick Pictures house telegram, dated June 18, 1920, reads:

FORGOT TO LEAVE WORD AT OFFICE TO GIVE YOU FLAPPER PRINT. WIRE ME AFTER VIEWING WHETHER OR NOT YOU LIKED IT STOP HAVING LOT OF TROUBLE AT STUDIO WITH DIRECTORS LABOR UNION ETC. A LITTLE ENCORAGEMENT WOULD HELP. DON'T WIRE ME IF YOU DO NOT LIKE PICTURE. ALL MY LOVE MYRON.

There is no wire in response to this telegram from Olive. Does this suggest she did not like *The Flapper* and as per Myron's instructions she did not wire? The last memo dated August 16, 1920 (four days after Olive and Jack left for Paris), and signed by the Chief Financial Officer of Selznick Pictures is an absolute bombshell! It reads:

A tinted lobby card for one of Olive's (center) most popular films, *The Flapper* (1920). Now available on DVD, it's one of the few Thomas films remaining in today's world.

Miss Sulger:

   Kindly note that Miss Olive Thomas is to be removed from the payroll until further notice.

J. W. Schleiff.

A memo of August 10, 1920, the week prior to the news that Olive was to be removed from the Selznick payroll until further notice, read:

Miss Sulger:

   Kindly deduct salary of Miss Thomas from payroll week of August 7, 1920. This is at the request of Mr. M. C. Howard.

J. W. Schleiff.

   Olive went from being advanced money, to having money deducted and then she was removed from the payroll altogether. But, despite the frequent cash advances, Olive was still Selznick's golden goose. Their accounting records were based solely on the profits that she generated on a weekly basis. She was notified of her contract renewal in July of 1920, the exact same time that the Talmadge sisters (Norma and Constance) ceased distribution of their popular films with the Selznicks. Coincidence? Probably not. It now seems the Selznicks optioned Olive for a third year strictly for financial reasons. With the Talmadge sisters gone, another major loss (and Olive's departure would have been just that) would have ruined them. Financially, the Selznicks needed Olive and after studying her bank records, it appears that Olive needed the Selznicks just as much.

There would be one major bump in the road in relation to Olive's final year with the company. She would be working back on the East Coast, at the new studios in Fort Lee, New Jersey, and because of this there would once again be an East Coast-West Coast conflict in Jack and Olive's marriage. By 1920 their relationship was on shaky ground, certainly not strong enough to maintain at a distance. Strangely, that fact didn't seem to faze Jack in the slightest. He failed to take his wife's new film contract into consideration when negotiating his next career move, and more importantly, he failed to see his mother's manipulation and ulterior motives in encouraging and starting a production company that would be anchored in California, thus causing Jack and Olive to be separated—again! Mother Pickford and Mary were hellbent on breaking up Jack and Olive's marriage from day one and keeping Jack on the west coast was their best possible chance of doing just that.

Jack's Goldwyn contract ($2,000 per week, equivalent to $20,000 today) expired on the very day he and Olive left for Paris (August 12, 1920). As previously mentioned, Jack Pickford Productions would be based in California. With Olive now bound to the Selznicks and their new East Coast studio for another year, she would be away from the Brunton Studios (and her husband) on the West Coast for months at a time. Clearly, Olive's stress levels were in overdrive by the time she left for Paris.

As a final point, it's evident that the once-close relationship (romantic or otherwise) between Olive, Myron and Selznick Pictures was waning at the time of her departure abroad. Which raises two important questions: Why was she removed from the Selznick payroll until further notice?—And did the Selznicks disapprove of her trip to Paris?

Just prior to Olive's fateful journey, pre-production was completed and several scenes of a film titled *Jennie* had been shot, with Olive starring. According to the *AFI Catalog*, this film was announced in January-February 1920 as Olive Thomas' next project after *Youthful Folly*; Alan Crosland and Roy Horniman were listed as the director and scenarist, respectively, at that time. In May 1920, after the release of *The Flapper*, the film was announced as being in production at the Robert Brunton Studios, and Selznick announced a release date of July 19, 1920—three weeks before Olive left for Paris and only two months before her death. However, no evidence that the film was finished or distributed has been located. The five-reel feature, a comedy-drama, was not included in a list of Olive Thomas pictures included in records of Select Pictures Corp., the distribution company. Its title is alternately spelled *Jennie* and *Jenny* in contemporary trade articles.

Did Olive walk out on this new feature and flee to Paris, causing the suspension? Or was the suspension a mere formality because she was traveling abroad, not working, and she would be put back on the payroll upon her return? It may be that simple.

A snippet about Olive's Parisian shopping spree was printed in *The Charleston* (West Virginia) *Daily Mail* on September 5, 1920, the very date that Olive took the mercury bi-chloride. Obviously word of Olive's hospitalization had not yet reached the U.S. The item read:

> Olive Thomas is expected to add greatly to her wardrobe while she is abroad on a short vacation. News that she is visiting Paris caused added action at her New York home, and clothes closets and cedar chests were being put in readiness for the deluge.

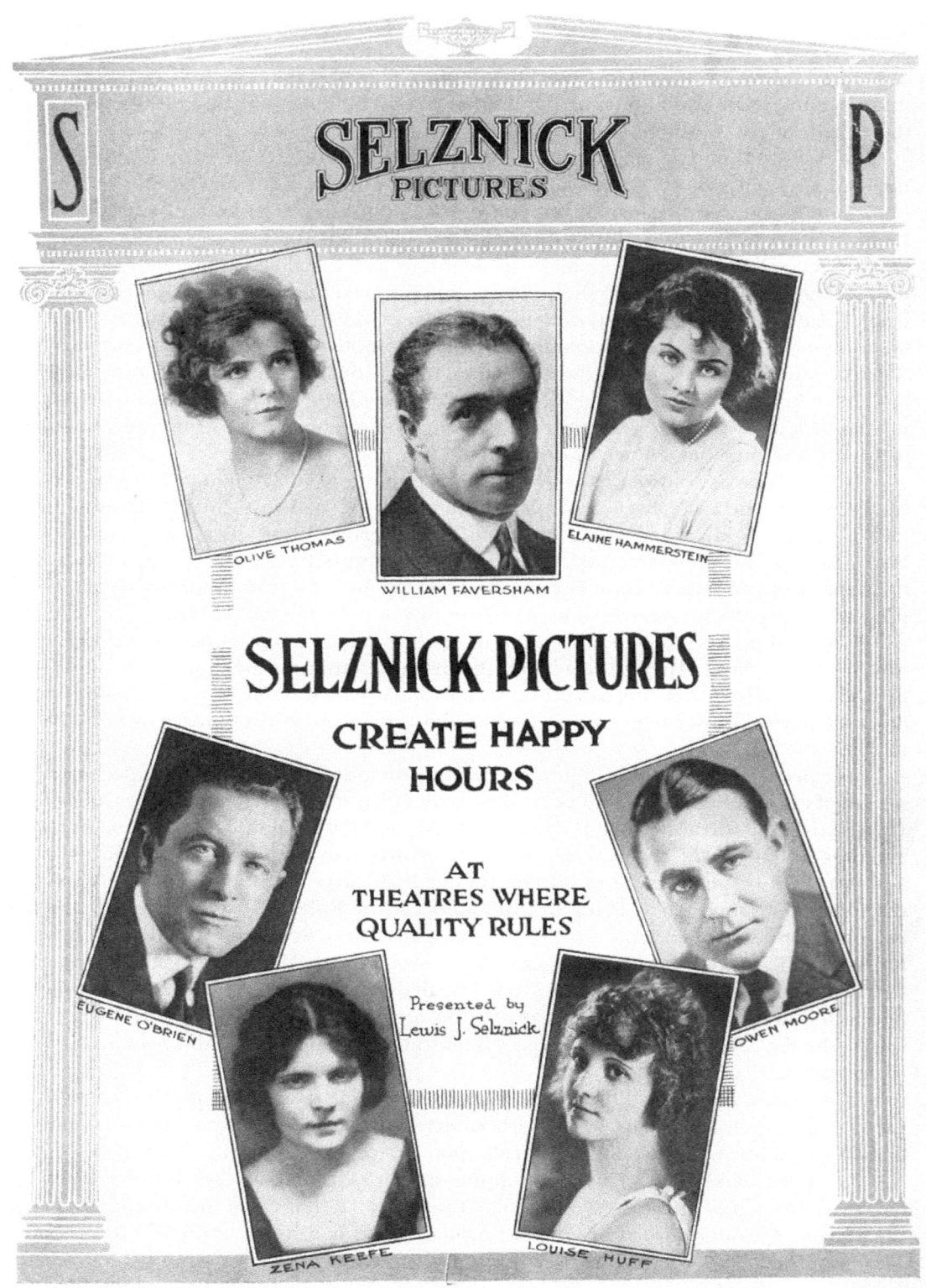

A full page ad released by Selznick Pictures to promote their stars.

It was public knowledge that Olive was traveling overseas to buy a new wardrobe. Other articles around the same time suggest that the new clothing was strictly for professional purposes, not personal. If these stories are to be believed, Olive left American shores with the knowledge that she was still a valued employee of Selznick Pictures.

Could the sudden news of being removed from the Selznick Pictures payroll have been a contributing factor in Olive's overdose? Jack and Olive sailed for Paris on August 12, the memo was issued August 16. It was an eight-day voyage; they arrived in Paris on August 20. Was word of her suspension from Selznick Pictures waiting for her at the Hotel Ritz? One way or another, she *had* to know about it—eventually.

A promotional glass slide for *The Flapper* (1920).

At the time of her departure to Paris, Olive had work troubles, financial troubles and marital troubles. To top it off, Olive was in California at the time of Mary's marriage to Douglas Fairbanks (March 28, 1920) but she did not attend the ceremony. Why? Because she wasn't invited! It's a telling sign that the tumultuous relationship between Olive and the Pickfords (especially with her sister-in-law Mary) was intensifying in the months prior to her death. Olive's journey to Paris was an escape from her very complicated life, on every level, back home. It is an understatement to say that, both personally and professionally, things were not going well for her.

Despite the relationship between Olive and the Selznicks being strained prior to her trip abroad, one thing's for certain; Olive generated a lot of money for Selznick Pictures Corporation and they were genuinely devastated at news of her death. In fact, it has long been rumored that David Selznick only added the O. as a middle initial (thus becoming David O. Selznick) after Olive's death in honor of her memory.

An undated *Motion Picture Classic* interview with Sue Roberts showcased Olive's easygoing persona along with her informal relationship with her boss Myron before things went awry:

> "Oh, dear," said Olive, "I do hope I won't have to see any more people today. I look such a fright!"
> Which started an argument on the impossibility or possibility of such a thing. At its very height Myron Selznick entered quietly.
> "When you two girls finish chatting," he said, "Cosmo Hamilton is waiting outside to see you, Olive!"
> "Oh, dear, what does *he* want?"
> "To talk over ideas for your next story. Surely you're not afraid of any mere man."

"Afraid?" said Olive, as she rose vigorously to her full height of five feet four. "Have you forgotten that I can beat both you and Jack at wrestling? Afraid of a man! I guess not. Any woman can get the best of a man if she wants to."

Myron and Olive stood side by side, both belonging in the bantamweight class.

"See *my* star," said Myron.

"See *my* manager," said Olive. "Haven't we got the 'littlest' company?"

"We won't have anyone in our company who is over five feet four, will we, Olive?" said Myron.

"No, siree!" agreed Olive. "Even Jack is in that class, so he can kinda belong. What I like is we're going to have just a little corner of a studio, but it's all our own. Isn't it fun? No one can boss *us*. Can they, Myron?"

"No, siree!" agreed Myron.

Roberts concluded the article with her own thoughts: "I had forgotten that my companion was Olive Thomas, a famous film star and the wife of the equally famous Jack Pickford. I had failed to remember that she used to be a favorite in Flo Ziegfeld's well-known Follies. To me she was just a jolly good fellow—just one of the girls."

It seems Olive's persuasive personality worked financially in her favor too. The Selznick file at the University of Texas shows several cash advances in Olive's name so whatever pay cut she initially took when signing with the company came with tidy cash bonuses whenever she (or Jack) needed to be bailed out of hot water. The Selznicks and their company were reliant on Olive's continued success so they did all they could to appease her every whim and wish. In hindsight, it may not have been a bad deal after all.

Given the fact that everything was riding on the success of Olive's films (she *was* Selznick Pictures), it's not surprising that the company took out a $300,000–400,000 life insurance policy on their one and only star. It's long been suggested that it was Jack who took out the hefty policy right before their trip to Paris. With constant financial problems plaguing him, it only added to the speculation that Olive's death may have been something more than a suicide or accident.

Olive was Myron and L.J. Selznick's first protégé at Selznick Pictures and they treated her like a princess. The frequent cash bonuses, personal travel costs and lavish clothing allowances more than made up for the lesser salary offered her. An April 12, 1920, Selznick Pictures receipt for Olive's clothing expenses lists the following:

> 1 Pair of black gloves (20 buttons)—$10.50, 1 Pair of shoes—kid—$9.00, 2 Shoes—destroyed—$52.00, 1 Dress—cream lace—$100.00, 1 Kimona—$40.00, 5 Pairs stockings—$30.00, 2 Hats—$25.00. A total cost of $266.50 (approximately $2500 today).

Upstairs and Down (1919) was the first Olive Thomas film produced by Myron Selznick, and the first film released by the new Selznick Pictures Corp. A March, 1919 issue of *Moving Picture World* printed an article entitled, "Rapid Work Done on *Upstairs and Down*." It read:

> Myron Selznick, president of the Selznick Pictures Corporation, astonished the New York Offices of the company this week by telegraphing from Los Angeles that all the scenes of *Upstairs and Down* had been photographed. This is the first production of the new corporation which has announced a series of eight features yearly, starring Olive Thomas.
>
> The quick work in turning out this first production is the more remarkable because the company had to begin building from the smallest detail and is a tribute to the organizing ability of Myron Selznick and Director-General Charles Giblyn. They went to

Los Angeles early in January and did not begin work until everything was in first class shape for continuous operations. As a result, the speed of the production, despite the handicaps of organizing a new corporation, was such as might be envied by producers who have been in the business much longer.

The thoroughness of the preliminary production plans is exemplified by the fact that Mr. Giblyn took with him to California flashlight photographs of the scenes of the Oliver Morosco production *Upstairs and Down* and complete descriptions of all the accessories of the play. The elaborate settings showing the servants' quarters and the living rooms of a big Long Island country house were reproduced in every detail for the Selznick production.

Released on June 8, 1919, *Upstairs and Down* had the working title, *Society People*. And, there was no expense spared in the marketing of the film, or Selznick's new star. A February 8, 1919, issue of *Motion Picture News* ran with a story entitled, "Electric Signs Advertise Selznick Pictures." It read:

> Olive Thomas receives great advertising through two big electric signs, advertising Selznick Pictures, which have been installed at Times Square. These carry the simple announcement:
>
> "Myron Selznick Presents Olive Thomas in *Upstairs and Down*, Direction Charles Giblyn."
>
> This is said to be the first step taken by Selznick Pictures Corporation in what is heralded as a nationwide campaign of advertising. One of these signs, 32 ft. × 34 ft., is located on Broadway between Forty-fifth and Forty-sixth streets and is of an especially novel, though simple design. The letters of the word *Upstairs* in *Upstairs and Down* run upwards on a diagonal, each letter standing on an outline of a step of stairs.
>
> The lettering in the sign burns steadily, only the outline of the stairs flashing on and off. Each step flashes separately, giving the impression of an ascending movement. The installation was worked out as a suggestion for exhibitors who will later be booking the picture.
>
> The other sign, at Forty-second Street and Seventh Avenue, is about the same size, but owing to the shape it was impossible to use the stairs design, which calls for an almost square area of illumination. Negotiations are now said to be underway for still a third Selznick Pictures sign. Arrangements have been practically completed for this structure, which when in operation will be the largest amusement sign of its kind in the city and will practically blanket Times Square with Selznick Pictures illuminations, so that from no point of this center of the world's theatrical life will it be possible to escape the Selznick advertisements.

The third sign was indeed erected and Olive Thomas and Selznick Pictures took over Times Square. The *Los Angeles Herald* (March 11, 1919) wrote that Olive had created history with three electric light signs situated in the immediate vicinity of Times Square. Norma and Constance Talmadge were her closest competitors at one sign apiece.

Myron discussed the upcoming release of *Upstairs and Down* in the March 8, 1919, issue of *Motion Picture News*, saying:

> "I am convinced," says Mr. Selznick, "that the public wants well-dressed plays. The stories of sordid realism, hunger, poverty, suffering and all that sort of thing are no longer popular. The most successful pictures are those which make audiences happy. I believe that in *Upstairs and Down* we have a combination of the comedy and romantic elements combined with luxurious settings and costuming that will make this one of the hits of the season."

In the film, Olive plays "baby vamp" Alice Chesterton. Some publicity stills and lobby cards have this working title imprinted on them which often confuses people into thinking it's a whole other film. They are one and the same.

An unidentified 1919 review of the film said:

> We awaited Olive Thomas' appearance in the Hattons' stage farce, *Upstairs and Down* (Selznick) with considerable anticipation. But alas! The thing has lost en route to the screen. The director, Charles Giblyn, keeps the players too far from the camera, for one thing. Moreover, Mr. Giblyn didn't seem to be able to get his action to hold the interest anywhere. The subtitles, remnants of the Hattons' lively dialog, alone carry the comedy.
>
> *Upstairs and Down* is a story of the Long Island idle rich and their servants below stairs, of the polo pony folk and their servitors. It preaches the philosophy that you must "treat 'em rough" to win a girl above stairs but that the same thing is deadly below. Thru it moves the (apparently) guileless baby vamp, Alice Chesterton, of course played by Miss Thomas. Her performance lacks verve, although she is piquant in her bathing suit moments. Robert Ellis reveals some possibilities as the hero, and Rosemary Theby and Kathleen Kirkham are both appealing in their roles. But *Upstairs and Down* lacks an elevator—of piquancy.

The Spite Bride, The Glorious Lady and *Out Yonder* were the final three 1919 releases with the newly formed Olive–Selznick partnership. Triangle still had *Toton, The Follies Girl, Prudence on Broadway* and *Love's Prisoner* up their sleeves. However, they were in such severe financial straits at the time, it was only a matter of months before Triangle Pictures would be no more. Creditors stepped in and subsequently held back on the release of Olive's last four films in order to cash in on the success of her move to Selznick Pictures. All four Triangle productions were released throughout 1919, giving Olive eight new releases in one year!

Variety, May 30, 1919, gave *Love's Prisoner* a less than flattering review, saying:

> It seems a pity that Triangle could not have found a better vehicle for Olive Thomas than this five-reel feature. E.

An original poster for the 1919 Triangle release, *Toton*. This rare U.S. one-sheet is more than likely the only one now in existence.

Magnus Ingleton is the author. Jack Dillon did the directing. The story is absurd, unreal and lacks entertaining qualities. The star takes the part of a young criminal, Nancy (Olive), whose father just before he leaves for a long term "up the river" designated her the "best little pickpocket in the city." On her parent's retirement, Nancy (Olive) has two younger sisters to provide for. These are left in the care of Jonathan Twist, a jeweler and also her "fence."

Nancy ostensibly secures a position as traveling saleswoman, but in reality she continues her career of stealing. Then follow many scenes with the heroine as a demonstrator in a drug store. Here she meets Lord Cleveland (Harvey Clark). What his lordship is doing in this country is not explained, but they get married and go to England.

Nancy returns to America after the death of her husband and divides her time between society, charity, and stealing. One day she is caught with the "goods," and the detective sent to arrest her falls in love with his prisoner. After she has paid the penalty of her crime, marries her, and it all ends with the usual clinch—and a sigh of relief from those who had to sit through it.

A promotional ad for *The Spite Bride* (1919).

Mechanically, the picture is all right, it is clear and sharp. The settings are in keeping and lighting good. But if anything, these technical advantages make the shortcomings of the story more pronounced.

Unfortunately, many of Olive Thomas' films are now considered "lost." The only print currently available of *Love's Prisoner* is missing the final reel. Almost half of Olive's films (all made between 1916–20) still exist in some form (not always complete) and are awaiting restoration in professional archives; other prints are most likely gathering dust and disintegrating in someone's attic without their owners realizing the significance of what they have in their possession. The reality is, the majority of Olive's work is lost forever.

A private collector has restored "Play Ball" (1916), an episode of the popular *Beatrice Fairfax* series starring Olive, and he sometimes makes it publicly available. *An Even Break* (1917) is currently undergoing restoration with the Library of Congress and a handful of copies are known to exist in private hands. Long considered "lost," *Out*

A promotional glass slide for *Prudence on Broadway* (1919).

Yonder (1919) was recently rediscovered and restored in the Netherlands. Its first public screening in over eighty years occurred on April 7, 2005, in Amsterdam.

The Flapper (1920) is now widely available on DVD. The George Eastman House has a print of it along with *Everybody's Sweetheart* (1920), Olive's final film, and *Broadway Arizona* (1917). These three films are available for viewing upon appointment; however, no copies will be made for private use from this source. A print of *Madcap Madge* (1917) was recently transferred (by the George Eastman House) from nitrate to safety film and a full restoration has recently been completed. Others, including *Indiscreet Corinne* (1917), *Betty Takes a Hand* (1918) and *The Spite Bride* (1919) only exist in snippets. The AFI is currently in the process of restoring what's left of *Betty Takes a Hand* (1918).

Footlights and Shadows (1920) and *Youthful Folly* (1920) were quickly followed by Olive's whimsical role of sixteen-year-old Ginger King in *The Flapper* (1920). The title helped give worldwide currency to the term which helped define the new, modern, liberated woman of what became known as "The Roaring Twenties," and it was Myron Selznick who was credited for making her a star.

Helen Rockwell, an *Exhibitor's Trade Review* reporter interviewed (January 6, 1920) Olive about her role in *The Flapper* (1920):

> We found "Ollie" having fun with a pile of dresses which might have been the result of a raid on a misses boarding school. Middy blouses (a woman's loose blouse with a sailor collar), tam o-shanters (a tight-fitting Scottish cap or beret with a pompom, tassel or feather in the center) and practical square-toed shoes perched brazenly on the top of a heap. A mackinaw coat (a short plaid coat made of wool) of many colors struggled for expression from the bottom of the pile. "Ollie" was getting ready to go on location.
>
> Once again she is allowed to play the sort of role dearest to her heart, the role of a schoolgirl. Ever since ever and ever so long ago when Olive played "Madcap Madge" for Triangle she has longed to do schoolgirl parts. She has pined for them. She has loathed herself as a debutante, herself as a wife and mother, been disgusted with herself as a fisher-maid—in short she's never been satisfied with any of her celluloid selves since dear old "Madge."
>
> "I made the picture three years ago," she will tell you earnestly, "and fans have never stopped inquiring as to when I'm to play a schoolgirl again. My fan mail is large, exceedingly large, and the one picture remains the favorite. Fans haven't forgotten it even after three years, and now Mr. Selznick has agreed to let me shorten my skirts again, put a bow in my hair and romp to my heart's content."

Our thoughts flew back to some of the dream creations we had seen Olive wear in recent photoplays, and we patiently endeavored to understand how she could look a Middy in the face and grow excited. You see we are feminine. Olive Thomas is not so much feminine as just a kid.

"But I want to create a certain role," she explained. "You see, Mary is the kid in pictures; Norma does drama; Constance is the flippant, flighty wife; Dorothy the hoyden; Nazimova is exotic and steeped in mystery, my Jack does boys, while I ... I ... why, don't you see, I am just nothing at all!"

She grew quite excited as she pursued the subject. "I have no fixed position. I don't mean a *definite* thing to anybody. Now you see if a fan wants to enjoy a comedy, he knows that he can pick Charles Ray or Dorothy Gish and get what he's looking for. If a fan is looking for a picture of youth he knows that he can walk in to see Mary Pickford or my Jack and find it. For a frothy affair of sophisticated

Olive as Betty Marshall in *Betty Takes a Hand* (1928).

humor, there is 'Conny' Talmadge. If it's drama that's wanted, well, drop in to see Norma. But how ... I ask you ... how can a fan know what he's getting when he pays his money to see me? He or she is likely to find me weeping through five reels because I haven't a child, or tripping the light fantastic as a chorus girl of questionable reputation. I grow to womanhood and am tossed back to the flapper type. I am nothing in particular. Don't you see?" And she spread out her hands with such an expression of utter hopelessness that we laughed right out.

And then she went on to tell us that she was to try her hand at school-girl roles again and if the public took to them she was to go on doing them for a while. She wants to create a sort of Booth Tarkington girl. She wants to be in the feminine line what "her Jack" is in the boyish way. She desires to be known as *something in particular*.

Her next story is to be *Sixteen* [working title for *The Flapper*] and is an original story by Frances Marion. "My Jack did *Seventeen* [1916] ... and as I'm just a year younger than Jack it's all right for me to do *Sixteen*. It's quite fitting, isn't it, that I should?"

After we had exhausted our enthusiasm looking over the various styles of Middy blouses which Olive fancies, we stumbled across the apartment and into a motion picture machine.

"I ran off a Charlie Chaplin last night," said Ollie. "I have a lot of fun with it. I can get a new film every day. I just shoot it up there on the wall and entertain my friends."

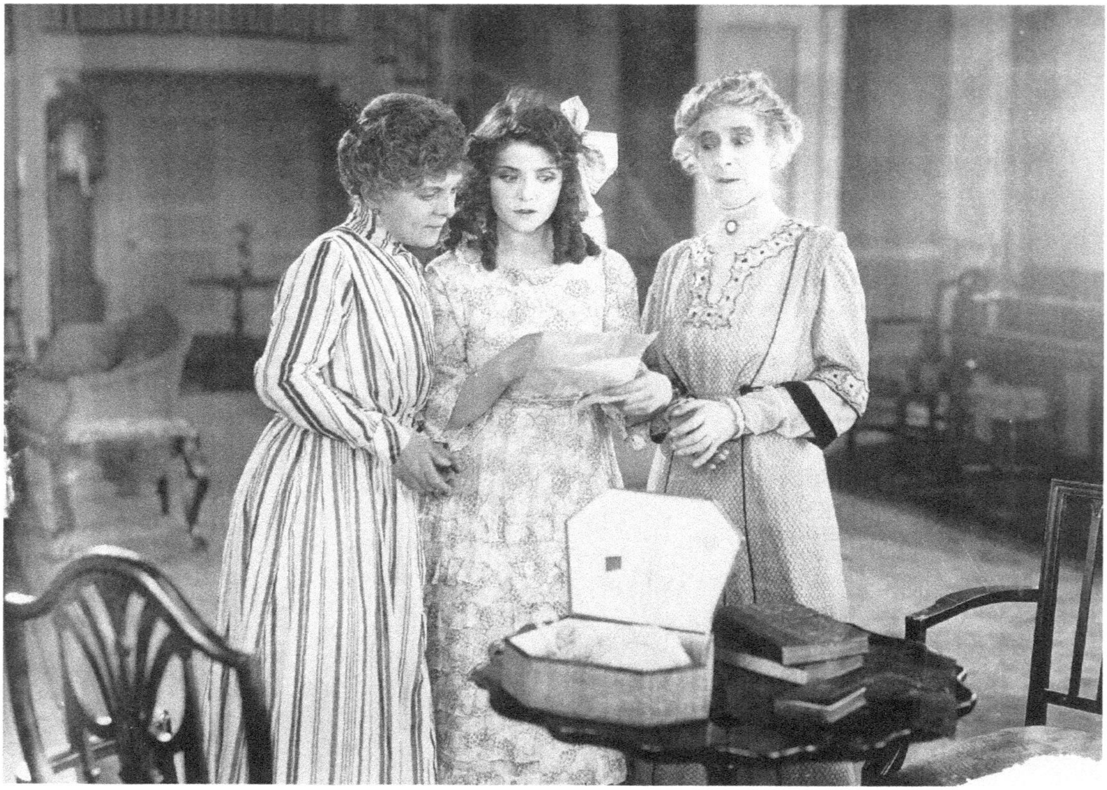

"Do you try out your new pictures?" we ventured.

"Heavens, no," replied our hostess sitting perilously on the edge of a table and swinging her legs. "I hate my pictures. What's the use of pretending I like my pictures when I don't. When they show me one of my pictures up at the Selznick projection room I can't get a person to sit with me. I 'pan' myself so hard they refuse to listen. I think I'm awful."

Now although you think Olive Thomas is all wrong and lacking in perception, you can't help liking her for it. It is good for the soul to meet a person, especially an actress, and more especially a young, pretty actress, who fails to enthuse particularly about herself, and who just loves Dorothy Gish, and raves about Connie Talmadge, and thinks Norma is a dream.

A promotional glass slide for *Darling Mine* (1920).

"Oh, sometimes I'm not so bad," she admits grudgingly, "but usually my face looks funny or my hair is not right or my tears look faked."

She is delightful when she shows you her books of "stills."

"This is a scene from my last picture. This pretty girl is Miss ____, Oh, she's lots of fun, such jolly company. And this was Mr. ____. He's an excellent actor. Been on the stage for eighteen years. And a charming person. This over here in the corner is my dog. Isn't the location pretty?"

Then with a flip of the head she turns the page and you discover she's been holding the book with her thumb smudged over her own portrait. She'd go through the entire book that way if you'd let her.

Like Peter Pan we can't imagine that Olive Thomas will ever grow up. She impresses you as being a delightful child, playing at grown up but actually uncomprehending the responsibilities that go hand in hand with ankle dresses. She skips, not walks, and would probably turn a cartwheel on the street if she felt like it. She embodies the spirit of youth and we can think of no one better suited to give youth to the screen than she. We hope she may be allowed to continue with her heart's desire and give us school days. In these days when to look into the future is to imperil your disposition for the season, it will be decidedly pleasant to look into the past through "Ollie" Thomas and remember the good old days when times were a little less hectic, and you were young.

Variety, May 21, 1920, reviewed *The Flapper* more favorably than they did *Love's Prisoner,* saying:

This is the fluffiest sort of fluff, but good summer booking just the same, though any but the best type of houses may find it lacking in dramatic meat. This is due to the delicacy with which Alan Crosland has directed Olive Thomas, who here continues her trip

Opposite, top: **Olive in a scene from** *Youthful Folly* **(1920).** *Opposite, bottom:* **Olive in a scene from** *Footlights and Shadows* **(1920).**

Olive in another scene from *Footlights and Shadows* (1920).

toward film fame. Photographic and laboratory work were of the high class Selznick has led us to expect in his pictures.

The story, moreover, is better than this firm's usual run. Frances Marion wrote it, and it concerns the escapades of a schoolgirl. Too strictly brought up, she gets into all sorts of innocent trouble when the chance comes. Some of the titles were humorous in the best sense. All were well thought out and phrased.

More interesting than any of the commercial phases of the picture is Miss Thomas herself. Her appeal is the sex appeal. Very sensibly her director has assented to the fact. Miss Thomas has too heavy a make-up in the first reel, and her dresses should not fit so tightly. This light, whimsical story remains, nevertheless, excellent market stuff for the more appreciative audiences.

Needless to say, Olive's death just a few months after the release of *The Flapper* gave the film (in some macabre way) a whole new appeal. There's no better publicity rivaling death that will catapult an actor, writer or painter to the heights of stardom ever achieved in life.

Thanks to Sarah Baker, Andi Hicks and Milestone Films, a pristine print of *The Flapper* was released (together with a documentary) on DVD in 2005. This continued dedication to film preservation is needed to ensure that Olive Thomas and her many contemporaries remain a moving image for generations to come, not just names and faces on still photographs.

Darling Mine (1920) was followed by *Everybody's Sweetheart,* a film released on October 4, 1920, just three weeks after Olive's death. Newspapers ran ads publicizing the film as her last picture: "The last opportunity you'll ever have to see America's prettiest

A promotional shot for *The Flapper* (1920).

screen star," said one ad promoting a screening at the Lyric Theater. Another ad stated, "The final appearance before the camera of America's captivating screen star, whose loss of life in the whirl of the shameless orgies of Paris, has aroused the world to the dangers of the sinful city." Audiences flocked to her films (many of which were re-released) and gasps were heard when they saw her name and pretty face, so full of life, on the screen in front of them.

As a result of her death, *Everybody's Sweetheart* tripled its business and past Olive pictures were re-released across the country. All three Selznicks attended her funeral with Myron acting as one of the pallbearers. A $22,000 (approximately $200,000 today) ivory inlaid limousine was provided by the Selznicks for Olive to ride in. After the funeral it was passed along to L.J.'s brother, Sol, in Pittsburgh, who was trying his hand at the automobile business. At the sale of Olive's personal effects, L.J. bought a $680 (approximately $6000 today) diamond and emerald ring to remember her by.

The *Indiana Evening Gazette* (September 20, 1920) ran a headline, "Broadway Throngs Gaze at Flashing Sign—OLIVE THOMAS." The article described the emotion of the crowds that would stop and stare at the flashing sign advertising her latest picture, saying:

> With the terrible death tragedy of Olive Thomas, American Motion Picture star, still fresh in their minds, Broadway's gay throngs gazed spellbound at a large electric sign high above the street which could be seen for many blocks. There, in white glittering letters in the center of the sign was the name "Olive Thomas," flashing the same as

A lobby card showing a scene from *Darling Mine* (1920).

usual, although the motion picture star was dead, a victim of accidental poisoning. Hundreds stopped along the street and watched the sign as though they expected its bright letters to fade away and go out like the life of the beautiful girl of the movies. But the sign continued to flash long after the theater and cabaret crowds had departed.

An unidentified 1920 newspaper article entitled, "Olive Thomas: Twice a Shadow to Film Fans," gave an account of what moviegoers' reactions to Olive's death:

Three o'clock in Paris this morning—empty, silent streets, save for the slow passing of a gendarme, the rattle of a market cart over the cobblestones. A few pale lights from the shadows, a city asleep, and somewhere in the midst of it the body of a young American girl, very still.

The same moment in Detroit, with the clock's hour hand pointing to mid-evening, and there were hundreds pouring into the blazing front of the Garden Theater to view for an hour or so the moving to and fro on the silver screen of the quiet still girl in faraway Paris.

The organ rolled through a stately march and rollicked through a mad melody of rag as the pantaloons in a comedy puffed and tumbled their plot, and then swung into a merry melody as the flickering blur of the title straightened out and in white fire letters announced the star and the play—Olive Thomas in *The Flapper*. So filled was the house with music that there was no way of hearing the comments, but from the far rear looking down over the audience one could see heads of couples suddenly draw close and faces turn as whispers were exchanged.

From out of a mass of shadows there sprung clear and distinct a stretch of lovely California garden, the glitter of a stream and the flying feet of little children racing across the lawn. Just behind them came a taller figure, head bent, curls flying, arms out held. Suddenly the head lifted and straight at the patrons laughed the eyes of Olive Thomas, quaint and elfin and very child-like.

Theaters across the country ran Olive Thomas features, both old and new. Audiences gasped when first she appeared on the screen and sat mesmerized throughout the film. As "The End" flashed onto the blackened screen, they stood and applauded. The only thing missing was Olive magically appearing and taking an appreciative bow.

For a moment it was as if it was all a cruel hoax. How could this vision of life on the screen be lying still, lifeless, in an empty Paris church, so far from home? Yet it *was* true. Death had lifted Olive to a pedestal, an increased public appreciation, never before seen for an actress.

Although he carries a last name that was instrumental in Olive's career, Daniel Selznick can only give his opinion on Olive's career and death. Daniel has no memory of Olive being spoken about within the family unit, saying, "Since Olive's career took place long before I was born, all I can do (knowing something of the relationship between my father and his brother) is to try and understand how enchanted Uncle Myron must have been taken with her, as a young man, and confirm how aggressively my grandfather Selznick wanted to create stars. I have seen two or three of her films, and while it's easy to recognize Olive's appeal, I also felt she projected astonishing immaturity.

"Her limitations as an actress were related to her youth; she was barely old enough to manage her own affairs, let alone consider starting her own family. I certainly have no reason to believe she might have been murdered, even though the evidence suggests that she could have been. Rather, I suspect that what happened was an accident, though being clearly impulsive, she might have attempted suicide if she'd had too much to drink and/or was tired or stressed."

Fame came quickly to Olive, perhaps too quickly. In a *Picture Show* article (August 2, 1919) Olive hinted at how tiring her hectic work schedule really was. "Jack and I have a fine house out in California and it's nice weather and all that. But there's nothing to it. I never see my home. All I do is work every day."

Daniel Selznick concludes with, "Think of the three Selznicks, heartsick at losing her, but also flush with cash thanks to her films. Selznick Pictures had arrived and Olive Thomas had helped them get there."

A title card for *Darling Mine* (1920).

After his father's company (Lewis J. Selznick Pictures, Inc.) closed in 1923 (liquidation was final by 1925), Myron Selznick worked for other studios, primarily as a production adviser. However, with his industry connections, aided by his brother's (David O.) rise to one of the most powerful film producers in Hollywood, he saw another business opportunity and set himself up as a talent agent. Partnered with Frank Coleman Joyce, the brother of actress Alice Joyce, they formed Joyce-Selznick, Ltd., the first Los Angeles talent agency. It became very successful but personal problems plagued Myron Selznick along with severe alcoholism. That lethal combination contributed to his premature death (March 23, 1944) in Santa Monica, California. He was forty-five years old.

✯ Chapter 5 ✯

PARIS

I'd like to get Olive and take a vacation.
—Jack Pickford shortly before their tragic trip to Paris

By March of 1920 Olive had made her way to New Orleans to wrap filming on her latest feature, *The Flapper*; from there the filming shifted to Lake Placid, New York. Since she was on the East Coast, Olive took the opportunity to spend some long-awaited quality time with Jack. She also took time out to watch her latest feature *Out Yonder* (1920) as a paying audience member. *The Los Angeles Herald* (April 19, 1920) reported that Olive was seen wiping tears from her eyes with a handkerchief when she thought nobody was looking. "Well, anyhow," she defended herself, "when I see myself on the screen I never seem to be watching me, for myself off stage and myself on stage are two utterly different personalities."

Both Jack and Olive had been working hard and had now been separated for close to four months. It was around this time that Jack was quoted as saying, "I'd like to get Olive and take a vacation" (*New York Times*, June 1920).

On August 12, 1920, they did just that. Jack and Olive sailed from New York to Paris on the luxurious ship, the *Imperator*. They referred to the vacation as their "second honeymoon," but they were both too busy with work to have a first honeymoon so the term wasn't exactly true.

It was an eight-day voyage with the ship docking in Paris on August 20. Many of their movie star friends were aboard the ship and Olive threw a lavish birthday party for Jack right there in the middle of the sea. He was thrilled. By all accounts the pair were in good spirits throughout the entire journey.

They arrived in Paris and checked into the prestigious Hotel Ritz. Opening on June 1, 1898, the hotel has long been synonymous with opulence, service and fine dining. The Hotel Ritz consists of the Vendôme and the Cambon buildings with rooms facing Place Vendôme and, on the opposite side, rooms overlooking its famous garden. The hotel became a favorite of many of the world's wealthiest people, with luxurious suites named for some of its notable patrons from the past. These include Ernest Hemingway for whom a bar in the hotel was named, F. Scott Fitzgerald, Marcel

A photograph postcard of the *Imperator*, the ship that took Olive on her fatal voyage to Paris.

Proust, King Edward VII of the United Kingdom, Rudolph Valentino, Charlie Chaplin and Greta Garbo. Couturier Coco Chanel made the Ritz her home for more than thirty years.

In 1979, the Ritz family sold the hotel to Egyptian businessman Mohamed Al-Fayed who refurbished it and in 1988 added the Ritz-Escoffier School of French Gastronomy. The hotel was where the owner's son Dodi Al-Fayed and his companion, Diana, Princess of Wales, had left from before their fatal car crash in the nearby Pont de l'Alma road tunnel. This tragic accident along with Olive's death years earlier have made the Hotel Ritz not only famous, but also infamous.

Soon after their arrival in Paris, Jack left Olive and took a brief trip to London. He later stated that he and his ex–brother-in-law, Owen Moore (Mary Pickford's ex-husband), had made the trip together to get fitted for some new clothes. Aside from leaving his pretty young wife alone in Paris, the relationship appeared to be trouble-free. It was no secret that Olive and Jack had a fiery relationship and those few trouble-free days was the calm before the storm. Everything would soon come to a crashing end. As turbulent as things often got between the pair, no one predicted the turn of events that would take place on the night of September 5, 1920.

The evening started out like any other. The couple had dinner with friends, Fred Nelson (actor), Cyril Gray (cameraman), Fred Almey, Lt. G. A. Ray (of the American Embassy), Wilfred Graham and Florence Wulfelt. Afterwards, Jack and Olive hit several nightspots in the infamous Montmartre party district. Some witnesses claim they were seen together all evening, while others stated they were partying alone. A November 2, 1920, article in New York's *The Olean Evening Times* ran a picture of actress Lois Meredith and said, "Miss Meredith was a close friend of Miss Olive Thomas, the movie actress, who recently died in Paris, and was with her on several parties shortly before the death of Miss Thomas."

Together or apart, there's no question both Jack and Olive had been drinking; and with the ease of availability of drugs in Paris at the time, it's safe to assume that Jack (not Olive) had scored his fair share of heroin and/or cocaine too.

Several contemporary publications have unfairly labeled Olive a drug addict because of her close association with Jack, who was without question an addict. However, there was no evidence then and there is no evidence now to prove that Olive Thomas was an addict. She was a party girl, she drank champagne, she may have used drugs occasionally, but an addict she was certainly not.

Charles Lockwood's book *Dream Palaces: Hollywood at Home* is one of the many publications that leads the reader down a mythological path. He solves the entire mystery of Olive's death in one paragraph, saying:

LAST PHOTOGRAPH OF OLIVE THOMAS

Does this look like a marriage in trouble? This was the last photograph ever taken of Olive Thomas (with husband Jack Pickford) shortly before their tragic trip to Paris. Friends said it was an attempt to patch up their marriage. Others insisted they were happy and looking forward to a long future together.

> On September 10, 1920, pretty Olive Thomas, ex–Ziegfeld girl, rising comedy star, and sister-in-law of Mary Pickford, committed suicide in her Paris hotel room. Olive, it turned out, was a heroin addict; she killed herself after she failed to score a large supply of smack for herself and her husband, Jack, who was also an addict. In the ensuing uproar, Jack was exposed as a hopeless philanderer as well. He went into a hospital for nervous exhaustion and offered no comment on these charges, but his sister, Mary, denied these "sickening aspersions" on his good name.

DeWitt Bodeen's *13 Castle Walk* comes up with one of the most bizarre conclusions for two of Hollywood's greatest mysteries. He states that Jack contracted syphilis from his affair with director William Desmond Taylor (bisexual rumors plagued Jack) so he shot Taylor to get revenge. He claims that Olive killed herself because she had contracted the disease from Jack and she couldn't bear to live with it.

In another instance, Kenneth Anger's scandal-laden book, *Hollywood Babylon*, dedicates an entire chapter to Olive's demise. It is within these few pages that the infamous Sable Cape story rears its ugly head. A valet used his passkey to enter the Pickfords' room with a breakfast trolley. "What he saw froze him in his tracks," writes Anger. "A sable opera cape was spread out on the floor, and on it lay a nude young woman. One hand still clutched a bottle of toxic bichloride of mercury granules. That young woman was Olive Thomas."

Anger's account of Olive's death has become Hollywood folklore. Honestly, there is no need to dramatize her death with an embellished version of events. In Olive's case, the truth (or attempting to find it) far outweighs the myth.

According to the police statement, Jack claimed that he and Olive arrived back at their hotel room, together, somewhere around 3 A.M. (hotel staff claim to have seen Olive returning alone, at 1 A.M.).

One of the shocking headlines published in American newspapers after Olive's death in Paris, France.

From this moment on there are a number of scenarios that could have logically happened and it's unfortunate that Jack was the only witness. Jack's night of excess with the consumption of alcohol and drugs, combined with the overwhelming shock of what she had done and the eventual grief of losing his wife, together with his lifelong track record for self-preservation makes his version of events less than credible. To further complicate the matter, after Olive was taken to hospital he was heavily sedated. He was too traumatized to continue his stay at the Hotel Ritz after the incident and the Hotel Crillion was his place of residence for the remainder of his stay in Paris.

All of these factors are logical reasons as to why Jack's story is at times inconsistent, yet a cloud of doubt still hovers over his head. There is a strong sense that the truth lies somewhere between what he said happened and what really happened. What we were left with then and what we're most certainly left with now (86 years later) is one of the greatest mysteries, and one of the greatest tragedies that Hollywood and the movie industry ever experienced.

For the first time in its short history, Hollywood's golden reputation was dragged through the mud. With the death of Olive Thomas, the public came to realize their matinee idols were mere mortals, just like them. The "powers that be" were forced to act quickly and the fingers of blame were promptly pointed in the direction of Paris, France. Yes, Olive and Jack were Hollywood stars but they were not under the influence of Hollywood at the time. They had been corrupted and drawn in by the sinful lifestyle that was sweeping Europe. Blame Paris! It was a long shot but eventually church groups and newspapers picked up on the topic and several articles were written about the sleazy Paris parties bursting with drugs, alcohol, orgies and corruption that were at fault for luring poor little Olive Thomas to her premature death.

But, as director Raoul Walsh explained, Hollywood wasn't confined to American shores; the motion picture industry fell under an international. "Hollywood," he said, "is a mythical abstraction without geographical boundaries. Whether its locations are in Manhattan, a western prairie in New Mexico, the High Sierra, Paris, London, the Alps or a converted orange grove in Los Angeles—they all form the total myth known as 'Hollywood'" (*100 Years of Hollywood*, Editors of Time Life Books, 1990).

If Olive's death was ever in danger of being forgotten, Hollywood's imminent future and the countless scandals that followed her demise jolted the moviegoing public back to reality.

Roscoe "Fatty" Arbuckle, William Desmond Taylor, Wallace Reid, Thomas Ince and Mabel Normand would all fall from their pedestals in the years to follow and the media had a field day convincing readers (who at the time believe almost anything that was put to print) that the curse of Hollywood, this city of sex and sin, was solely responsible. Paris could no longer be blamed because these new scandals occurred on home turf. All eyes were now on Hollywood and there was no one to point the finger at this time. The death of starlet Virginia Rappe (exactly a year after Olive) and the lengthy court trials of Arbuckle bumped Olive's story from the papers, but until then, innuendo about Olive's life and speculation about her tragic death continued to be written about on an almost daily basis.

Olive curled up with a book during a quiet afternoon at home. This photograph was taken three months before her death.

Initial newspaper reports strongly suggested that an emotionally delicate Olive had committed suicide. *The Los Angeles Examiner* (September 11, 1920; relayed from London, September 10, 1920) reported the following:

> Olive Thomas, broken-hearted and temporarily unbalanced, who died in the American Hospital at Neuilly today from mercurial poisoning, was convinced that she could never again bring herself to live with her husband, Jack Pickford. Such is the story that came to London today in a letter to an intimate friend from a screen star on close terms with Pickford and his wife who was in Paris the night Miss Thomas took the bichloride of mercury.
>
> According to the letter, the pair were enjoying an unbelievably happy "second honeymoon" when an interruption came. Jack made a hurried trip to London, August 25th. When he rejoined his wife in Paris, Olive, the letter said, had told Jack that further life with him would be abhorrent and impossible. Then, the letter continued, came the wild party of Saturday night. The letter declares that Miss Thomas took a large dose of cocaine immediately preceding the swallowing of the bichloride of mercury.
>
> She did not have medical attention until sometime afterward. A friend of hers, who had spent some time with the pair, said they were like a couple of kids, calling one another "papa" and "mamma." She said apparently their past quarrels had been forgotten.

Despite suggestions of Olive taking cocaine before ingesting the poison, the physician's statement does not concur with these claims. On September 19, 1920, C. F. Bertelli of *The Los Angeles Examiner* relayed an article to the American public that was originally printed in Paris the day before. Rosika Dolly of the famous Dolly Sisters, spoke of her friend Olive's last moments:

> I knew Olive Thomas very well. In fact, I was invited to the party on the fatal night," Rosika Dolly ... told me in discussing the death and the conditions in Paris which are held in part responsible for it.
>
> "I was not able to go and did not see Olive until afterward at the hospital. She was devoted to Jack and he was devoted to her. As she dragged out the agonizing hours before her death she kissed his hand repeatedly and told him how much she loved him. Personally I am certain that Olive could not have committed suicide while normal and therefore I do not really believe she committed suicide."

Bertelli (Paris correspondent of Universal Service, reporting for *The Journal*) relayed many reports back to America during the controversial days leading up to and surrounding Olive's death. Graphic stories about the wild parties that lured Americans to Paris and now Olive Thomas to her death threatened to slander the name and reputation of a beloved star the public came to know as "Everybody's Sweetheart."

Bertelli gave accounts of priceless champagne rivers flowing as if it cost nothing, and of waiters impersonating slaves serving food and women, yes women, some nude and others nearly nude on silver trays. After linking Olive Thomas's name to these wild twentieth century reproductions of Greco orgies, fellow reporter Johnny O'Connor set out to restore Olive's reputation. O'Connor angrily debunked Bertelli's slanderous claims in his popular column *Stage News of the Week*:

> *The Journal* has done much to Americanize America. Apparently satisfied that they have completed their mission at home, *The Journal* is now, through the efforts of Mr. Bertelli, trying to Americanize Paris.
>
> In trying to Americanize Paris, Bertelli in order to be convincing and smack of reality coolly stigmatizes the reputation of one of the sweetest little characters who ever registered on the screen. We don't know Mr. Bertelli, nor do we ever care to. But the orgy

he depicts in his article, suggests that Bertelli knows his way around the dumps he describes, for in one paragraph he admits playing the role of guide to the "shockeries" for visiting friends.

Bertelli sensationalizes his story and heartlessly attacks the name of little Olive Thomas in such a manner that it carries all the stench of a direct accusation. And, *The Journal* proceeds to blast forth the story under a four-column scarehead; while the body of little Olive Thomas is speeding across the ocean on its journey to her last resting place.

What a beautiful story to find its way into the home of hundreds of thousands of Olive Thomas's admirers. What a nice thing to comfort those nearest and dearest to her in this, their hour of bereavement. And what a nice smear to throw on the illusions of the picture fans who knew little Olive Thomas as they viewed her on the screen. At least *The Journal* might have considered some of these things before publishing such blasphemy.

June 1920. Olive looking at a portrait that Harrison Fisher painted of her five years before.

But, little Olive Thomas had many friends and those friends know better than Bertelli that this little child was not a frequenter of the holes Bertelli speaks of from his intimate knowledge. The motion picture industry and the motion picture public will remember Bertelli for the deed he has done. And they will always remember Olive Thomas, as she lived, one of the sweetest characters ever born to this earth.

There's no doubting it, whether it be in Hollywood or Paris, Olive and Jack were always ready for a party. But, the industry wanted the American public to read about Olive Thomas, Victim, not Olive Thomas, Party Girl, who got what was coming to her.

Jack never denied that he and Olive went to various night spots on the evening in question; he even admitted to the consumption of alcohol. Forbes W. Fairbairn of *The Los Angeles Examiner* published Jack's version of events on September 13, 1920. Just days after Olive's death he had flown back to London with his ex–brother-in-law Owen Moore in an attempt to escape the growing media circus in Paris:

> London, Sept. 12—[Pickford and Moore] arrived in London by airplane this afternoon from Paris for a few days. Pickford gave me the following interview regarding the

death of his wife, Olive Thomas, who died Thursday from the effects of poison swallowed early Sunday morning, a week ago. "Olive and I were the greatest pals on earth," said Jack. "Her death is a ghastly mistake. We both canceled work in America to take a belated honeymoon. We were the happiest couple imaginable. Coming over she gave me a big birthday party aboard ship. When we arrived in Paris her only thought was that she had to buy some dresses and then get back home to complete her picture contracts so that we could settle down to have a home and babies.

"I went to London to buy some clothes for myself and arrived back in Paris the fateful Saturday night. We had dinner with a few friends and went to the cafes. We arrived back at the Ritz hotel at about 3 o'clock in the morning. I had already booked airplane seats for London. We were going Sunday morning. Both of us were tired out. We both had been drinking a little. I insisted that we had better not pack then, but rather get up early before our trip and do it then.

"I went to bed immediately. She fussed around and wrote a note to her mother. It read:

"'*Mamma dear: Well and having a nice time. Leaving here September 11. I will cable you from the boat and will tell you all the news when I arrive. Olive. Love to all.*'

"She was in the bathroom. Suddenly she shrieked: 'My God!' I jumped out of bed, rushed toward her and caught her in my arms. She cried to me to find out what was in the bottle. I picked it up and read: 'Poison!' It was a toilet solution and the label was in French. I realized what she had done and sent for the doctor. Meanwhile, I forced her to drink water in order to make her vomit. She screamed, 'Oh, my God, I'm poisoned!'

"I forced the whites of eggs down her throat, hoping to offset the poison. The doctor came. He pumped her stomach three times while I held Olive. Nine o'clock in the morning I got her to the Neuilly Hospital, where Doctors Choate and Wharton took charge of her. They told me she had swallowed bichoride of mercury in an alcoholic solution, which is ten times worse than tabloids. She didn't want to die. She took the poison by mistake.

"We both loved each other since the day we married. The fact that we were separated months at a time made no difference in our affection for each other. She even was conscious enough the day before she died to ask the nurse to come to America with her until she had fully recovered, having no thought she would die.

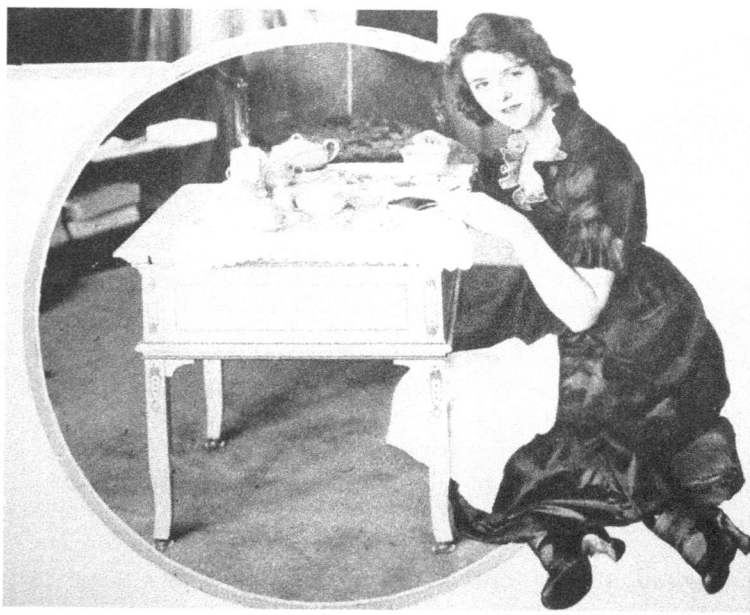

In June 1920. Olive has afternoon tea.

"She kept continually calling for me. I was beside her day and night until her death. The physicians held out hope for her until the last moment, until they found her kidneys paralyzed. Then they lost hope. But the doctors told me she had fought harder than any patient they ever had. She held onto her life as only one case in fifty. She seemed stronger the last two days. She was conscious, and said she would get better and go home to her mother.

"'It's all a mistake, darling Jack,' she said. But I

knew she was dying. She was kept alive only by hypodermic injections during the last twelve hours. I was the last one she recognized. I watched her eyes glaze and realized she was dying. I asked her how she was feeling and she answered: 'Pretty weak, but I'll be all right in a little while, don't worry, darling.'

"Those were her last words. I held her in my arms and she died an hour later. Owen Moore was at her bedside. All stories and rumors of wild parties and cocaine and domestic fights since we left New York are untrue. I am leaving for home Saturday with Olive's body. Her burial will be in New York."

Contrary to medical reports, Jack maintained that Olive had continued to verbally communicate with him up until her death. Highly unlikely

June 1920. Olive at home with her record player.

given the fact that she had first ingested the poison and vomited some of it back up, thus burning her vocal cords both times. With an investigation into what happened undertaken immediately, had Olive been able to speak, the first person questioned by police would have obviously been the ailing victim. Olive was never able to give her version of events, to anyone.

In order to avoid the embarrassment of confessing to being a victim of syphilis and needing the mercury bichloride as a treatment for the disease, Jack emphatically stated that Olive had mistakenly drank a "toilet solution." Back in Hollywood he was known as "Mr. Syphilis" so it was no secret as to why he would have mercury bichloride in his possession. Still, Jack was Jack. Even with the reality of his young wife dying in front of him, he was still trying to cover up as best he could.

Before the advent of antibiotics, syphilis was frequently treated with mercury bichloride. The use of the substance for the treatment of the sexually transmitted disease gave rise to the saying, "A night in the arms of Venus leads to a lifetime on Mercury."

Once absorbed into the bloodstream, this highly toxic and corrosive substance

Despite her death at the dawn of the flapper era, Olive was the first flapper before the term was even known to the public. Here she is dressed like one.

combines with proteins in the plasma or enters the red blood cells. It does not readily pass into the brain (often giving the victim the ability to speak until death) but it fiercely attacks other major organs. All mercury absorbed from the stomach and intestine is carried through the blood directly to the liver. It accumulates in the kidneys and often causes severe damage.

Ingestion may cause severe gastrointestinal irritation, renal failure, and death with acute lethal doses in humans ranging from 1 to 4 graines. The toxic effects are usually evident within 10–15 minutes of ingestion. Death can occur within 24 hours, resulting from shock, renal damage, and severe gastrointestinal damage or kidney failure. Chronic symptoms include increased salivation, bleeding gums and loosening of the teeth.

On June 10, 1913, Dr. William J. Robinson wrote a letter to the editor of *The New York Times* (published June 16, 1913) about the spate of poisoning deaths linked to bichloride of mercury, saying:

> Since the somewhat dramatic death of a Southern banker from accidental poisoning by a tablet of bichloride of mercury, many suggestions have been offered with the purpose of minimizing the possibility of such accidents. One suggestion is to make all poisonous tablets of a peculiar shape, triangular or octagonal, etc., which will render them for harmless tablets unlikely.
>
> Another suggestion is to have them colored in a peculiar manner, still another is to have each tablet wrapped separately in wax or parchment paper, or enclosed in a gelatin envelope; still another is to have all such poisons dispensed in a peculiar bottle, with a prickly surface, or with a tinkling bell attached to it, etc. All these suggestions are good as far as they go; but they do not go far enough, because they do not go to the root of the evil.
>
> Those who make the suggestions all assume that such poisons as bichloride of mercury (corrosive sublimate) or carbolic acid are necessities in the household, and being necessities, we simply must surround their use with certain safeguards. This is an erroneous idea, and I wish to declare in the most emphatic manner possible that not only is bichloride of mercury and carbolic acid not necessities in any household, but there is *no* excuse for their ever being in any home.
>
> The only way to avoid deaths accidental or deliberate, by these violent poisons is to prohibit their sale absolutely, except in small quantities on a physician's prescription, as is the case in most European countries.

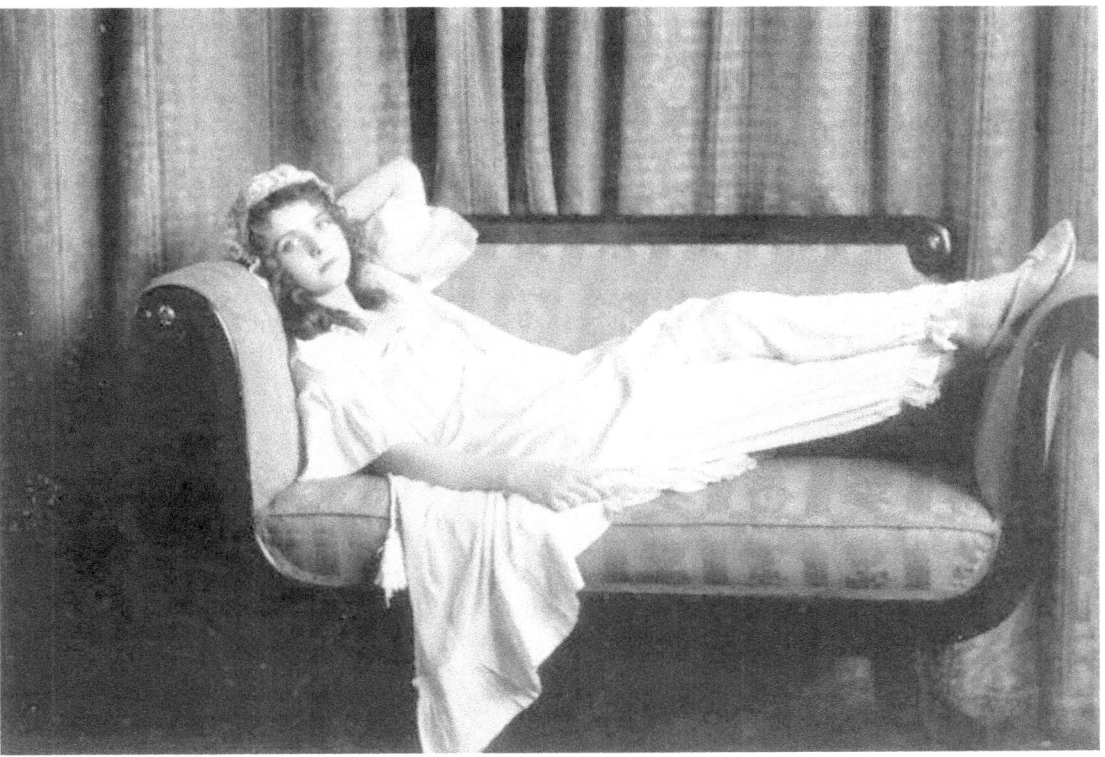

Taking it easy.

I am not given to sensationalism, but I am convinced that hundreds and hundreds of accidental deaths from bichloride and carbolic acid occur annually which never reach public notice. The death has taken place, the heart-breaking tragedy is there and cannot be undone; the greatest wish then is to avoid neighborhood and newspaper notoriety, to escape the unpleasantness of an autopsy, and the friendly family physician is called in and gives a certificate testifying to death from natural causes. All these tragedies could be avoided by forbidding the sale of strong poisons for which there is absolutely no need, no justification.

Less than two weeks later, a June 26 letter to the *Times* suggested several ways to prevent further unnecessary deaths as a result of ingesting the poison by mistake. Edward Swallow wrote:

I presume the recent case of poisoning by taking mercury bichloride tablets instead of some kind of tablets for internal use can only be accounted for by the fact of the poisonous tablets being the same color or probably the same size as some other harmless ones, which the unfortunate person happened to have kept on the same shelf with other medicines used in the house. This is a practice common with the public, who knows practically little of poisons, the very reason one might think for taking extra care how they store and handle them.

Bichloride of mercury tablets are manufactured in blue color as well as white, the natural color of the well-known antiseptic, and it would probably be a good idea if the law forbade the sale of the latter variety, and made it compulsory for each blue tablet to be stamped "poison." Also, bichloride of mercury tablets should only be obtained on prescription from a doctor, thus preventing the sale of the antiseptic in original bottles.

The Bridgeport Telegram (Friday, September 10, 1920) published a direct quote from Olive's treating doctor about what happened on the night in question, saying:

> Doctor Joseph Choate of Los Angeles who is chief physician for Miss Thomas today gave the following account of the incident of the condition of his patient, "At 4 o'clock Sunday morning, Olive Thomas, by mistake took a large quantity of alcoholic preparation containing twelve graines of bichloride of mercury. It is estimated that she received at least six or eight graines (or grams) of bichloride. Realizing the mistake she called to her husband. It was only through the efforts of Jack Pickford in giving first aid that Miss Thomas is alive today.
>
> The effect of the poison was rapid because it was in alcoholic solution. The usual acute nephritis occurred within 21 hours. The first specimen (blood test) showed two and one half grams of albumin (the main protein in human blood) per liter and the second and third specimens each ten grams per liter, which constitutes a world's clinical record. Thereafter, it was impossible to make tests, there being a complete suppression for four days. The very best medical talent has been called on the case. Her condition is most serious but there is still hope."

Actually, Olive's family had already been notified that there was absolutely no hope of recovery. The poison had taken its toll and Olive had gone deaf and blind before lapsing into a coma. Acute nephritis ended her suffering on the morning of September 10, 1920. Dorothy Gish (younger sister of Lillian Gish) and her mother had canceled their ongoing travel plans to stay by Olive's side. They were with her when she died, as was Jack.

The *New York American* (September 12, 1920) reported that Olive's brothers had been told of Olive's imminent death but they chose to keep the grim news from their mother until she arrived to meet them in New York from her Philadelphia home. They had underestimated the media coverage surrounding their sister's condition and then her death. The article "Olive's Mother Got Sad News on Train" read:

> Mrs. Harry Vankirk, mother of Olive Thomas, arrived here yesterday morning from her home in Philadelphia, after a summons from her sons to come to New York at once. She had been advised daily of her daughter's condition, but had not been told of her death when she started for this city. First word of the tragedy came to her on the train. She glanced over the shoulder of a man sitting in front of her and read the headlines in a morning paper telling of her daughter's death.
>
> So greatly was she affected that she had to be helped from the train when met at the station by her sons. Her first demand was, "Is it true she is dead?" The young men, to avoid immediate shock to her, told her the cables were in error and that the end had not come. Later, when Mrs. Vankirk had been quieted down in her daughter's apartment, she was told the poisoning had proved fatal. She collapsed and was put under the care of a physician.
>
> William and James Duffy, brothers of the actress, made absolute denial of the reports of serious domestic trouble between her and her husband, Jack Pickford. The Duffys added, "Petty troubles there might have been, but they certainly were not of a nature that would be likely to cause Olive to take her life. Besides, she was not at all of that temperament, and couldn't have done it even had she tried."
>
> Asked if they knew of the $300,000 (approximately $2.75 million today) life insurance policy for which, it is said, Mrs. Pickford applied, the brothers replied they knew nothing of it until they read the newspapers.

Dr. Choate (who reportedly did Olive's physical for the life insurance policy before she left for Paris) was quoted as saying that Olive had not spoken since she was stricken (contradicting other reports that she did indeed speak several times). The doctor's version of events are merely "facts" told to him by others ... or what he was paid to say. Corruption in France was rampant at the time and it's highly likely that money is the reason there are so many holes in the case, both then and especially now. Bribe or no bribe, the contradictions of what happened leading up to Olive taking the poison and the days afterward continued to unfold as the days rolled by.

Jack's statement was the most publicly circulated but others were interviewed and gave a different version of events. Fellow actress and friend Mae Murray stated that Olive was high on drugs when she saw her last, yet former brother-in-law Owen Moore stated that Olive was in "fine spirits." The Dolly Sisters agreed with Moore. Some even claimed they witnessed Olive partying alone, *without* Jack. Mae Murray was far from a reliable source (she fled to Spain a few days before Olive died) but she refused to believe that Olive would ever commit suicide. After Olive's death, she never spoke to Jack Pickford again. In her autobiography *The Self Enchanted* (Jane Ardmore with Mae Murray, 1959), Mae claims that Olive told her that Jack didn't want her on the trip at all and it was only at her insistence that he allowed her to join him at the last minute. Mae said that Olive in Paris was distraught and tense and crying. Jack had left her the minute they arrived and she hadn't seen him in almost three weeks. Mae and Robert Z. Leonard, her husband, offered to take Olive out for dinner at the Ritz at 8 o'clock but Olive phoned to say Jack had returned at last and was throwing a big party at Zelli's, a nightclub. Everybody went to Zelli's. Jack ignored Olive and she became hysterical, running out into the night.

With so many unknowns in retracing Olive's footsteps on the night she took the poison and beyond, it's important to touch on what *is* known. The one common factor leading up to Olive taking the poison was that no one seemed to be able to account for Jack and Olive, together or apart, after 10 P.M. There are five unaccounted hours between 10 P.M. and 3 A.M., the latter being the time that Jack stated they *both* got back to the hotel room. None of the so-called "friends" who Jack said came to their room in order to get them to rejoin the partying were ever identified or came forward to give statements.

Other reports suggest that Jack and Olive went their separate ways for most of the evening. As the early morning hours passed by, Jack grew increasingly angry at his wife for not being back at the hotel with him. When she did creep back in at 4 A.M., the inevitable confrontation began and shortly after, Olive was poisoned. *The Los Angeles Herald* (September 10, 1920) reported the following:

> It was on Sunday night that Olive, accompanied by several of her friends, set out to "see real old Paris," went for the last time to the famous "Dead Rat" of the Montmartre

OLIVE'S MOTHER GOT SAD NEWS ON TRAIN

Summoned Here by Sons, but They Hid the Fact of the Death in Message.

The tragic headline about Olive's mother receiving news of her daughter's death while on a train.

A reflection of Olive. The photographer can also be seen in the mirror.

district. [Despite its high-class appearance, the "Dead Rat" was a notorious hangout for gangsters, drug dealers and the like.) All of them in the highest of spirits—on the surface at least—the hilarity at the Montmartre resort waxed greater and greater until, with the closing of the "Dead Rat" at 1 A.M., Olive Thomas and her crowd started on a taxicab round of the clandestine resorts which are always open to the magic sesame—gold. But even the most maddening of hilarious nights must pass with the dawn, and when the Follies dancer and star of the Los Angeles studios crept back into her suite at the Ritz at 4 A.M., she found her husband, Jack Pickford, deeply resentful.

Extremely excited as a result of the round of Montmartre resorts, a fit of deepest despondency seized her when her husband attempted to remonstrate with her. Olive went into the bathroom where she drank three-quarters of a bottle of bichloride solution prescribed for face external use. Whether she drank this intentionally or by mistake is a question yet unanswered.

In the consideration of mercury bichloride, excessive use and "accidental death" as a result of using the agent in the latter part of the 1800s and the early part of the 20th century (for many conditions) caused the medical industry to eventually declare that its deleterious influences greatly overbalanced any possible good that could result from its use as a cure, thus deciding to exclude it entirely from the list of medical agents.

The widespread manufacture of penicillin after WWII allowed syphilis to be effectively cured for the first time and to this day, the primary treatment for syphilis is penicillin. Thanks to the advances in modern medicine a steady dose of the antibiotic ranging from several days to several weeks will cure the disease. In 1920, at the time

Jack (and possibly Olive) was using the mercury bichloride for syphilis, the usual length of treatment was up to three years.

Jack's version of events surrounding Olive's death varied over time but the one consistency to his story was that his wife's death was nothing more than a tragic accident. *The Los Angeles Examiner* (September 12, 1920) ran an article that strongly disagreed:

OLIVE THOMAS, MOTION PICTURE ACTRESS, DEAD

The headline that shocked the world!

> Dr. Warden, famous poison specialist, who had charge of the case toward the end, declared a police investigation into the circumstances under which Miss Thomas died would be of the utmost value in revealing the facts. "It would show," he said, "whether Miss Thomas committed suicide, as the medical evidence indicates, or whether she took the stuff by mistake, as claimed. Personally, I am convinced that if she had taken a sleep potion in the same quantity as she took the poison she would be dead just the same."

Owen Moore gave his own statement to the press (*The Bridgeport Telegram*, September 10, 1920):

> Olive was extremely unwell when she left America. As soon as she arrived in Paris a doctor was called. She was prescribed a sleeping draught that she was to take at night when she was unable to sleep. However, she did not heed the doctor and Saturday night she insisted on going out to a party. Contrary to rumors, her husband went with her. They returned to the Ritz Hotel early Sunday morning and that is when the tragedy occurred. It is my belief that Olive, being extremely high-strung and nervous, took the subliminate by mistake for her sleeping draught. I do not believe she tried to commit suicide. Jack has been splendid throughout.

Moore was not the most neutral of sources either. Having just divorced Mary Pickford (at her request so she could marry Douglas Fairbanks), he would still do all that he could to remain in her good graces. That included giving positive statements to the press about Jack and Olive's relationship, playing down any scandalous suicide reports that would blacken the Pickford name and taking care of his fragile ex-–brother-in-law and friend, Jack, in her absence. Moore was in damage control mode, not just for Jack's sake, but for Mary's too.

The squeaky-clean Pickford reputation wasn't all it was cracked up to be. It seems the entire family had addictive personalities, even Mary. She started drinking heavily in the early 1930s. In Charles Lockwood's *Dream Palaces: Hollywood at Home*, fellow actress May McAvoy said:

> After dinner (at Pickfair), the men would go off by themselves—I thought it was rude and crude—and Mary would take us up to her room. She'd go into the bathroom and take a big slug of something, then rinse her mouth out with mouthwash.
> Jack supplied Mary with all the hard liquor she wanted during Prohibition. One day, he and director Eddie Sutherland were drinking and they ran out. "Jack said not to worry, and we drove over to Pickfair," Sutherland recalled years later. Mary wasn't home, and Jack went right up to her room and into her bathroom. "Gin or whiskey?" he asked. "The hydrogen peroxide bottle's gin, the Listerine bottle" Scotch." We sat down in the bathroom, Jack on the tub, me on the commode, and finished off both bottles. I was worried about Mary. I know what it's like to go looking for a drink and not find it. But Jack said it was okay, there was plenty more where that came from.

Mary's beloved mother Charlotte died in 1928, Jack died in 1933 (age 36) and her sister Lottie died in 1936 (age 42). She was slowly losing her husband, Douglas Fairbanks, to his womanizing ways and by 1933, at age 41, she would make her last film. But, prior to these personal woes, Charlotte Pickford would regularly share decanters of alcohol with her three children, Mary, Jack and Lottie. They all drank, all the time, in good times and in bad. Now that they were gone, Mary was left to drink alone.

In the eyes of the public, Mary Pickford was still the little girl with the curls; she was still America's Sweetheart. Yet, behind the sacred doors of Pickfair, Mary had lost her family, her husband *and* her career. Alcohol was now her only comfort.

Mary Pickford's innocent, somewhat puritanical reputation was part of the Hollywood myth that the public was led to believe, but, in reality, she was just another Pickford who used a substance to numb the pain. Unlike her siblings and despite her alcoholism, Mary lived a long life, dying of a cerebral hemorrhage on May 29, 1979. She was 87 years old.

★ Chapter 6 ★

THE INVESTIGATION

That's the first time I ever had to watch anybody die.
—Jack Pickford referring to Olive's death

The official morgue report stated that Olive's body arrived at 6.35 P.M. on September 11. Her name, age, place of birth and other personal information is filled out correctly, but the space for occupation states, "no occupation."

The "type of death" is listed as "poisoning" yet the "presumed cause of death" is listed as "unknown." The time between her death and her arrival at the morgue is given as "one day." Her transport between the American Hospital and the morgue was in a police truck. The column for "suicide or homicide" is left blank, implying her death was accidental. The morgue report lists exactly what Olive was wearing when she arrived at the American Hospital; these items were also shipped to the morgue along with her body and itemized. There was a garland of flowers made of pink fabric, pink garters, white stockings, white satin low-cut shoes, a white slip, a white dress with trimmings and a white towel.

The day after Olive's death, the September 11 edition of *The Mansfield News* (a newspaper based in Ohio) ran the headline, "The Officials Order Autopsy to Ascertain the Exact Cause of the Death of Olive Thomas." The article goes into further detail, saying:

> Paris, Sept. 11—The judicial authorities tonight ordered the body of Miss Olive Thomas, American motion picture actress and sister-in-law of Mary Pickford, deposited in the morgue for an autopsy on Monday to determine the exact character and amount of poison which caused her death in the American Hospital at Neuilly yesterday. The Thomas case took this sensational turn after apparently having been closed. The judiciary refused to accept the report of Police Commissionaire Catrou that Miss Thomas' death was accidental. The judges held that the evidence was insufficient.
> The initial determination of death was based mainly upon the testimony of husband Jack Pickford who said that his wife had drunk a quantity of mercury bichloride solution by mistake after returning to her apartment at the Ritz last Sunday after a gay night among the Montmartre dance resorts.

Three days after Olive's death, a September 13, 1920, Paris edition of the *New York Herald Tribune* reported on the impending autopsy that would be undertaken on the body of the petite actress that afternoon:

> An autopsy of the body of Miss Olive Thomas will be held at the Paris Morgue today by Dr. Paul, who has been commissioned by M. Pamart, the examining magistrate, to determine the cause of the film actress' death.
>
> While dismissing any suspicion of foul play, the police authorities wish to make a thorough investigation before permitting the remains to be sent to America for burial. It is said that the examination is being extended to certain Montmartre resorts and is linked with the case of Captain Spalding, formerly of the United States Army, who was recently sentenced to a term of six months imprisonment here for bringing cocaine into the country. The examination of the body at the American Hospital at Neuilly-sure-Seine revealed only the discolorations which are always produced in cases of mercurial poisoning. [It was rumored that Olive's name was listed in Captain Spalding's book of "customers" who regularly purchased cocaine and heroin.]
>
> Mr. Jack Pickford, the husband of the dead actress, in replying to the questions put by police commissioner, M. Catrou, denied reports of marital difficulties. His version of accidental poisoning and of the immediate efforts to summon aid for his wife was borne out not only by the employees of the Hotel Ritz but also by the physician who attended Miss Thomas at the hospital. During his wife's consciousness at the hospital, Mr. Pickford made an identical account of the incident, and Miss Thomas implied the accuracy of the account by the smile of confidence with which she regarded her husband.

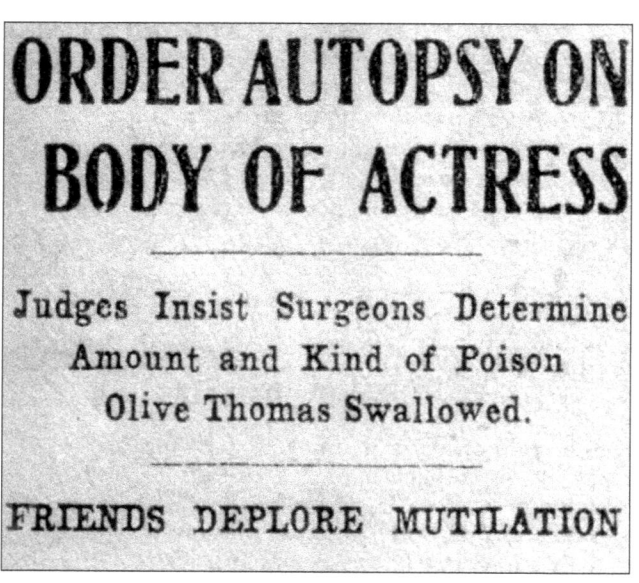

French and American newspapers ran headlines similar to this for days after Olive's death.

At the time, Paris was the sleazy, carefree city that Americans would travel to for the abundance of drugs, booze and wild parties. While Jack's drug use (both cocaine and heroin) was widely documented, Olive became a drug addict by association, not necessarily because she was a user. No evidence suggests that Olive ever went beyond a wild party and too much champagne.

During the late teens and early twenties, many Americans were arrested for drug smuggling in Paris and the newspapers documented these arrests on an almost daily basis. While the French papers blamed the Americans for "corrupting their country," the American papers blamed the French for the temptations of a sinful city that took the life of "Everybody's Sweetheart," Olive Thomas. After Olive's death, fellow actress Mae Murray said in her autobiography, "Paris lost its charm after that."

On September 14, the day after the autopsy, the Paris edition of the *New York Herald Tribune* published the findings of the coroner:

6. The Investigation

93

A photograph postcard of the *Mauretania*, the ship that brought Olive's body back to the United States of America.

Accidental death due to mercury poisoning was the result arrived after the autopsy of the body of Miss Olive Thomas yesterday. No trace of violence was discovered and a burial certificate was issued.

No funeral service will be held in Paris, but the body will be taken to the Church of the Holy Trinity at three o'clock this afternoon to remain until Saturday, when it will be taken to America in the Mauretania, accompanied by Mr. Pickford and several close friends. The last rites will be performed in the United States.

The *Mauretania*, carrying Olive's body, finally docked in the United States on September 24, two weeks after her death. The day after, the *New York Clipper* ran a story (relayed from Paris, September 17, 1920) about Jack being sued for $30,000 (approximately $290,000 today) for fifty dresses and two fur coats (one ermine and seal and one mink) that Olive had ordered a week preceding her death. She had only had two fittings and no clothes were delivered, but the heartless claimants argued that the orders were definitely given and even threatened to seize Jack's luggage as surety unless he paid. A mutual understanding was swiftly arranged and the disagreement was eventually settled without further incident.

The Mansfield News, based in Ohio, followed up their initial report (in a later edition) on Olive's autopsy results, saying:

The death of Miss Olive Thomas, beautiful young American motion picture actress, who died in the American Hospital at Neuilly from mercurial poisoning was accidental, it was announced today by Police Commissionaire Catrou who conducted an official investigation. Mr. Catrou said he would make a report to the judicial authorities to show that Miss Thomas was the victim of an accident and that she had not intentionally committed suicide. The investigation was conducted at great speed and the police official said at noon that it was virtually completed.

He examined employees from the Ritz Hotel where Miss Thomas was living and doctors who attended her and her husband, Jack Pickford.... The body of Miss Thomas will

A rare lobby card for *Everybody's Sweetheart* (1920). Incidentally, the title of the film has nothing to do with the story line. It was changed to capitalize on Olive's death.

not be exposed to the view even to her friends. The face was horribly contracted by pain and badly splotched by the deadly poison.

Pickford protested against reports that there had been a disagreement between his wife and himself. He branded them as untrue. Testifying at the inquiry the young husband said he returned to the Ritz hotel at 3:30 o'clock Sunday morning after spending the night dancing at Montmartre resorts with his wife. He declared that both he and his wife were sober.

"I went to bed and my wife entered the bathroom," continued Pickford. "She took a bottle from the table and drank from it. Then she threw the bottle upon the floor in alarm and called for help. I jumped from the bed and ran into the bathroom where my wife was standing in the middle of the floor and the broken bottle was lying at her feet. I saw that she had taken bichloride of mercury and I tried every antidote that was available. I called in the hotel employees and sent for four doctors. My wife was taken to the hospital."

The body of Miss Thomas will not be embalmed until the inquiry is completed and a medical examination is made. It is expected however that the body will be shipped to the United States next week for burial. A sensation was caused by Miss Thomas' death and many prominent American residents united in denouncing the Babylonian revels of Paris.

Miss Thomas took poison after a gay night in the Montmartre restaurants followed by a visit to clandestine places of entertainment which are operated in defiance of police

A scene still from the lost film *Everybody's Sweetheart* (1920).

regulations. Her friends said she was much excited over the sights she had seen and was in an extremely nervous condition when she returned to her hotel on Monday. They assume that she took poison by mistake while in this excited condition.

The Rev. Dr. Beekman, pastor of the American Church in Paris who has been conducting a campaign against vice ever since the war, described conditions as "deplorable." He declared that many Americans came to Paris and fall victim to the lures of Babylon. "Thousands stay long enough just to lose their souls and then return home broken in health and spirit and unfit to lead a clean life," said the clergyman.

The *Syracuse Herald* (Sunday, October 31, 1920) ran an explosively graphic article about the wild, drug-induced sideshows that were then considered "entertainment" in the various restaurants and nightclubs of Paris. This in-depth article, entitled "What Olive Thomas Saw in Gay Paris Before She Killed Herself," gives a first-hand account of the type of reckless atmosphere that Olive and Jack were exposed to during their stay abroad. It read, in part:

> What happened in the four hours between midnight of that September Saturday night and 4 o'clock Sunday morning, when Olive Thomas, the young American actress and wife of Jack Pickford, arrived home at her apartments in Paris, swallowed the fatal poison and sank to the floor sobbing: "This is what Paris has done to me!"
>
> It may never be known exactly what Olive Thomas saw and did or exactly what nightlife resorts she visited, but the tragic death of this young actress has served to focus world-wide attention on what the Rev. Dr. Beekman calls "the lure of Paris," and a

movement is now under way to force the police authorities of the French capital to clean out the notorious amusement places which are a disgrace to the city.

If the simple-minded Americans who help maintain by their money the vicious dens of Paris knew the real facts which surrounded "the lure" of these tawdry places and the people in them they would not be so easily victimized.

In leading Americans to patronize these resorts, a very dangerous and important role is played by a host of disreputable noblemen, some of French birth and others recruited from the nobility of every country in Europe. They have lost their position in their own circles through some misdeed and now make a living by steering wealthy American and other tourists to the disreputable haunts of Paris. And the renegade noblemen are paid a large commission by the proprietors on all money spent in these places.

In their own country Americans would not allow such men in their homes, and abroad they are easily misled by social pretense. These noblemen are usually of authentic title, but actually they have fallen to the lowest state of degradation and are trafficking in vice and crime by means of their titles and pretended rank. In reality, their social status is lower than that of the waiters and the cabmen who honestly take their fees, whereas the others are only masquerading as "gentlemen." They are distinguished-looking noblemen, with gloved hands and waxed mustaches—the Princes and the Counts—who insidiously guide the unsuspecting American into the most dangerous and costly dens of Paris. They are permitted to enjoy social intimacy with the wives and daughters of respectable Americans, who too often feel deeply honored by their attentions.

The cable dispatches have emphasized the fact that Olive Thomas spent part of the fatal night at supper in the Café du Rat Mort, at Montmartre. After that a veil seems to have been drawn over the places she visited and the scenes she witnessed. The variety of entertainment offered in all-night Paris is endless. Did Olive Thomas visit some of these places which moved her to feel utter disgust with life and mankind?

The Café du Rat Mort—the Café of the Dead Rat! The name is somewhat suggestive of putrefying pleasures, but this restaurant is, in fact, one of the better restaurants of Montmartre. It is a very luxurious and expensive establishment. It is only as a stepping stone to the innumerable haunts lying within a stone's throw that it belongs within the circle of demoralization.

Here one can obtain exquisite wines and liqueurs and delightfully cooked dishes. No drugs or semi-poisons are dropped into the drinks, as at some places. Of course, the diner may throw a dash of other into his own or his companion's gin and thereby make a mixture of maddening intoxication. That would be his own affair, not that of the establishment.

The Rat Mort has always maintained a peculiarly excellent Tzigane or gypsy orchestra. Some of these men are wonderful violinists, and deliberately set themselves to fascinate a woman visitor whom they perceive to be especially susceptible to music. Many an American has been led into rash actions, which she could never have committed at home, by these designing, if artistic scoundrels.

At all the fashionable Parisian restaurants a young girl goes around to the tables offering bouquets which the men diners are invited to buy for their companions. Whenever she thinks it safe the flower girl will sprinkle a dash of cocaine, from a tiny silver pepper pot, upon the bouquet before handing it to the customer. For such a bouquet the exorbitant price of ten to twenty francs is asked.

A girl who sniffs cocaine in the course of an exciting and fatiguing evening is likely to conceive an irresistible attraction for the drug. Many an American woman has started the deadly cocaine habit in restaurants of Paris.

The disreputable young noblemen already described play a great part in spreading the drug habits among American women. Most of them carry an imposing outfit of gold and silver receptacles for drugs, attached to a key chain at the waist. Often they are drug addicts themselves. Among their outfit is usually to be found a box of cocaine and an atomizer, with which they can squirt a dash of liquid morphine into a friend's drink.

6. The Investigation

This selection of posters was published in an *Exhibitor's Trade Review* book sent out to theaters. The manager of the theater would order the posters for his lobby to promote the newly released film. Interestingly, the only original title here is *Love's Prisoner* (1919); the other titles were eventually changed before the film's release.

Of similar standing to the Rat Mort is the establishment generally known to Americans as "the Abbey," but properly called the Abbaye de Theleme. It is within half a block of the other restaurant on the Place Pigalle. It is named after that Abbaye de Theleme. It is a place filled with men and women intent not upon religion, but upon enjoying themselves in every possible sensual way that pleased them.

The "Abbey" is a large and imposing place. It boasts a stage under a dome where a vaudeville performance goes on while the diners eat and the orchestra plays. Such appropriate performances as the "danse du ventre" (the stomach dance) have been given during dinner. This establishment has always been a favorite night resort with spendthrift Russian grand dukes and wealthy South Americans and Cubans.

As one steps out of either of these establishments on the Place Pigalle, there are within a few minutes drive hundreds of places where every kind of entertainment is offered that perverse imagination can invent to stir the senses.

On the Rue St. Lazare, just opposite the great St. Lazare railway station, there is a nameless establishment which has always been remarkable for its strange entertainments. The house furnishes exquisite dinners and suppers to parties who always order and engage a room in advance. Some of the rooms are large enough to allow space for a vaudeville show.

The proprietor of this place prides himself that he can always furnish a new thrill for the most dissipated patrons. At a recent supper party the proceedings opened by the waiters carrying in an immense basket of flowers which they placed on the table.

Immediately it opened up and a pretty young girl, almost entirely undraped, stepped out, began to run around the table and dip her feet in the plates just before supper was served. Several of the men guests tried to bite her little toes.

This entertainment proved so popular that it has been many times repeated, but other bizarre performances have been given. Latterly the house has been distinguished by the "whipping dancers" which have been given there. Since the great upheaval in Russia, Paris has been overrun by Russian dancers, often women of great talent and beauty, who on account of their distress are willing to give any exhibition that may be asked of them.

At this place the Russian dancers give a supper performance in which they go through the maddest gyration and end by lashing one another with whips until their backs and necks are marked with great welts and they sink to the floor exhausted.

Many of the Parisian resorts, understanding that their spectacles will cause embarrassment to American women, insist that they shall be masked. As the woman visitor passes the front door an attendant steps forward and arranges a mask on her face, observing: "Madame will kindly wear this mask. Perhaps she would not like to be recognized in this place."

Why should American men and women of respectability at home go to such places? One important influence, the insidious ether cocktail and the bouquet sprayed with cocaine, will be explained later on.

But in leading visitors to depart from their home standards of refined behavior the disreputable noblemen already mentioned exert a great influence. The assurance by men of such apparently high rank that it is the proper thing to do this or that produces an overpowering effect on Americans, both women and men.

The ultimate object of every entertainment is to exact an exorbitant charge from the spectator—usually in the form of an innocent looking bill for supper. Perhaps the American visitor will utter a roar of protest. The manager will suavely remark: "Our clients never complain. It is a perfectly proper bill. Is monsieur prepared to be sued, after he has enjoyed such entertainment?"

This disguised threat usually brings prompt payment. The escorting noblemen often takes a hand in bringing about a settlement. Perhaps he may consider it wise to reach out a lordly hand for the bill and remark: "Don't let's make a fuss. I will pay the bill."

A proud American will rarely allow a noble guest to pay for his entertainment. If the noblemen does suffer any loss, the house reimburses him. If the bill is paid by the American the titled guide collects half the next day.

One of the newest and most fashionable night resorts of Paris is conducted by an American, Harry Pilcer, and is called L'Oasis. The same criticisms cannot be made against this place as against the others mentioned here.

6. The Investigation

A close-up shot (taken in 1911) of the menacing entrance to L'Enfer, or "Hell" in English. It was one of the popular Parisian nightclubs in the region where Olive and Jack partied.

L'Oasis is an open-air dancing place in a beautiful garden laid out by Paul Poiret, the eccentric dressmaker. In fact, it is in the rear of Poiret's establishment on the Avenue d'Antin, Harry Pilcer used to dance at the Apollo and his chief claim to fame is that the late Gaby Deslys was fond of him.

Gaby left him a small fortune, with which he has started a syndicate of dance establishments, with jazz bands from New York's East Side and professional dancers from Broadway. He is trying earnestly to Americanize the nightlife of Paris. Poiret's models parade there his latest creations, and hence it offers a very legitimate attraction to every American woman.

From the Place Pigalle to the Place de Clichy stretches the Boulevard de Clichy, and nearly every building along this big boulevard offers some queer entertainment. Here stood the notorious old Moulin Rouge, which was pulled down some years ago and replaced by a magnificent building called "the Moulin Rouge Palace."

Every Saturday night the palace used to hold a raffle, at which some very valuable object was given as a prize, such as a thoroughbred horse or a diamond necklace. Once among the minor prizes was a little white pig which was beautifully manicured and perfumed.

A lively party carried the little pig into a café in the nearby Place Blanche and made him intoxicated with champagne. He provided so much amusement that a little drunken pig has been the feature of the Saturday evening entertainment at this place ever since.

It would be hard to catalogue all the odd resorts that infest the Boulevard de Clichy and adjoining streets. For instance, there is an establishment called "Le Ciel" (Heaven), which has been decorated by an artist of florid imagination to represent the abode of the blessed as he imagines it. The attractive girl attendants are dressed as "angels" in bright, airy costumes, and do their utmost to make the visitors enjoy themselves in "Heaven."

When a man is tired of "Heaven" he can go to "L'Enfer" (Hell), which is just next door. Another artist has decorated this place, perhaps with better information, to represent the abode of the lost. The attendants are dressed as devils and many infernal amusements are provided. Of such freaks there is no end.

Perhaps the most brutal of the innumerable nightly entertainments of Paris is one in which a negro fights a big rat and eats it alive. It is a popular after-supper place in the Rue de Grenelle. One would think this entertainment rather a poor aid to digestion, but strange to say, it is very popular with women and judging from their clothes, they belong to the wealthy classes.

The human combatant is a big, powerful, heavy-jawed Martinique negro. His face marked with numerous scars of former combats. One of the large, fierce rats, for which Paris sewers are noted, is selected as victim. The man takes the rat by the tail and places it on a little stand.

He faces the animal and slowly prepares to eat the beast alive. He gives it a good chance to fight, but takes care to prevent it from running away by holding its tail. The cornered rat always fights fiercely and inflicts many severe bites on the huge, terrifying negro jaws that slowly close upon it. After a horrible struggle the negro eats up the big rat with a crunching sound and grimaces suggestive of pain and discomfort.

Once the cornered rat succeeded in biting through the negro's carotid artery, causing him to bleed to death. But another negro was quickly found and the entertainment goes on as usual.

A fight between two women, known as "a wild cat combat," used to be a popular feature at Madame Rappette's bar in the Rue St. Honore, long the most fashionable bar in Paris, but now passed away. Other "wild cat combats," however, may be seen nightly in other resorts.

The original "wild cat combat" occurred accidentally when a Belgian beauty called "L'Ooleau" (the Bird) and a French woman named Alice Dauvray had a serious disagreement. They fought and scratched one another until their faces were dripping with blood and their clothes were torn off their backs.

A select gathering of American millionaires, English noblemen and Parisian boulevardiers was present. Some of them found the exhibition so entertaining that it was repeated with other women combatants. Since then it has been repeated in many of the night resorts of Paris. No rules of fair play are enforced and all kinds of fouls are applauded. The clothes-tearing is an exciting feature of the combat that cannot be found in any fight between men. The peculiar noise caused by the ripping of a lace-trimmed garment evidently gives the greatest satisfaction to the spectators.

Madame Rappette's bar helped to popularize the most sinister and dangerous of Parisian drinks—the ether and brandy cocktail. Every kind of deadly drug could also be obtained there, whether cocaine, morphine in any form or hasheesh.

Ether and brandy was first made fashionable as a drink by a wealthy American woman resident in Paris, Mrs. Harvard, who asserted that it gave her a beautiful still.

Who, but an insane person, would pay an exorbitant price and enjoy seeing a brutal-faced creature bite to death a struggling rat?

What person in his right senses would relish seeing a biting, scratching, hair-pulling struggle between two abandoned women?

How can such repulsive exhibitions in the all-night resorts of the "gay" French capital be a "lure," as the Rev. Dr. Beekman calls it?

One explanation which is pointed to by the proprietors of these places is the ether and brandy cocktail and the cocaine, which are thoughtlessly or unwittingly indulged in by visitors before they start their round of midnight visits.

This Mrs. Harvard used to go on morphine sprees, and to save herself from becoming a morphine addict she would change off to brandy and champagne mixed. Then to break the brandy and champagne habit she took to brandy and ether. In this way she said life became one round of agreeable intoxication.

A New York physician, who is visiting Paris, when consulted concerning the effects of ether and brandy said: "I have no doubt that this mixture produces about the most dangerous form of intoxication known. I have had some experience with ether drunkenness in New York and found it difficult to cure, but the mixture with brandy further complicates the problem. The effect of ether is greater on the nervous system, but less on the digestive organs than that of plain alcohol. In the long run, however, the destructive effect of ether and brandy on the nervous system caused an even more hopeless condition than that of the simple alcoholic."

One disadvantage of ether and brandy is that it gives a very offensive

April 30, 2006. A modern glance at the exact location where Le Ciel and L'Enfer stood almost a century ago. Today, these notorious nightclubs are replaced by a sushi bar and various sex shops.

and unmistakable odor to the breath. To obviate this the Parisian drink-mixers are adding essence of violets and other perfumes to the mixture.

One well versed in the attractions of Paris states that a cocaine spray, an ether and brandy, an "apertif" of dry vermouth, and then dinner with white and red wine, a bottle of champagne, some three-star brandy and a glass of Benedictine will fortify the American to start the evenings and face all the sights of Paris.

Suicides are extremely common among foreign visitors to Paris, and they are often committed in the places where the victims have lost their money and ruined their health. Parisians love to tell the story of a man who ordered the best dinner procurable at the best restaurant on the Avenue de L'Opera. Having received the bill, he wrote on the back: "I regret I cannot pay the bill, but I will give you as little inconvenience as possible." Then he took out a revolver, held it a considerable distance from his head, so as not to make an unseemly wound, and shot himself.

On the other hand, a ruined youth entered a notorious establishment on the Rue Royale and shot himself before he had taken a drink. The scrubwoman who cleaned up the stain observed: "Imbecile! He should have had some fun first."

It would be interesting to know what was the scrubwoman's conception of "fun"—the antics of a drunken pig, the negro and the rat combat, the revolting battle of the women, or the stupor of a drug debauch? Are the wealthy patrons of these "lures" of the mental and aesthetic caliber of a scrubwoman of the dives?

The prevalence of drinking in Paris adds enormously to the dangers that await the unsophisticated American girl visiting Paris. Such deadly drinks as that described and all kinds of wines and liquors are obtainable at prices, which are, of course, exorbitant. European women, even of the highest class, are accustomed to drink, and this fact often leads American women to alcoholic excesses they would not dream of committing at home.

There is practically no legal restrictions, such as America enforces, to the use of dangerous drugs in France. Morphine indulgence by women in cafes and public places is not only common but rather old-fashioned. The maddening habit of eating hasheesh, or Indian hemp, has lately become very fashionable.

To the woman who has eaten hasheesh, every sensation changes its normal character. She thinks that her beauty is irresistible. She thinks that she charms multitudes when she opens her mouth. She thinks she is a bird and can fly over the treetops. She takes a ride in a taxicab and believes she has been to the moon. She listens to a street person and weeps because it sounds like heavenly music. The after-effect of hasheesh eating is an irresistible impulse to kill somebody. In consequence, many of the confirmed hasheesh eaters of Paris have to be accompanied by attendants.

There is something fresh to do at every hour of the night in Paris, and hence the destructive character of its appeal. If one has spent the whole night visiting the various resorts, and the dawn has found one still awake, there remains still a new and appropriate recreation. This is a visit to one of the charming and expensive restaurants of the Bois de Boulogne and "a glass of fresh milk."

One of the most fashionable of these places is the Cascade. It keeps its own cow or cows in an adjoining field. It hurts the business sense of a Parisian restaurateur to sell milk alone, but there is a certain daring incongruity about it. The charge for the "fresh milk" is enormous and you are expected to order something to eat at the same time.

So it happens that at dawn there is always a sprinkling of weary pleasure-seekers dropping asleep over their glass of milk. After that they go to bed and come to life again sometime between the mid-day "apertif" and sunset, when they are ready for another round of pleasure.

Many earnest French men and women have thoroughly realized that the good name of France is endangered by the lure of Paris. The Duchess d'Uzes, wife of the premier member of the old nobility, has publicly declared it a disgrace to France that the allurements of Paris should be the cause of ruining young women of foreign nations.

Olive Thomas was not the only American girl who might truthfully repeat her words: "This is what Paris has done for me." Just where Olive Thomas went and what she saw in the early morning hours may never be known. But her tragic death may not have been in vain if the influences now at work shall prevail to wipe out the plague spots of Paris.

Despite the coroner's conclusion that Olive's death was accidental and with all evidence of foul play or suicide ruled out, the American media were hell bent on blaming Paris for Olive's death; even if it meant accusing her grieving husband of murder. Swirling rumors that Jack had taken out an insurance policy on Olive's life were splashed across the front pages of American newspapers across the country, eyebrows were raised and rumors began. When murder was ruled out, Jack was blamed again; this time for her suicide. Jack had passed syphilis on to his wife and that was the reason Olive killed herself, they claimed.

In hindsight, it appears that Olive's "accidental" death was due to the fact that she wandered into a darkened bathroom, tired and with a headache that wouldn't go away, she decided not to turn on the light for fear of waking her sleeping husband. Jack had already complained that the lamplight on the desk where she was writing a letter home to her mother had disturbed him. Thinking the only medication in the bathroom cabinet was her sleeping pills (earlier she had made sure the mercury bichloride was in the other room to avoid the deadly mistake that was about to happen), Olive thought nothing of taking the medication sight unseen. Moments after taking the pills, Olive realized there was something terribly wrong.

The sleeping pills were where they were supposed to be but it appeared the bottle of mercury bichloride had been placed on the shelf next to them. It's suspected the maid cleaning the room earlier in the day had spotted the mercury bichloride in the bedroom and, innocently thinking the pills belonged in the bathroom, she did her job and put them where she thought they ought to be. During the investigation the maid admitted to placing a bottle of pills back in the bathroom cabinet but she insisted the pills were sleeping pills, *not* mercury bichloride. Either way, Jack could be blamed for Olive's death on all three counts, with a fourth theory being thrown into the equation as a "possibility."

1. Suicide because he gave her syphilis and she couldn't accept living with the disease—Jack's fault!
2. Murder to cash in on the life insurance policy that he was rumored to have taken out before their trip—Jack's fault!
3. A tragic accident due to Olive picking the wrong bottle of pills in a darkened room so as not to wake him. Had Jack not complained about the lamp disturbing him earlier, Olive would have turned on the bathroom light before taking her sleeping pills (some reports suggest it was a sleeping potion), thus avoiding the deadly mistake that would eventually take her life—Jack's fault!
4. There are several conflicting newspaper accounts on how Olive ingested the mercury bichloride. Some articles suggest she took the pills directly while other reports suggest she dissolved the pills in alcohol (as it was topically prescribed to treat syphilis) and ingested it that way. This is believable for a suicide but taking a solution of mercury bichloride by "accident" is unlikely given that it would have to be mixed and prepared which would give the person enough time to realize the "about to be" deadly mistake. Another logical theory that is entirely possible but not publicly discussed

A modern view of the location where the infamous "Dead Rat" nightclub once entertained throngs of movie stars and notables from around the world. The seedy atmosphere of days gone by has not changed in this Parisian district. As the photograph shows, the building that was once the home of the "Dead Rat" is now a sex theater.

until now is my own: Given the fact that Jack had already gone to bed, it's possible that he may have mixed and used (topically, as prescribed) part of the bichloride-alcohol solution before going to sleep and neglected to throw away whatever he didn't use. Innocently thinking the solution was water (once mixed, the solution was colorless and odorless), Olive may well have taken her sleeping pills (as prescribed) and washed them down with the remaining poisonous solution.

Jack's desperate attempts to induce Olive to vomit with glasses of water, milk and eggs would cause her to bring up the undissolved sleeping pills, thus leaving no trace of them in her system at the time of her autopsy. With that said, failing to dispose of the unused mercury bichloride solution leads to Olive's death being—Jack's fault!

Jack was never a strong person; is it any wonder that he climbed to the top deck of the *Mauretania* as he sailed back home (with Olive's body) with thoughts of ending it all by jumping overboard? No, not really. Film director Allan Dwan was on the same ship and talked Jack out of his suicidal thoughts. How could he think of doing such a thing? His death would cause such dreadful heartbreak to his beloved mother, sister Lottie and of course his favorite sister, Mary. "Think not of yourself," Dwan said, "think of them!" (*Pittsburgh Press*, October 1920).

Then Jack had an epiphany. Somehow he knew Mary would already be going into damage control mode back home. Mary fixed everything. She *always* fixed everything and this would be no exception. If Jack ever needed saving, it was now. By the time he hit American soil, Mary would have the press wrapped around her little finger and Jack Pickford, grieving widower, would avoid public and media scrutiny—not right away, but eventually. Everything would be fine. Mary wouldn't have it any other way.

The *New York Telegram* gave a touching account of Olive's funeral service. The September 28, 1920, article entitled, "Throngs Honor Olive Thomas: Thousands Mourn As Funeral of Movie Star is Held," started with the following poem:

> There is a door to which I have no key.
> There is a veil through which I cannot see.
> Some little talk awhile of Me and Thee.
> There was—and then no more of Me and Thee.

The article continues:

> Olive Thomas has passed. The beautiful face that smiled so bewitchingly across the lights or sent its wistful gaze out from the screen is hidden from mortal view. The human Olive has returned to the dust from whence it came.
>
> Never, in the history of stage or screen, has such a tribute of love, respect and sorrow been paid to a star as was given to the memory of the youthful wife of Jack Pickford at St. Thomas' Episcopal Church this morning.
>
> The hour for the burial services was fixed at ten o'clock. Long before the appointed time, moving picture fans from every section of the city and suburbs, from every walk of life, from every nation and every creed, surged through surrounding streets, packing the entrance to St. Thomas' solidly to the police lines and rippling out for blocks in all directions.
>
> In the picturesque and impressive edifice itself there gathered such a congregation of men and women as never before have come to sorrow. Practically everyone of importance

Opposite: **A superimposed image of the facade of the "Dead Rat" nightclub's entrance over the modern-day entrance. It is well documented that Olive, Jack and a handful of friends dined at the "Dead Rat" just hours before she took the fatal dose of poison.**

in the theatrical world today except such as were barred by distance came to pay their last tribute to Olive.

There were the girls from the Follies, that famous garden of beauty wherein Olive bloomed the fairest flower. Today they were not gay butterflies, swirling through the calcium meadows of pleasure. They were just girls who had lost a pal and whose hearts were bowed down at the parting. If their step is heavy this morning when the lights glow, if there is a sob in their voices, it will be for their friend, the human bud who was a credit and a joy to their beauty bouquet—Olive Thomas.

There also were film folk. Not only brilliant stars whose names twinkle electrically from the fronts of theaters. They were present, of course, sad that one so bright among them should be dimmed in death. There was also the cameraman, the property boy, the wardrobe woman, the extra girl, the carpenter—every studio helper upon whom Olive had turned the warmth of her smile, and she missed no one.

There were managers, producers, directors, and authors. There were artists whose brushes had sought to portray the sunny soul of Olive through the fairness of her face. There were models who had romped with her through careless studio days. There were capitalists and clerks. There were men and women with toil-hardened hands, and there were men and women from high ranks of society. Olive knew and loved them all.

Shortly after ten o'clock when more than 4,000 people packed St. Thomas' to the outer doors, a male choir of thirty-six voices sang the processional. They entered from the left of the edifice, proceeded up the altar steps and took their places in the choir stalls.

Immediately thereafter the voice of Rev. Ernest M. Stires, rector of the church, was heard repeating the Episcopal burial service, with Bishop James Henry Darlington, of Harrisburg, Pennsylvania, bishop of Olive Thomas Pickford's home diocese. He proceeded the bower of orchids in which was borne the earthly remains of Olive. The blanket of orchids trailing and trailing ferns entirely concealed the metal casque. It was made up of lavender orchids with a cross of white and gold orchids, the gift of the husband, standing directly over the lovely eyes now sealed in death.

Following came the honorary pallbearers—Owen Moore, Harrison Fisher, Thomas Meighan, Myron Selznick, Alan Crosland, Gene Buck, William Skelton and Harry Carrington.

One among them, Mr. Moore, former husband of Mary Pickford, sister of Jack Pickford, the bereaved husband, was in Paris on that tragic night when the high-spirited American girl made the fatal mistake of swallowing poison under the impression she was taking a sleeping potion. Mr. Moore has remained with Jack Pickford through all the harrowing scenes attendant upon the death of the girl who put up such a brave fight for life. He accompanied Mr. Pickford and the body of his wife home from France.

Harrison Fisher, one of the country's foremost artists, first recognized the beauty of Olive Thomas when she came a small-town girl from a village near Pittsburgh, to seek fame and fortune in the great city. Mr. Fisher had perpetuated her beauty by pen and brush.

Behind the ushers came Jack Pickford supporting the grief-bowed figure of Mrs. Harry Van Kirk, Olive's mother. Mrs. Pickford walked with Mr. Van Kirk, Lottie Pickford with Mr. Fred Almey. The two brothers of Olive, James and William Duffy, brought up the rear of the family group.

Jack Pickford is a pathetic figure. Sorrow has bent his shoulders. The corners of his lips droop with sadness. His eyes are dim with tears. He is no longer the youth who capers so delightfully across the screen. His is a husband broken in health and in spirit by the parting with his beloved.

As the casket was borne down the aisle after the brief but impressive service, a hush fell over the mourners and sobs were heard. It seemed as though every woman in the church had a handkerchief to her eyes. Many of them sobbed, "Poor Mary" (as in Mary

Pickford) as the casket was carried through the aisle. Following the reading of the service, the choir sang, "Abide with Me." The services were concluded with the choir singing, "Hark, Hark, My Soul."

As the pallbearers began leaving the church and the casket was carried out, many of the audience crowded down the stairways from the balcony and the side pews in an effort to reach the entrance. The crush was so great that hats were broken and several of the ushers, including Irving Berlin, William Collier Jr., and John O'Meara, with the assistance of four policemen, attempted to hold the crowd in check. Their efforts were futile, the crowd surging and splitting up the eight pallbearers who preceded the casket. Additional help had to be given by Lieutenant Brady before it was possible to carry the casket through the aisles of humanity down the steps of the church to the hearse.

Eight motor carriages were used to convey the members of the family and friends to Woodlawn Cemetery, where the body was placed in a vault, to remain there pending completion of a mausoleum.

About three hundred and fifty floral pieces received from friends and relatives had been placed on the altar, and in the front part of the church. Flowers still were arriving at the church after the service. A dozen automobiles were needed to take flowers to the cemetery. One floral piece of roses, orchids and lilies was from Mary Pickford. One of the largest pieces was a wreath with flowing white ribbon bearing this inscription—"From the stage hands of the Selznick force."

Various other departments of this company sent handsome floral designs. Dudley Field Malone sent a large design with a pigeon. The "60 Club" sent an enormous piece inscribed "60." One design was inscribed, "Our Pal Ollie."

An unidentified September 29, 1920, article titled, "Riot at Church Door Mars Funeral of Olive Thomas," gives a more graphic account of just how bad things got amongst the grief-stricken crowd:

> Several women fainted, pallbearers jostled, and a near-riot caused by unruly souvenir seekers who gathered in front of St. Thomas' Episcopal Church, Fifth Avenue and 53rd Street yesterday morning where funeral services were held for Olive Thomas, motion picture star, who died in Paris of bichloride of mercury poisoning. Thousands who knew her on the screen repeatedly broke through the police lines to snatch handfuls of the floral tributes that were being carried through the streets to vehicles waiting to take them to the cemetery.
>
> Four mounted policeman and twenty-five on foot could not keep open the lane through which mourners entered the church. As the service progressed, women stormed through the crowds, eager hands reaching for anything which they could carry away as a souvenir of the occasion. When the funeral cortege began leaving the church, the crowd became still more unruly, and the pallbearers were pushed aside. For a while there was danger of a serious accident, but the police finally succeeded in clearing a passageway for the casket and re-establishing their lines.

A similar article (*The Moving Picture World*, October 9, 1920) entitled, "Women and Girls Storm Church to Attend Funeral of Olive Thomas; Many Tears in the Vast Audience," reported similar scenes of grief amongst the out-of-control crowd:

> Never before in the history of funerals in New York City did the police have to cope with such a tremendous crowd as gathered to witness the funeral of Olive Thomas at St. Thomas' Church at Fifty-third Street and Fifth Avenue on Tuesday morning, September 28th.
>
> Fifth Avenue from Fifty-fourth Street to Fifty-third was packed solidly with women of all descriptions and ages, and the police that had been sent there to preserve order and keep the people in check, found themselves powerless to stem the tide of frantic, struggling women who made dash after dash to enter the church. Above the noise of passing

motors could be heard the hysterical cries of women and children who were being crushed by the mob. The police time and again were rushed and hundreds would reach the doors of the church, literally bowl over the ushers and gain admittance to the church which was already crowded to capacity.

The lieutenant of police in charge sent a call for some mounted men, and for the first time in many years New Yorkers were treated to the sight of mounted police on the sidewalk trying to push back the crowds. When the services had been concluded inside of the church and the coffin was carried out, the crowds again broke through the police lines and the pallbearers became hopelessly entangled in the mob.

When the mourners led by Jack Pickford, his mother-in-law and his brother-in-law emerged from the church, the crowd had gotten beyond the control of the police and the mourners became separated. Only by Herculean efforts on the part of the police and the ushers were the mourners literally borne to the automobile and safely seated.

Inside the church were other scenes that have seldom been witnessed in New York. As far as the eye could reach, the seats were crowded with women of all ages and descriptions. A constant buzz was heard throughout the edifice, and as each motion picture celebrity entered the church the name would be bandied from mouth to mouth.

As the services started and the orchid-covered coffin was carried into the church, preceded by the ushers, women and girls who did not have a seat of vantage jumped on the benches and fought one another to get a glimpse of the mourning party. The solemnity of the occasion apparently did not seem to occur to them. But there were many in the vast audience who sincerely mourned the passing of one of screendom's shining lights.

Each branch of the industry and the stage was represented. And those in the audience who had known "Ollie" made no pretense at hiding their tears and their hearts went out to Jack Pickford.

"Ollie" Thomas Pickford is now at rest, but she will ever remain green in the memories of those who know the ever-smiling vivacious girl, who was a friend to all and who brought sunshine to many through the medium of the screen.

The Moving Picture World (September 25, 1920) published a heartfelt tribute to Olive written by her boss, Lewis J. Selznick. He said:

Following the tragic death of Miss Thomas in Paris I feel it is due to her memory that something should be known of the real woman. To the majority of you these words are superfluous, for you knew her. It is to the others that these lines are addressed.

Olive Thomas was one of the happiest, most cheerful persons I have ever met, and to know her was to love her. She enjoyed her success, but was always simple and unaffected, never touched by the least suggestion of pride or vanity. She was big-hearted and money meant nothing to her except the means for doing good and gratifying the wishes of others. She never thought of herself, but her one desire was to make everyone around her happy. She lived for her family and friends.

Any of the hundreds of personal friends will tell the same story—Olive Thomas was a persistent optimist, always cheerful, always determined that everyone about her should be the same. In her business relations her word was as good as any contract ever written. She was looking forward to the coming year's work with the greatest enthusiasm. Never in my life have I met anyone with a higher sense of honor and a finer character than Olive Thomas.

Exhibitor Trade Review called Olive...

... a sparkling effervescent gem of joyousness and gaiety. She cast a ray of sunshine over the world wherever she went. As pure and beautiful in soul as in body, she was the supreme personification of light-hearted girlhood. No unclean thought had a dwelling place in her mind; no word of anger ever passed her lips. Lovable to a degree, she was a friend to rich and poor alike, and everyone with whom she came in contact was the cleaner and better for the association.

She was the Soul of Honor, truth and unselfishness—gentle, sensitive and emotional in every way. Olive Thomas has passed, but the place where she has trod is cleaner and finer for her having been with us for even so little a time. A great artist has been taken, but while memory holds a place in human hearts, her fame, her personality, and her charm will live on until the curtain is finally rung down on the world's stage.

Selznick Pictures collected their hefty insurance policy on Olive but in order to avoid further rumors of Jack's monetary gain from Olive's death, it was widely speculated that Mary "advised" him to hand over the $37,094 (approximately $380,000 today) from her estate sale to his mother-in-law, Mrs. Lorena Van Kirk. A July 15, 1922, *Telegraph* article reports on the sale:

Olive Thomas, first wife of Jack Pickford, who died September 10, 1920, through mercury poisoning while in Paris, left a gross estate of $37,094, according to the appraisal yesterday by the Tax Commission. The property consisted almost entirely of jewels and personal possessions. It was revealed by the papers that Jack Pickford has relinquished all claims to any part of the estate in favor of Mrs. Lorena Van Kirk of St. Louis, mother of the dead film star. Miss Thomas' jewels were her particular pride. She owned gems in a quantity to make a queen jealous. Her furs and other belongings were also worth thousands. On November 22, 1920, an auction on the larger part of her property realized $26,931 [approximately $245,000 today]. The most persistent bidders in the sale were Mabel Normand, Lewis J. Selznick, Mrs. Stuyvesant Fish and Mrs. Jerome Bonaparte. Samuel Marx was the auctioneer. The public auction notification read as follows:

Samuel Marx, Auctioneers will sell by public auction at his salesrooms, 115–117 West 23rd Street, New York City (West of Sixth Avenue), Monday, November 22nd, and Tuesday, November 23rd, 1920. Commencing at 2 o'clock pm each day. By direction of Nathan Burkan, Esq., Administrator. All the personal effects belonging to—The Estate of Olive Thomas Pickford, deceased, comprising: Jewelry, Furs, Wearing Apparel and Automobiles.

The description of some of Olive's personal effects were listed as follows:

Jewelry: Rings—Star Sapphire and Diamond, Cabochon Sapphire and Pearl, Pearl and Diamond, Solitaire Pearl, Solitaire Diamond (about 10K).
Necklaces: Diamond, Oriental Pearl, Pearl and Sapphire, Jade.
Bracelets: Diamond, Diamond and Sapphire, Pearl and Sapphire.
Brooches: Diamond, Pearl and Sapphire.
Trinkets: Crystal and Diamond Watches, Gold, Diamond, Platinum and Crystal Cigarette Cases, Green Gold Combination Watch and Cigarette Case, Chatelaine, Beaded Bags, Gold Mesh Bags, also one 14K Gold Toilet Set.
Dresses: The entire wardrobe of Mrs. Olive Thomas Pickford, deceased, in Brown, Blue, Green and Black Velvet, Taffeta, Spangle, etc., handsomely trimmed.
Furs: Silver Fox Neck Pieces, Hudson Seal Coatee, Muskrat Lined Cloth Coat, Stone Marten Stole, Stone Marten Scarf, Stone Marten Cuffs, Kolinsky Robe, Full Length Russian Sable Coat.
Automobiles: Locomobile Town Car, 38 H.P., No. 13392, wire wheels. Cadillac Town Car, 1920, Mode 59A, Motor No. 278.

Mabel Normand bought a 14-carat gold cigarette case for $50 (approximately $450 today), a twenty-piece toilet set for $1425 (approximately $13,000 today), a diamond pearl brooch and sapphire pin for $500 (approximately $4500 today) and a platinum set with star sapphire for $425 (approximately $3800 today).

Olive is buried at Woodlawn Cemetery in the Bronx, New York. She's situated in the Wintergreen section, in a crypt built for two. To this day she lies there alone. Her only identifying marker on the now decaying concrete mausoleum is "PICKFORD."

The Pickford file in relation to Olive's internment at Woodlawn Cemetery spans a sixteen-year period. The last communication was May 8, 1936, three years after Jack Pickford's death. The Superintendent of the Cemetery writes to Mr. Dennis F. O'Brien, Jack's lawyer, requesting notification in the form of an affidavit, listing the heirs of Jack Pickford. It reads as follows:

> Dear Sir:
>
> In reply to your letter of April 30th and also in confirmation of our phone conversation in regard to lot #14851 and mausoleum thereon, our records show that this lot stands in the name of Jack Pickford.
>
> At the death of Mr. Pickford the title of this lot and mausoleum passed to his next of kin, and as we do not have an affidavit on file stating who the heirs are, we would appreciate it if you will have the enclosed affidavit completed and return two copies to us for our records.
>
> In regard to the condition of the mausoleum, we find that it requires a thorough overhauling, some of the joints require repointing and the building should be cleaned. For a complete job the cost will be approximately Eighty Dollars ($80). For the repointing of the bad joints only, the cost will be Forty Dollars ($40).
>
> To provide for the weekly interior cleaning of the mausoleum and special care to the turf thereafter, the cost will be Sixty Dollars ($60), per season.
>
> The turf on the lot, however, is not in very good condition and should be regraded and seeded. This would involve an additional expense of Forty-five dollars ($45).
>
> We are enclosing two cards which we would ask you to please sign and return to us if the above estimates meet with your approval.
>
> Very truly yours,
> The Woodlawn Cemetery.

The letter went unanswered. In fact, it's the last communication received by the cemetery in relation to Olive's mausoleum. Ironically, the cemetery's reply was in response to an April 30, 1936, letter initiated by Jack's lawyer, Dennis F. O'Brien. It read:

RIOT AT CHURCH DOOR MARS FUNERAL OF OLIVE THOMAS

Women Faint and Hats Are Broken When Souvenir Seekers Storm Through Crowds to Snatch Handfuls of Floral Tributes From Casket.

Olive's funeral created mass hysteria. The thousands of people that attended were held back by policemen. Fans scurried to grab flowers from the casket, people were crushed, and women fainted.

6. The Investigation

Funeral of Olive Thomas, Screen Star, Is Attended by 15,000

A headline mentioning the astonishing attendance at Olive's funeral.

Dear Sir:

Would you kindly inform me in what part of the Woodlawn Cemetery is located the Olive Thomas mausoleum? Miss Thomas was the wife of Mr. Jack Pickford at the time she died.

Please inform me also as to its physical condition and the condition of the uncovered portion of the lot, and if the mausoleum appears to be neglected, what you would recommend done to it and what the same would cost.

Thanking you for this information, I am,

Very truly yours,
Dennis F. O'Brien.

That letter was written a little over three years after Jack died. Jack had no children; there were no heirs. Mary was his next of kin and she tied up all the loose ends in relation to her brother's death. As for Olive, she was a distant memory. Mary had little interest in maintaining her former sister-in-law's final resting place so it's no surprise that the cemetery's response to Mr. O'Brien's letter was ignored.

It's been seventy years since Olive's file at Woodlawn Cemetery was active. Back in 1936, when the letter to Jack's lawyer was sent out, Olive's mausoleum needed repointing and cleaning. This was sixteen years after her death and fifteen years since she was placed in the crypt. With only periodic spot repairs in the years that followed, it's now estimated that a full restoration on Olive's mausoleum will cost somewhere in the region of $25,000. What this would involve is a complete cleaning that includes repointing of the mortar joints (something that needed doing seventy years ago) and

The newspaper clipping under that headline.

packing the roofline with lead wool. This would ensure the mausoleum is kept completely dry for at least fifty more years. In addition, the exterior would be treated with a biocide that would keep it from "turning green" from the biological growth. Included in the cost is $4000 for the restoration of the bronze door. The Woodlawn Cemetery is now in the process of raising the funds to return Olive's mausoleum back to its best.

A chronological timeline for the Olive Thomas Pickford mausoleum based on the files at Woodlawn Cemetery are as follows:

9/10/1920	Olive Thomas Pickford dies in Paris, France—"Accidental Poisoning" is listed as cause of death.
9/28/1920	Remains of Olive Thomas Pickford brought to the Woodlawn Cemetery.
	Undertaker E.M. Speer—Funeral scheduled to arrive at 11:45 A.M.
	Casket placed in Catacomb #525 of the New Receiving Tomb.
10/2/1920	Jack Pickford of Los Angeles, CA purchases Lot 14851 Wintergreen Plot, Section 108/121 in the Woodlawn Cemetery. The Lot consists of 600 sq. ft. and costs $2400 (approximately $25,000 today).
10/5/1920	The Woodlawn Cemetery receives a payment of $1000 (approximately $11,000 today) for Lot 14851.
6/21/1921	Farrington, Gould & Hoagland, designers and builders of monuments, mausoleums and statuary, submit plans and specifications for the construction of the Pickford Mausoleum to the Woodlawn Cemetery.
7/13/1921	Note in cemetery file that Mr. Rumsey will be at the Pickford Lot at 4 P.M. for the purpose of laying out the lines where foundation work is to be built for a small mausoleum.
8/23/1921	The Woodlawn Cemetery receives a payment of $1400 (approximately $15,000 today) for Lot 14851.
9/16/1921	A planting plan for the Pickford Lot is submitted to Mr. John W. Rumsey of 33 West 42nd St., NYC.
9/22/1921	A letter written by Jack Pickford (from the Biltmore Hotel in New York City) to the Woodlawn Cemetery reads as follows:
	Gentlemen:
	This is to authorize you to remove the casket containing the remains of OLIVE THOMAS PICKFORD from Catacomb No. 525 in Receiving Tomb No. 3 to the PICKFORD mausoleum on the Wintergreen Plot, Park Avenue, Woodlawn Cemetery, to be placed in the upper catacomb of said Mausoleum, the transfer to be made on Sunday, September 25th, 1921, in time for committal services at 3:30 P.M. on that date.
	Yours very truly, Jack Pickford
9/25/1921	Remains of Olive Thomas Pickford moved from the Receiving Tomb to Lot No. 14851 Catacomb #2. Committal Service scheduled for Sunday afternoon at 3:30 P.M.

A heart-wrenching photograph showing the crowd of mourners looking on as Olive's flower-laden casket leaves the church on the day of her funeral.

5/23/1922   Mr. Dennis O'Brien of O'Brien, Malevinsky & Driscoll, representing Jack Pickford, writes to Mr. Fred Diering (landscape designer for Woodlawn Cemetery) to ascertain if Mr. John Rumsey of the American Play Company has made arrangements to have a lawn and shrubbery put around the mausoleum of Mrs. Jack Pickford. He advises Diering that Pickford will be here for a few days and is anxious to have the matter attended to.

5/25/1922   The Woodlawn Cemetery writes to Mr. Dennis F. O'Brien to advise him that a planting plan for the Pickford Lot has been submitted to Mr. Rumsey but there has been no response to the proposal.

6/22/1921   Specifications detailing the construction of the Pickford Mausoleum are received by the Woodlawn Cemetery. Construction is to be done by the firm, Farrington, Gould and Hoagland, Inc. of 258 Broadway, NYC. The specifications identify that the building is to be constructed of granite with a white marble interior of Vermont Marble.

10/13/1922   Note in the Pickford file indicates that Mr. Rumsey, of the American Play Company would like an estimate for landscaping the Pickford Lot.

4/9/1923	The Woodlawn Cemetery writes to Mr. John Rumsey of 33 West 42nd St., NYC and provides a planting plan for the Pickford Lot.
9/13/1923	The Woodlawn Cemetery writes to Miss Katharine McCarthy of 100 West 59th St., NYC with a planting scheme for work to be done on the Pickford Lot. The cost of the proposed work is $350 (approximately $4,000 today).
4/30/1936	Attorney Dennis O'Brien writes to the cemetery requesting a report on the condition of the Pickford Mausoleum and cost estimates for making improvements to the site if it looks neglected.
5/8/1936	The Superintendent of the Woodlawn Cemetery writes to Mr. Dennis F. O'Brien of 152 West 42nd St., NYC requesting that the attorney provide the cemetery with a completed Heirship Affidavit identifying the heirs of Jack Pickford, the legal owners of the mausoleum and lot. In addition, the Superintendent reports that the mausoleum requires repointing and should be cleaned at a cost of $80 (approx. $1,125 today). The cemetery also recommends that Mr. O'Brien provide for weekly interior cleaning of the mausoleum as well as regrading and seeding of the surrounding turf.

Despite Jack's subsequent marriages (he was unattached at the time of his death), Mary Pickford eventually admitted that Olive was "the love of his life." An admission that was better late than never but it was too little, too late. Ironically, it was at the insistence of Mary that Jack be buried in the Garden of Memory at Forest Lawn Memorial Park in Glendale, California. In fact, all the Pickfords are there. Mother Charlotte (died 1928), sister Lottie (died 1936) and of course Mary (died 1979).

Jack and Olive were one of the unluckiest lucky couples in Hollywood history; to be joined in death would have seemed like the appropriate end. But Olive and Jack spent most of their married life separated on the East and the West Coast and the finality of death was no exception to the rule.

A November-December 1995 article written by Stuart Oderman for *Films in Review* summarized the position and condition (at the time of the writing) of Olive's final resting place:

> Olive's mausoleum doesn't face the road. It's hard to locate and once you find it, you realize the stones have not been washed in decades. The window is almost concealed in cobwebs.
> Mary [Pickford] wanted it that way.

★ *Chapter 7* ★

WHAT JACK TOLD MARY...

[Olive] fought a hopeless battle, dying in my brother's arms.
—Mary Pickford

"Jack had not been himself," Mary Pickford insisted, since Olive's death a dozen years before. She indulged him endlessly, panicking when his dissipation led to breakdowns, paying his considerable legal fees, and financing several movies for him. Then, when his films did only middling business, she blamed her own fame for curtailing his. Mary tried to keep his mind off Olive by giving him co-directing jobs on *Through the Back Door* and *Little Lord Fauntleroy* (both 1921) but the extent of Jack's contribution was suggesting a gag or two—and that was on the days he bothered to show up. He indulged in a wild wake, painting the town red and flying his plane in swoops over Los Angeles. One day when Mary was talking with a journalist, she heard a familiar sound above the studio. She ran outside screaming, "Oh, Jack, you promised!" Jack tipped a wing in recognition. And Mary shrieked, "Stop! You'll kill yourself!" (Eileen Whitfield: *The Woman Who Made Hollywood*).

The fact is, Jack wallowed in a world of alcohol- and drug-induced self-pity and grief (or was it guilt?) for two and a half years after Olive's death. Yes, he married Marilyn Miller on July 30, 1922, but professionally he did not return to the screen until *Garrison's Finish* in January of 1923. It was far from a comeback. Aside from a cameo appearance in the "spot the celebrity" eight-reeler, *Hollywood* (1923), *Garrison's Finish* was Jack's only starring role of the year. He returned to the screen a year later as Jed McCoy in *The Hill Billy* (1924), and again it was his only film of the year. From 1925, in the eight years that Jack had left to live, he made just seven more films. In the days when stars could conceivably churn out a new film every six weeks, it's obvious that Jack had lost interest in his career, and life in general.

Jack was a raging alcoholic and drug fiend for most of his adult life. But his increased alcohol consumption and wildly destructive behavior after Olive's death appears to have been a crutch to make living with Olive's demise a little easier. There were so many unanswered questions surrounding the lead-up to her death and Jack held many (if not all) of those answers. Unless he had ice water running through his veins, the weight of that burden would have been difficult to endure without the help of a bottle of something stronger than lemonade.

When you analyze the few years that Jack had left to live after Olive's death, everything, on every level, began to fall apart for him. His career, two more marriages, his health. Finally death came to him in the very hospital where Olive died thirteen (unlucky number?) years before. The old saying, "What goes around, comes around," seems to be extraordinarily appropriate when it comes to describing the life of Jack Pickford.

> Many harsh things were once said and written about my brother. The fact is he suffered a devastating loss as a young man. I am convinced it was the memory of Olive Thomas, the only woman he deeply loved, that pursued Jack to the end.

They were the candid words of Mary Pickford in her sugarcoated 1955 autobiography, *Sunshine and Shadow*.

Thirty-five years after Olive's death and twenty-two years after her brother's death, Mary Pickford once again attempted to defend her brother and clear his name. Portraying him as a martyr, she tells the story of what happened in the hours leading up to Olive's death and in the days after. She continued with, "I am ready to take an oath that Ollie's death was an accident. Jack told me so and Jack would not have lied to me."

According to Mary, Jack told her that he and Olive embarked on their ill-fated journey to Europe in August of 1920. With them, several friends of a similar age and temperament looked forward to a carefree time away from making movies. Ironically, one of those friends, Bobby Harron, would meet his own tragic end (at age 27), just one week before Olive. Mysterious circumstances surrounded his death too.

It was officially determined an accident, but those who follow that theory believe that Harron, who was by this time back in New York on September 2, 1920, for the premiere of D.W. Griffith's *Way Down East*, which was scheduled for the next day, purchased a revolver from an unidentified man who needed money, put it in his dinner jacket pocket and forgot about it. Later he took the dinner jacket from a trunk, the gun fell to the floor and discharged, striking him in the left lung. Those who continue to believe that Bobby's death was a suicide claim that he was extremely despondent when Griffith bypassed him for the lead role in *Way Down East* in favor of his new protégé, Richard Barthelmess. The real nail in the coffin (no pun intended) was his unrequited love for Dorothy Gish; her rejection of his affections had left him heartbroken.

Paris Police Want Testimony of Jack Pickford, Dead Actress's Husband.

One of the many controversial headlines that caused the public to think that Jack Pickford knew more than he was letting on about Olive's death.

A September 25, 1920 article in *The Moving Picture World* said:

> Bobby was looking forward to attending the opening of *Way Down East*. His dress clothes had just arrived from California, and after he tumbled out of bed on the morning of the accident, in a hurry to keep a studio appointment, he picked them up, intending to give them to the hotel tailor to be pressed. It is said that it is a custom to

carry a revolver in California because of the danger of encountering highwaymen at night on some of the less frequented roads. Bobby had left his revolver in the dress suit and it fell out onto the floor, the cartridge exploding. The bullet penetrated the right lung. Bobby staggered to the telephone and called for help from the hotel office. A policeman decided to put him under arrest (for suicide) before a thorough investigation was made.

His death was officially ruled as an "accidental" gunshot wound. Despite having appeared in close to two hundred films, Harron, like many of his contemporaries, is virtually forgotten today.

According to Mary's recollection, Jack repeated the story of what happened in Paris so often that over three decades after it happened she could still visualize it every step of the way.

Jack had told his sister that on the night in question, he and Olive had been doing the local nightspots. Several friends including the Dolly Sisters, Dorothy Gish and Owen Moore (Mary's ex-husband; she married Douglas Fairbanks just twenty-six days after their divorce was finalized) were with the couple for most of the evening.

At one o'clock in the morning, Jack suggested they turn in for the night since they were both scheduled to make a 7 A.M. flight to London. Olive agreed to go back to the Ritz Hotel, but just as they were undressing for bed more friends came by and tried to get them back into their clothes for another round of partying. They both insisted they were far too tired and the crowd left the room. Incidentally, these "friends" were never identified.

Jack went right to bed but Olive decided to write a letter home to her mother. After some time had passed, the light from the desk had awoken Jack and he was surprised to see Olive still up.

"Please, come to bed, darling," he said, "It's so late, and I can't sleep with that light on."

Olive answered petulantly. "You don't care that I can't sleep, do you? I've got an awful headache." Olive turned out the offending light and went to the window overlooking the street.

"Why don't you take an aspirin?" Jack mumbled as he focused on Olive and drifted back to sleep. The next time he awoke it was to a crash and a blood-curdling scream. Olive was standing in the darkened bathroom as Jack rushed to see what was wrong.

"Quick, Jack," she said, "turn the light on and see if the bottle with the bichloride of mercury tablets is in the cabinet."

Jack did as she said. "No, Ollie, only the aspirin bottle is here."

America's sweetheart and Olive's sister-in-law, Mary Pickford, circa 1916.

"Then I've taken poison!" she screamed.

Olive had supposedly put the mercury tablets elsewhere to prevent this fatal mistake from happening. The maid had evidently straightened the room and placed the bottles, which were of the same size, side by side on the shelf of the medicine cabinet.

Jack tried to flush the poison from Olive's system by first giving her at least twelve to fifteen glasses of tepid water. He then raced downstairs to fetch melted butter and milk but given it was the middle of the night, everything was locked. The night watchman helped Jack obtain the butter and milk while at the same time contacting the American Hospital by telephone. As Jack ran back to the room the squealing sounds of an ambulance siren could be heard approaching the hotel.

Precious time had been lost and Olive lingered for almost a week before her eventual death. Mary remembered Jack telling her that the doctors praised him for thinking quickly and administering the water, milk and butter when he did. Had it not been for his quick thinking, she may have died immediately. In hindsight, it would have been kinder to let her do so. "It was a week of agony for the poor darling. She fought a hopeless battle, dying in my brother's arms," said Mary.

The inevitable investigation immediately began into what caused her death. Was it suicide, accident or murder? The French authorities questioned Jack repeatedly. His story changed from time to time, but Mary always put this down to the grief and distress that he suffered as he helplessly watched his beloved young wife die in agony.

After days of investigation and an eventual autopsy, Olive's death was declared an accident (due to lack of evidence) and her body was embalmed and prepared for the long voyage home.

As Jack crossed the ocean with Olive's body, he later confessed to putting his jacket and trousers on over his pajamas and going to the top deck to climb over the rail when something inside him said, "You can't do this to your mother and sisters. It would be a cowardly act. You must live and face the future."

Author Stuart Oderman interviewed Minta Durfee, first wife of comedian Roscoe "Fatty" Arbuckle, for a 1995 *Films in Review* article on Jack and Olive. In it she remembered how overly protective Mary was of her little brother:

Going by this early scene still, Mary Pickford protected her brother Jack both on and off the screen.

7. What Jack Told Mary...

Mary's little brother, Jack, was always in some kind of trouble, but she always looked after him and she was much nicer to him than she was to her prettier and more talented sister, Lottie, who should have had a better career. Jack was always given the second chance, no matter what kind of scrape he was in; women, liquor, drugs. Jack knew he had the magic and power of the Pickford name to rely on and anything was okay, so long as there was the willingness of Mary and her mother Charlotte to appear at the right time and talk to the right people to bail out their little boy.

[Olive and Jack] were married in secret," Minta explained. "She was a nice girl. She wasn't very intelligent and she didn't have too much business sense, but he didn't have much intelligence or business sense either.

Ollie was a Follies girl and if you were a Follies girl, it meant you were very glamorous and beautiful. A lot of men were naturally attracted to her. When you're that pretty, men fall all over you and give you diamonds and fancy cars and everything. Ollie certainly had her pick of millionaires and society playboys. The one she settled on was Mary's brother, Jack.

Mary never approved of Ollie and her mother never approved of her either. They used to tell Jack that Ollie was a cheap little chorus girl who came from a poor mining town.

Well, Ollie did come from a poor coal mining town, but the Pickfords weren't what you would call society. They came from nothing and made a lot of money and they *became* society.

Mary didn't like the way Ollie and Jack were married. You know, secretly. I guess she forgot she married her first husband, Owen Moore, secretly. It's funny what a little money can do to people. You think you can rewrite your own history, but you can't when your contemporaries are still around.

Still, you have to feel sorry for poor Jack. He was never allowed to do anything on his own or be his own man. All his life he was dominated by two women; his mother Charlotte and his sister Mary.

In her autobiography, Mary remembered the first time she saw her brother upon his return from Paris. She was waiting at their mother's house in Hollywood. A car drove up and Jack stepped out ahead of a few other people. Dressed in deep mourning, his shoulders drooped, his head bowed, a broken man approached her. She suddenly had a cold, clutching feeling in her heart that it would not be too long before he and Olive would meet again ... in death.

Her inclination was right; it would not be too long, not too long at all...

✯ *Chapter 8* ✯

A BROKEN MAN AND HIS WOMEN

The past cannot be changed, the future is in your power.
—Mary Pickford

Mary Pickford admitted in her autobiography that in Jack's heart, no one could ever take the place of his his darling, Ollie. Maybe so, but in the years that followed her death, he attempted marriage twice more. Not at all unusual given the fact that Olive's death made him a widower at the tender age of twenty-four.

Jack's next two wives were also Ziegfeld girls. Two years after Olive's death, he met Marilyn Miller. At the height of her career, she was starring in the Ziegfeld show, *Sunny*. Her $3,000 per week (approximately $35,000 today) salary made her the highest paid musical comedy performer to date at that time. In 1918, just two years before Jack became a widower due to Olive's death, Marilyn was widowed at just twenty years of age when her husband of one year, fellow actor, Frank Carter, died in an automobile accident.

Once again, Flo Ziegfeld's pattern of lavishing gifts and attention on another pretty young girl was in full swing. But Marilyn only used him for the good that it could do her and Ziegfeld's hopes were dashed when Carter, a handsome young comedian-dancer with the build of a professional fighter, swept her off her feet.

They were married in May of 1919. But, love came at a price. Embittered by Marilyn's rejection and blaming Frank for it, Ziegfeld cut him from the Follies show immediately. Marilyn responded to the news by threatening to quit (he threatened her with a breach of contract suit) and throwing a diamond bracelet, a gift from Ziegfeld, back in his face. Despite the blow-up she continued to stay in Ziegfeld's employ. After being let go from the Follies, Frank went on the road as the lead player in *See Saw*. Not used to being separated, the newlyweds would telephone each other constantly.

Desperate to see his wife, Frank called Marilyn after his Pittsburgh show had ended for the week and informed her that he was "dog-tired" but he was insistent on driving to New York that very night to be with her.

"Honey, no. I don't want you driving when you're tired. Wait until next week when the play is in Philadelphia. Please dear, you'll need the rest," Marilyn begged.

"Wait for me!" Frank shouted down the phone. Those were the last words the couple spoke to each other (Marjorie Farnsworth: *The Ziegfeld Follies*).

Shortly after that phone call, news of Frank's death arrived just minutes before Marilyn was due to go on stage. Their brand new royal blue $10,000 (approximately $90,000 today) Packard, driven by Frank, had crashed just outside of Maryland. Frank had lovingly inscribed the doors with their initials (MM & FC); the car and the inscription was a surprise first anniversary gift for his bride.

After seeing the luxurious car at the annual automobile show, Marilyn instantly fell in love with it. Frank purposefully disapproved of such an extravagant purchase (the standard Packard sold for $3,500—approximately $32,000 today) but it was all a front. He

Jack Pickford's second wife, Marilyn Miller, circa 1930.

secretly went back the next morning while Marilyn was still sleeping to put a down payment on it, for her.

Driving conditions, especially at night, were treacherous in those days. Many of the roads had little or no illumination, except for the car's headlights. It appeared that Frank misjudged a sharp curve, the car spun out of control and overturned, leaving him pinned under the front seat. At just 28 years old he was killed instantly. Just minutes after she was told the devastating news, Marilyn, a true professional, gave a flawless performance in the play, *Sweet Sixteen*. Ziegfeld then excused her from the show and agreed to give her an extended break so that she could come to terms with her grief.

Marilyn was devastated. She even somehow managed to blame Frank's death on herself, saying, "When I first saw that stunning new Packard that he meant to surprise me with, I felt even worse. Frank was dead, but the car was little damaged except for a dented roof and cracked windshield. I couldn't get over the feeling that it all might not have happened if I'd never raved about that car to Frank in the first place. I should have realized he'd rush out and buy it for me. He was always so impulsive and generous that way" (Warren G. Harris, *The Other Marilyn*).

Two days after the accident, funeral services were held at Campbell's Chapel on

Newlyweds Marilyn Miller and Jack Pickford, ca. 1922.

upper Broadway in New York City. The service was officiated by the same clergyman who married the couple just eleven months before. Florenz Ziegfeld sent the biggest spray of flowers but due to his lifelong aversion for funerals, he didn't attend the service.

Before too long, rumors that Ziegfeld attempted to pick up with Marilyn where they left off were rife. Marilyn even claimed publicly that she was forced to keep her dressing room door locked in order to keep Ziegfeld out! She insisted that he was desperately in love with her and would marry her if only his wife, Billie Burke, would agree to a divorce. It was constant scandal and embarrassment such as this that Billie endured throughout their entire marriage.

Just as he was with Olive, Jack Pickford was once again the thorn in Ziegfeld's side. The young widower met and fell in love with the young widow and Ziegfeld was again on the outside.

Upon news of the courtship, the Hearst publicity machine took full advantage of the budding romance. An article and pen-and-ink drawing (*American Weekly*, 1921) of Marilyn being courted by Jack in the middle of Woodlawn Cemetery was published in particularly poor taste. The cartoon showed the couple cuddling on a bench amongst the tombstones and the article claimed they met each other while paying respect to their recently deceased spouses, Frank Carter and Olive Thomas. The story read:

> Finally, on a day when the cold winter weather was setting in, Jack pressed Marilyn's hand and felt an answering squeeze as they bent over the grave of Olive Thomas. Both gave expression to the thoughts that had formed the silver lining to their cloud of grief. "I am sure they would want it this way," said Jack. He looked tenderly at the tomb of Marilyn's husband and then at the tomb of his wife. "I'm sure they would," said Marilyn.

Incidentally, the files at Woodlawn Cemetery suggest there could be some truth to this cartoon after all. Frank Carter was placed in receiving vault crypt #539 on May 12, 1920. He was moved to private crypt #400 on June 16 and moved again to the new receiving mausoleum crypt #534 on May 12, 1921. On October 9, he was placed in the mausoleum that he's still in to this day. During the time that Frank and Olive were in "storage," the cemetery was in the process of building a new receiving vault, hence his frequent moves. The lot owner was required to sign off before each move so Marilyn would have been required to be at the cemetery for this purpose. As it happened, Frank Carter and Olive Thomas were placed in their final resting places within two weeks of each other. It's entirely possible that grief and the peaceful surrounding of Woodlawn Cemetery brought Marilyn and Jack together.

Ziegfeld couldn't believe his luck. Jack was back in the picture and ready to steal another one of his headline performers away with marriage and promises of bigger and better things. Still embittered by Olive's death, Ziegfeld sent Marilyn letters attacking Jack's character in the hope that she would see the light and call off the impending marriage. He went as far as hiring a private investigator to dig up all that he could on him. The dishonorable discharge from the Navy, the drugs, the alcohol, the countless women and more importantly, Ziegfeld's opinion about the death of Olive Thomas. Ziegfeld was convinced that Jack destroyed Olive by getting her hooked on drink and drugs and then infecting her with syphilis. According to Ziegfeld, this triple combination led her to deliberately swallow the poison in order to end her misery.

Marilyn Miller and Jack Pickford in happier times, circa 1923.

Despite the smear campaign, Jack never uttered a word in his own defense. But Marilyn wasn't shy about doing so. Several newspaper accounts quoted her as saying:

> Ziegfeld is nursing an old grudge against Jack Pickford. He has done everything in his power to discredit Jack in my eyes. His attack on Jack is a perfect parallel of his attack on Frank Carter, which was less conspicuous because Frank wasn't as widely known as Jack Pickford. But in both cases, Ziegfeld wasted his spleen. He failed with Frank Carter as he failed with Jack Pickford. I shall marry Jack in spite of his ravings and rantings of a regiment of Ziegfelds and I am only too eager, too proud, and too happy to do so.

Marilyn and Jack were married on July 30, 1922, at Pickfair, the lavish home of golden couple, Mary Pickford and Douglas Fairbanks. As they were pronounced husband and wife, a low-flying plane released a blanket of orchids over the bridal party and those in attendance. It was the wedding event of the year. Near riots were reported outside the Pickford home as sightseeing buses caused roadblocks and those on foot attempted to scale the private walls surrounding the estate in order to get a better view.

As Ziegfeld got word that Marilyn and Jack had wed, he fired off one last jab in the form of a telegram, copies of which the media also received and printed. It read, "I pray that all your expectations will be realized and that God has happiness and prosperity in store for you in taking the step your honest friends consider the mistake of your life. Good luck my dear, Marilyn.—Flo."

Bide Dudley, poet laureate for the *New York World*, celebrated the occasion by writing the following congratulatory tribute:

> Oh, Marilyn, oh, Marilyn,
> You now are Mrs. Jack,
> And hearts are glad and hearts are sad,
> From Newfoundland to Yak.
> Oh, Marilyn, sweet Marilyn,
> It's joy we wish you, dear.
> We're all worked up; we lift the cup
> And drink to you near beer!

All the hype and hoopla in the world did nothing to ensure that Marilyn and Jack lived happily ever after. Like the tumultuous relationship between Jack and Olive, this one was even more so and it was five years of bust-ups and make-ups before Marilyn decided that enough was enough. She divorced Jack in Paris (in 1927) on the grounds of desertion and neglect.

With her marriage to Jack behind her, bygones were bygones and Ziegfeld once again had Marilyn's full attention. He set out to make her the star of his upcoming show, *Rio Rita*, and following its smashing Broadway success she went on to star in the equally successful, *Rosalie*.

By 1928 she became engaged to actor Ben Lyon; that fizzled out before she could tie the knot for the third time. Two years later she became engaged to Irish sportsman, Michael Farmer (who later went on to marry Gloria Swanson) but that too ended as quickly as it began. Don Alvarado and Fred Astaire were two other rumored fiancés before she finally settled on stage manager, Chet O'Brien, as husband number three. Justice of the Peace Leo Mintzer married the pair on September 1, 1934. Marilyn gave her full name as Marilyn M. Pickford, declaring she was twice widowed.

The February 1920 edition of *Photoplay* magazine. Olive once again had graced the cover.

By the late twenties, Jack Pickford was ailing. Still in his early thirties, he had the appearance of a much older man. Occasionally he needed assistance to walk and stand and on bad days he'd make use of a wheelchair. Years of drugs, alcohol and the ravages of syphilis had taken their toll.

Despite his worsening health, in late 1932 he insisted he was strong enough to take a European trip. His body had other ideas. He took sick in France and coincidentally he was taken to the American Hospital in Paris (the same hospital Olive died in) where he was immediately diagnosed with acute multiple neuritis.

Olive and one of her many furry friends.

By 1930, Jack had married yet another Ziegfeld girl, Mary Mulhern. "I'm the luckiest man in the world," said Jack. "I'm the luckiest girl in the world," said Mulhern (*New York Times*, 1930).

But the bride grew afraid of Jack within three months. He spent whole days abusing her and whiled away the others in drunken silence. At the time of his hospitalization (late 1932) the marriage was already in ruins and divorce proceedings were pending. In court, Mulhern related how Jack once tried to break her door down, and then chased her outside where she cowered in the bushes. "Mr. Pickford was a mighty nasty man," agreed the maid. "He sure is a hard man to get along with" (Eileen Whitfield: *The Woman Who Made Hollywood*). Their divorce was finalized in 1932.

In a cruel twist of fate, Jack soon found himself alone in Paris, gravely ill and in the same hospital that Olive died in years before. Desperate and scared, he made one last request to see second wife, Marilyn Miller, saying, "I'd like to see Marilyn one more time, if she isn't mad at me" (Marjorie Farnsworth: *The Ziegfeld Follies*).

According to Farnsworth's account, Marilyn agreed to visit with Jack but passport problems halted her journey in England before she was able to cross the Channel to Paris. After hanging on for as long as he could, Jack opened his eyes one last time and muttered to his nurse, "After all, I've lived more at thirty-six than most people have in a lifetime" (*Los Angeles Times*, January 6, 1933).

Marilyn never made it to his bedside. Jack Pickford succumbed to acute multiple neuritis (age 36) on January 3, 1933, in the American Hospital in Paris, France.

Upon news of his death, fellow actor and Biograph veteran Donald Crisp bluntly stated, "Jack was a drunk before he was a man" (*Motion Picture Weekly*, February 1933).

Jack's lifeless body would make the same lengthy sea voyage home just as Olive did thirteen years before.

Three years after Jack's death, Marilyn Miller would meet her own tragic end. Having realized she'd made yet another mistake in love with her hasty marriage to

Chet O'Brien, she filed for divorce. Marilyn's unexpected death (April 7, 1936) gave her a permanent escape before the divorce could ever be finalized.

An operation to correct a reoccurring sinus condition that plagued her for years was scheduled in March of 1936. Shortly before she checked into the hospital, she was walking down Fifth Avenue in New York City with a friend. According to Marjorie Farnsworth's book on the history of the Ziegfeld Follies, a pretty blue dress caught her eye. "Oh, I must have it," she said to her friend.

"For a special occasion?" her friend inquired.

"Very special. I'm going into the hospital tomorrow—"

"And you want to wear that dress when you leave? I don't blame you, it's lovely."

"Yes. When I leave. I want to be buried in it. I am certain I won't leave the hospital alive."

Three weeks to the day later, on April 7, Marilyn Miller died at Doctors Hospital of a toxic condition following surgery. She was 37 years old. There were whispers that she was also plagued with symptoms associated with syphilis. Marilyn and Frank Carter are buried side by side (a worn and tattered velvet cushioned seat separates them) in a large crypt (costing $35,000 in 1920; approximately $320,000 today) at the sprawling four hundred–acre Woodlawn Cemetery in the Bronx, New York.

The money from the sale of the Packard went towards the elaborate marble mausoleum that was built to resemble the little white country cottage they both dreamed about retiring to in their old age. Marilyn was laid to rest in an elaborate $5,000 (approximately $65,000 today) silvered copper casket.

Over one thousand people packed the St. Bartholomew's Protestant Episcopal Church on Park Avenue in New York City and a crowd of five thousand more crammed the streets outside. A staggering twenty-five thousand grief-stricken fans had paid their respects in a single file procession past her open coffin the day before. One hundred policemen were brought in to control the crowds and to allow the hearse and the ten additional cars, filled only with flowers, to take Marilyn to her final resting place in the Bronx. Her will stated that upon her death she be interred next to Frank and the crypt sealed forever.

Despite identifying herself as Marilyn M. Pickford before her marriage to Chet O'Brien, strangely her crypt inscription does *not* bear the Pickford name.

It reads: Marilyn Miller Carter O'Brien.

No living family members are left to maintain the crypt and the once impressive mausoleum is

A giveaway photograph of Olive Thomas to readers of *Picture Show* magazine.

now in a state of rapid decay. Woodlawn Cemetery now has a restoration program underway to fix many of the "celebrity graves" that have fallen into disrepair. Despite their inhabitants' wealthy lifestyles, out of the thousands of monuments within the peaceful green pastures of Woodlawn Cemetery, these "celebrity graves" are in the most need of work.

June Haver played Marilyn Miller in the not-so-accurate musical biopic, *Look for the Silver Lining* (1949) and Judy Garland played Marilyn in *Till the Clouds Roll By* (1946), a film based on the life of Broadway pioneer, Jerome Kern. Garland was pregnant with daughter Liza Minnelli at the time of production and was forced to stand behind stacks of dishes when singing the signature song "Look for the Silver Lining" in order to hide her growing baby bump.

According to Mary Pickford's romanticized autobiography, Jack purposefully chose to spend his last days (he was an inpatient months before his death) in the American Hospital in Paris in a bed where he could see the window of the hospital room where Olive had died thirteen years before. He did all that he could to forget the tragedy for more than a decade, yet ironically, in the days leading up to his death, by his own wishes, he forced himself to remember.

Years of opportunities and temptations were handed to him and Jack greedily took them all. In the end, his inability to say "no" was his ultimate downfall. It cost him his life, and ultimately, it broke his sister Mary's heart. Throughout his brief life, "little Mary" (as she was also known) had saved him time and time again, yet death was something even she was powerless to save him from. Jack lived fast and died young. Upon news of his death, family, friends and fans shed tears for a life that was cut way too short. Yet according to his nurse, Jack shed no tears for himself. He passed away with a contented smile on his face.

✭ *Chapter 9* ✭

MEMORIES OF A LOST LOVE

Olive wasn't happy, even with all the money she was making.
—Bernard Krug Thomas

    Almost eleven years after Olive's death, her first husband, Bernard Krug Thomas, gave *The Pittsburgh Press* (May 4, 1931) a lengthy interview about his life with her. It is mostly a self-serving tale, filled with selective and embellished thoughts about the dream girl he once loved and lost to bigger and brighter things; but, it does give insight into Olive's whimsical, somewhat impulsive personality.

    This interview is especially important because it appears to be the last time that Thomas was sought out by the media to speak about his life with Olive. He slipped into oblivion soon after, living out his days in McKees Rocks, Pennsylvania, and dedicating his life to taking care of his ailing, widowed mother. He died some time in 1968.

    When Olive Thomas worked as a wrapper girl at a Pittsburgh Department store she dreamed of luxuries her salary could not buy. Olive had been working at Horne's Department store for two and a half years when she met Bernard Krug Thomas as she and a friend, Helene Wise, were going into the Star Family Movie Theater in McKees Rocks Fraternal Hall. Helene knew Krug (as he was known), and asked him to sit with them in the show. On the way home, Helene told Olive that Krug Thomas had won the dancing prize at the latest Coney Island contest and was one of the best dancers in McKees Rocks. Olive was interested in him because she'd rather dance than do anything else.

    For the next six months, Olive and Krug went to a dance or a movie nearly every night of the week, and on Sundays, Olive was a guest at the Thomas home. She liked the quiet family life. Here, Bernard Krug Thomas breaks his silence on his courting days and subsequent marriage to Olive.

    "It was just another phase of her nature which was a counterpart of a Dr. Jekyll and Mr. Hyde story. Half of her wanted the real things of life, and the other half wanted the glitter of a make believe world."

Thomas met Olive frequently after the store closed. Often on her pay day she was crying because her $3 a week had gone to pay her bill at the soda fountain. If there was anything she liked after dancing and clothes it was chocolate sodas. Then Olive's family moved to Forest Groves, about eight miles from McKees Rocks and she and Thomas couldn't be together often because it was quite a drive for horse and buggy. Thomas continues:

"She was lonesome and in March she wrote me a letter telling me how lonely she was, she ended it with, 'Krug, let's get married!'" On April 1st, 1911, Thomas and a friend drove to Forest Grove.

"Olive was ready with her little black satchel packed and a suit box filled with dresses all tied securely with a rope. We drove into Pittsburgh for a license and were married. I was 21 and Olive was 16. For the first six months of our marriage Olive was happier than she'd ever been. She liked to cook and when she wasn't busy in the kitchen she was singing or dancing to phonograph music. She was never quiet a minute. It was impossible for her to be lazy even when she was ill and in bed. She kept her hands busy with fancy work. My mom said that Olive had the sweetest possible disposition but she worried about Olive's growing dissatisfaction with life."

When Krug gave her a small diamond ring she confided to her mother-in-law, "Oh, if for only a big diamond," and then one day she said, "Mother, do you know that I have never been satisfied with anything—why is it?"

At the close of her first year as a wife, Olive was going to dances again, every night. When Thomas was too tired after a day's work she went alone or with another girl. By now they had their own apartment.

"I earned $90 a month as a clerk," said Thomas. "I gave Olive $75 a month to run the house. Well, at the end of the month there'd be the bills but no money. She would cry and finally tell me that she had met some girls downtown and bought their lunch or she'd seen the prettiest dress and just couldn't resist buying it.

"Well, you could be as mad as a hornet at Olive for a while, and I did take to leaving the house for two days at a time, staying at the Americus Club. Then she would call me on the phone and tell me she had baked a lemon custard.

"Some days I would get home from work and Olive would be downtown. Then she'd come flying in all excited and probably wearing a new dress, but she could hustle a dinner together in no time. The house was always as neat as a pin, so was Olive. She could prepare a dinner in her best dress and when it was on the table she looked as fresh as a flower.

"We had a lot of fun, we both liked to dance more than to eat, [and] that was about the time the Tango and the Bear Dance were in style. 'Everybody's Doin' It' was the big song hit and we spent nearly every cent we had on dancing and good times.

"Olive liked to go to Billy Hammer's restaurant in the Jenkins Arcade. Gee, she certainly was a beautiful girl and could be the most gracious kid in the world but her nature demanded flattery. I'd be dancing with her when all of a sudden she'd ask me why I didn't tell her that she was beautiful, because the other boys did, and I guess they all thought she was because when we walked down 5th Avenue to the Grand Theater on Saturday night all the fellas in front of the pool room would elbow their way to the front to look at Olive and that pleased her.

"It was on a Saturday or a Sunday night dance that she was sitting on the porch with some friends admiring pictures of a group of Ziegfeld beauties. When her friends left she went to her room and looked at herself in her mirror and decided she was prettier than any of the girls in Ziegfeld's groups. She would go to New York and become famous too.

"When she told me I said, 'No you aren't. I'm going to New York instead, you can charge me with desertion and then you'll be free to make a career.' She didn't want to do that but it was the best thing for the both of us. I knew she'd never be satisfied with life as it was. I went to New York and got a job in a bank, Olive filed divorce proceedings against me and came to New York herself and got a job as a model for such illustrators as Harrison Fisher and Haskell Coffin. I don't know how she did it but before I knew it she was living in a beautiful apartment on West 81st Street, she had fine clothes and everything.

"She called me up one day and asked me out for dinner and we began going around together at the same time the divorce was being considered in Pittsburgh. I was at her apartment the night someone called to offer her a place in the chorus of Ziegfeld's Midnight Follies. Shortly after this she asked me to dinner and insisted on taking me to an expensive nightclub. We danced until 2 A.M. As I was leaving her apartment she took my hand and said, 'Goodbye ol' dear, our divorce was granted this morning. You'll meet a thousand girls, Krug, please, don't like any of them.'

"Olive wasn't happy, even with all the money she was making. She wrote to me that some mornings when she returned from a party she was sick of it all and couldn't stand the sight of the men in the crowd in which she traveled. She was continually asking me to accept an auto or some other gift, because, she said, it would make her happy to give me something. I later learned from her maid that she cried the first Christmas that we were apart when she received many expensive gifts from admirers but not even a card from me. She told her maid that one little card from me would mean more to her than all of the other gifts put together because she knew I really loved her.

"Some months after I came back to Pittsburgh and Olive was making good on the stage I was told by a mutual friend that Olive wanted to come back home. I shook my head and said, 'She can come back to Pittsburgh any time she wants to, but she can never come back in my home.'

"Myron Selznick, the producer, saw her in the Frolic and believed she was a potential star for the motion picture screen. He gave her a long-term contract and prepared to star her in elaborate society productions in which she would wear gorgeous gowns and be seen in vast company. But, Olive was really the ingénue type like Mary Pickford and her most successful pictures were *Footlights and Shadows, Youthful Folly, The Flapper* and *Darling Mine,* in which she played innocent girl parts."

The first picture that Thomas saw Olive in was *Upstairs and Down.* "She wasn't very good in it but it did give me a thrill to see her on the screen," he said. "It seemed as if she was always saying hello to me and after that her acting began to improve but she never was a great actress, she knew it and wrote me a letter saying she knew it was her beauty and not her ability that was making her a success.

"Her professional work in Hollywood brought her into the society of Jack Pickford and he proposed to her. I don't know whether Olive loved Mr. Pickford but I believe she was thinking more about having a famous star like Mary Pickford as a sister-in-law than having Jack Pickford as a husband.

"Anyhow, she married him without delay and his mother, Mrs. Charlotte Pickford, hinted that Olive wasn't good enough for a Pickford. When she wrote me a card while on her honeymoon she said, 'I often think of you and still love you.'

"The last time I saw her to speak with her was shortly after her marriage to Jack Pickford. I was sitting at a table in the Americus Club when Olive, Jack and two men came into the dining room. As she skirted past me she said, 'Why hello there, Krug.'

"I was walking down 5th Avenue when I saw the bulletin of Olive's death over the press office; it was a shock but not a surprise. It just seemed as if she had been born to live within a flash and to die in the same way. Anything else wouldn't have been like Olive.

"In 1923 I returned to New York and the first place I went was Woodlawn Cemetery. There was a big Irish policeman at the entrance. When I asked him for directions to Olive's grave, he said, 'Sure, me lad. I've been watchin' that grave for three years and not a single flower has been on it.'"

Bernard Krug Thomas placed a single red rose at her grave. He said, "Anything else wouldn't have been right for Olive."

✯ *Chapter 10* ✯

GHOSTLY ENCOUNTERS

The New Amsterdam Theatre has a long and colorful history. As with many other legitimate theaters during the Depression years, it was converted to a movie house in 1937. The Nederlander Organization purchased the theater in 1982 but major structural problems, combined with the uncertainty of the city's economic health (which had the Times Square redevelopment project in fits and starts), repeatedly delayed the reconstruction. New York State purchased the New Amsterdam in 1992 and subsequently resold it to the Walt Disney Co. for $29 million. The complete reconstruction of the theater between 1995–97 signaled Disney's confidence in Times Square and anchored the further redevelopment of the area.

Disney's restoration is stunning, both from the outside, where Times Square now bursts with a scrubbed-up neon glow, and on the inside, where the overdone baroque decor from the days of the Ziegfeld Follies has been lovingly returned to its former splendor. In the lobby, which contains elevators to take you to the mezzanine levels, you'll be greeted by uniformed ticket takers who look like they stepped out of a 1930s movie. To your right is a spacious and well-stocked refreshment area. The New Amsterdam Room downstairs, a broad round space connecting the men's and lady's lounges, is reached by grandly carpeted spiral staircases and features deluxe upholstered benches on which you can wait for the rest of your party to take care of business in the restrooms or at the inevitable (but elegant) souvenir stand. The grand reopening of the New Amsterdam took place in May of 1997, with a concert staging of *King David*. Later that year, a stage version of the highly successful full-length animated feature *The Lion King* was presented at the New Amsterdam. *The Lion King* went on to win the Tony Award for best musical in 1998 and has been playing to capacity crowds since its opening (www.nyc-architecture.com).

But, as the applause dies and the crowds disperse for another evening, it's what goes on after dark that continues to intrigue even the staunchest of skeptics. Robert Viagas wrote an article for *PlayBill* magazine entitled "The Ghosts of Broadway," in which he gave a first-hand account of the "other" performances that occur after the main shows have ended and the audiences have gone home.

In his article, Viagas mentions a "ghost light," the term for the lonesome light left to burn on an empty theater stage when everyone has gone home for the evening. The practical advantage of such a light is obvious—safety. It's there so the last person out of the theater and the first person into the theater won't fall into the orchestra pit in the dark.

There wasn't always a ghost light in theaters. Aside from the safety issue, there are several more colorful stories as to why the tradition began.

The urban legend is that a burglar who had broken into a theater one night, before the advent of a ghost light, had fallen off the stage, breaking his leg. Although he was trespassing, he sued the theater for creating an unsafe workspace and won!

Another theory is that leaving a dark theater makes ghosts think the theater has been abandoned and they cause accidents to happen on the set. The ghost light keeps them company overnight and assures them that it is indeed an active theater. Others say ghosts are afraid of light and would cause even more mischief than they usually do if the stage were left in complete darkness.

Lastly, New York City had an old fire code which required a theater to be lit on the stage when it was vacant to allow firefighters to see where the stage stopped and the orchestra pit started. Again, the ghost light was there for safety purposes. Whatever the reason, the tradition continues to this day and the subtle, if not eerie ghost light illuminates the stage of most working theaters throughout the night, including the New Amsterdam Theatre.

A pretty postcard portrait of Olive in her prime.

Dana Amendola, the man whom the Disney Corporation appointed to oversee the restoration of the New Amsterdam Theatre, was awoken by a 2:30 A.M. phone call during the lengthy restoration process. It was the security guard hired to patrol the theater; he was hysterical. During his nightly rounds, he crossed the stage and his flashlight illuminated a very attractive young woman whom he at first thought had gotten herself locked in the theater. She was wearing an old-fashioned green beaded dress with fur cuffs, a sash and a headpiece and she appeared to be holding a blue bottle (reportedly a poison bottle). As he called to her she smiled, blew him a kiss and left the stage—by walking straight through the wall onto 41st Street! It was the ghost of Olive Thomas!

There were numerous sightings of Olive's ghost by other theater employees previous to this encounter. Upon further research, the staff came across a book with a photograph of Olive wearing an outfit similar to what the security guard had described. After being shown the photo, the watchman positively identified the woman he saw on stage as her.

"This security guard had no theater experience, was not a costume designer and had never seen the picture," Amendola said. "We found out there were several observations of her from those who worked in the theater, and they all say the same thing" (www.foxnews.com). The security guard insisted he would only work days after this incident and the theater instituted a policy of scheduling their guards in pairs.

Amendola is still the vice president of operations at the theater and he has several stories involving workers who have seen Olive's ghost. Workers who renovated the theater for its 1997 re-opening have stated that she appears almost exclusively to men, even flirtatiously saying, "Hi, fella!" to some. One worker who was standing in the lobby heard a voice say, "How are you doing, handsome?" yet as he turned to see who was there, the lobby was empty. He quit immediately. Several workers had confessed to seeing Olive walking aimlessly around the theater as the renovations were being done. One time, they were so spooked they collectively dropped their tools and ran from the building!

Aside from her innocent flirtations, Olive's shown no consistent signs of mischief-making and prefers to appear when audiences have departed. To be on the safe side, two portraits of her hang backstage and everyone who works at the theater make a point of saying, "Good morning, Olive!" when they arrive for work and "Good night, Olive!" when they leave. It's a superstition that supposedly keeps Olive happy, for they are mere guests in *her* theater. It's the very least they can do.

She appears to be most upset by the annual Broadway Cares/Equity Fights AIDS benefit where the few surviving Follies girls are invited to take part in an Easter Bonnet competition. One particular year the sets began shaking violently for no reason and another year the light bulbs in one of the office floors burned out simultaneously without an electrical problem being detected. In life and death, it's apparent that Olive likes to be the center of attention.

The only marker identifying Olive's grave is "Pickford" at the top of the crypt. The tomb was designed so that Jack Pickford could one day be interred with her but given the fact that he married and divorced two more times, he was buried with the rest of the Pickford clan at Forest Lawn Memorial Park in Glendale, California. Olive lies alone in a space built for two.

Many people who have caught a better view of her say she's wearing a sash with "Olive" written on it. Upon further investigation, photos have confirmed that she did indeed wear a green costume that bore a gold sash during her Ziegfeld days.

The *New York Times* reported that other workers had seen Olive in a white dress trimmed in silver. She was crying and carrying what appeared to be a champagne glass. The *Times* identified her as Olive Thomas, who they said had been buried in a white dress trimmed in silver.

As recently as 2005 Olive was seen in the abandoned upstairs space that was once the New Amsterdam roof. She was walking through the air, unsupported. Of course, back in its day the roof once housed the innovative glass stage where the Follies girls could perform and the audience members got a better view—of everything. It makes sense that Olive was back there performing. In her short life the theater was the place she was happiest and she shows no sign of leaving any time soon.

Hollywood historian and author of *Hollywood Haunted* (Angel City Press, 1999), Laurie Jacobson, explains the phenomenon of some of Hollywood's most famous ghosts along with Olive's "comeback" at the New Amsterdam Theatre:

Deep in thought. It was said that Olive was never truly happy or satisfied with her life. Even with the fame and fortune that her successful career gave her, her first husband, Bernard Krug Thomas, said she had an emptiness that was never really fulfilled.

> Ghosts or spirits stick around or return for very human reasons: They're attached to a person, place or thing; they died unexpectedly and left unfinished business; they were murdered or the circumstances of their death never explained and their spirits seek justice or revenge. Those reasons describe Olive Thomas all over. Her life and her career were suddenly cut short. At 25, she certainly had unfinished business. Though she was making films in Hollywood, New York was Olive's kingdom and the New Amsterdam Theater her throne. It's natural for people to return to a place they love. When Lucille Ball's longtime home in Beverly Hills was being razed, her ghost was seen at the property's edge watching sadly. The Pantages Theater in Los Angeles regularly experiences a female spirit who sings alone on stage late at night and who has, over the years, joined live performers during a show. They believe it's the spirit of an ardent fan who died in the balcony in the 1930s while watching a musical. So Olive has returned in one of her best costumes to take the stage again where she knew her greatest success. Why is she seen carrying the blue bottle of poison? That's puzzlement. Superman actor George Reeves' death, written off as suicide, was most probably murder. His spirit has been seen in the house where he was shot carrying his instrument of death, a German Luger pistol. Perhaps Olive is also bound to the instrument that caused her death.
>
> Olive was mostly seen in the New Amsterdam during major renovations. Renovations notoriously kick up ghosts. They hate it—as most of us do. It's noisy and dusty and strangers are traipsing through. During renovations at the Hollywood Roosevelt Hotel in the mid '80s, the place was swarming with annoyed spirits who pushed maids into closets, bolted people out of their rooms and rang the switchboard from rooms with no phones. Spirits prefer for the place to remain the way it was in their lifetime. That's why people see ghosts walking through walls. Those walls weren't there when the spirits

were alive. Others have seen spirits without feet or from the knees up. These spirits were walking on the original floors of the building, often a foot or more below the new floors. Olive's spirit was spotted walking through mid-air, unsupported in the abandoned upstairs space that housed the New Amsterdam roof. Research shows that the roof once sported a notorious glass-bottomed promenade where, evidently, Olive still parades for her admirers.

Ghostly activity is wide and varied. Some spirits repeat the same action over and over, as if in an endless tape loop, unaware of the new inhabitants. The tour of the reconstructed New Amsterdam supports this theory with witnesses reporting to have seen Olive wandering the theater calling for "Ziggy," Florenz Ziegfeld's nickname. She is oblivious to those around her. This is a perfect example of the loop or replay explanation. This may not be a ghost, but residual energy from a dramatic or often repeated event—like the image of Marilyn Monroe seen in a mirror she once owned or the ghosts of former studio guards seen still covering their beat.

If Olive were only seen on the promenade, we might be able to say that's all there is to it. But Olive also participates with the living. She appears to them, flirts with men, sometimes speaking directly to them. She responded to the stage manager who told her she must leave. She has a fit when one of her peers comes to the theater and she lets people know when she's upset. Her spirit craves the attention, the limelight and the men—just as she did in life. She no doubt adores the ritual greeting and farewell from the current inhabitants. Olive's spirit is in the present, continuing with the life and success in the theater of which she was robbed that terrible night in Paris.

Clearly, Olive was not ready to give it up, had not nearly had her fill, so she continues to seek it long after her death. The very fact her spirit has been seen is a clue about the mode of her death. The ghosts of suicides are rare; they wanted out. No, Olive didn't go by choice. So, was it an accident or something more sinister? Olive was careless, reckless even, but enough to have accidentally swallowed all those pills? Personally, I think, during an alcohol-fueled argument, she threatened to leave Jack. He forced her to swallow the poison, then regretted his actions and tried to save her. Even if that is true, Olive's spirit seems uninterested in revenge or justice. After all, Jack got his in the end. His career ground to a halt not long after Olive's death and he quickly spiraled into destruction and death. Justice was served. Anyway, Olive was never one to be concerned with right or wrong. Her spirit remains true to that which was most important to her in life—her beauty, her allure and her fame.

A 1924 newspaper clipping, just four years after Olive's death, started with the headline: "Movie Star's Death Affects Grandmother: Aged Verona Woman Passes Away in Home." The rest of the story read:

The tragic death of Olive Thomas, motion picture star and wife of Jack Pickford in Paris a few years ago from poisoning, is believed by friends and relatives to have hastened the death of Mrs. Oliveretta H. McCormick, 79 years old, her grandmother; whose funeral will be held tomorrow afternoon. She was found dead in her home, 473 Center Avenue, Verona on Thursday morning.

When a relative broke in the door the aged woman was found in bed. Hanging on the walls and on the mantelpieces were several large photographs of the dead motion picture star.

Deputy Coroner John Aldisert learned Mrs. McCormick had reared Olive Thomas from the time she was 4 years old until she entered filmdom at the age of 16. The deputy learned Mrs. McCormick's health began to fail rapidly after Olive's death. From one neighbor the deputy learned Mrs. McCormick was reluctant to believe Olive was dead and often remarked that the film star would some times come to see her.

****

Given the numerous sightings of Olive's ghost, the old woman may have been right about her granddaughter's posthumous visits...

The New Amsterdam Theatre is located at 214 West 42nd Street, New York, NY, 10036. It runs daily tours that include stories about the various sightings of their resident ghost, Olive Thomas.

EPILOGUE

Olive was a dancing sunbeam suddenly snuffed out like a candle.
—David O. Selznick

Variety (September 17, 1920) published a poetic tribute to Olive that was written by a former Frolics colleague who was mourning the loss of a friend. The author is only credited as "M.F."

In Memory of Olive Thomas

Words cannot express my sorrow,
As I think back a few years ago,
When I worked on the roof with "Ollie,"
(As we called her) and loved her so—
Her generous ways in those good old days,
Kind thoughts and good wishes for all,
Will live in the memories of her pals
As the "roof days" they recall.

M.F.

As far back as actors go, and even with actors today, it takes a rather dramatic, complex individual to do what they do—act. Angelina Jolie confirms this in the August 15, 2005 issue of *Star*, "If I didn't have my films as an outlet for all the different sides of me, I would probably be locked up."

A particular personality type is required to be in the arts, in any form, and those intricate qualities often spill over into real life too; however there isn't always a chance for a second take when things go horribly wrong away from the safety of a sound stage.

With that said and in relation to Olive's early demise, it seems she was completely capable of a suicide "attempt" in order to scare Jack and bring his attention back to her (they both repeatedly accused each other of infidelities). But mercury bichloride is not a drug to be used in an attention-grabbing suicide bid. There is simply no going back after ingesting the caustic substance the way Olive did.

Lon Chaney's wife, Cleva Creighton, attempted suicide with mercury bichloride but before ingesting the substance she dissolved it (it was meant to be administered as an antiseptic) in water or alcohol first. The dosage was too weak to kill her and permanent damage to her throat was the lasting mark of her desperation.

In Olive's case, some accounts suggest that she ingested the coffin-shaped pills (produced that way as a warning) directly. Dissolving on the way down, they eroded her insides as they went. However, other media reports of the day wrote that Olive ingested the already dissolved pills in an alcohol solution (as it was meant to be topically administered) and the quantity taken was enough to kill several people. Either way, the amount of poison taken, in either form, was more than enough to take the life of the petite movie star.

Olive and Jack may have argued about something before he went to bed, but they *always* argued. Olive stayed up a little longer to write a letter home to her mother. By the time she finished writing she had an awful headache and because of a flight scheduled for early in the morning she knew she desperately needed some rest to alleviate her aching head.

In the few hours of sleep time that she did have left, quality hours were necessary. Mistaking the mercury bichloride (incidentally, the label was written in French) for her sleeping potion caused her to suffer days of agony before her inevitable death of acute nephritic inflammation on September 10, 1920. Her time of death was 10 A.M., Paris time.

Had her terrifying screams not awoken Jack (ironically, she decided not to turn on the bathroom light for fear of waking him because had already complained about the desk light shining in his eyes as she was writing the letter to her mother) he would not have been able to force Olive to ingest the water, eggs and milk. This desperate attempt to save her not only caused her to linger in agony for days but the constant regurgitation of the the additional fluids combined with the dissolving poison resulted in such severe chemical burns to her face, neck and throat that a closed casket was the only option.

With all of that said, darkened bathroom or not, taking a whole bottle of anything in a medicine cabinet will most likely cause imminent death and it's conclusive that Olive took the whole bottle. It's clear that Olive Thomas was the only person who could tell us exactly what happened but four days before her life was tragically taken away, the poison robbed her of her voice. Without Olive's statement of events, there are too many holes, too many versions and too many people who had careers and a way of life to lose to prompt them to tell the truth about what happened to the small town girl who dreamed of stardom, found it and lost it and her life just as quickly.

In an interview a little over a year before her death, Olive seemed eerily blasé about fate and mortality: "I think that you die when your time comes and not until then. I feel the same about other things as I do about death. I don't think you can change anything that is going to happen to you any more than you can change anything that has happened to you" (*Motion Picture*, June 1919).

Perhaps it was a mere coincidence but Olive was not the only Ziegfeld girl whose life came to a tragic, early end. In 1916, when Olive was entrenched in the glamour of the Ziegfeld world, she and five of her fellow Ziegfeld showgirls vowed to one day return to Broadway for a reunion of sorts. They promised to meet for supper in twenty years time. Churchill's restaurant was to be the place where the reunion would take place. When the day arrived Churchill's was no more, and one woman sat in the nearest café and drank a toast to the missing five.

Madelin Blitzstein of *Every Week Magazine* wrote about the misfortunes of the five women who didn't make the reunion and interviewed the one woman who did. The date that the plan was made was June 2, 1916. The place was the dressing room of the old New Amsterdam Theatre in New York. The time was the first night of the call for chorus girls for Florenz Ziegfeld's new edition of the Ziegfeld Follies.

And the dramatis personae were six beautiful young girls, five of them not yet out of their teens, each looking forward to a life of fame and luxury which Broadway holds out as a promise to all newcomers.

But there was one sour note in that scene of youthful ambition. It was struck by an old, poverty-stricken hag who seemed to sound a warning note as she looked at the gay young girls with her tired, sad eyes.

Glancing back at her, the girls decided that they would meet together 20 years from that night, at exactly 8 o'clock, at Churchill's restaurant, to discuss what had happened to them in the interim.

Jump ahead twenty years: On June 12, 1936 at 8 P.M., a lone customer sat at a table. It was Kathryn Lambert, one of the six girls who made the promise to meet her friends two decades before. It wasn't that her five friends forgot their pact. None of them could make it because all of them were dead!

"We were all famous, I guess," Kathryn said as she sat drinking a toast to her departed companions. "But death plays no favorites... The Follies that year, 1916, were perhaps the most famous of all. It included such stars as W. C. Fields, Ina Claire, Allyn King, Sam Hardy, Fannie Brice, Ann Pennington, Kathryn Perry and Ethel Delmar. We six were only girls in our teens, eager and bursting with ambition.

"Five of us were sitting in a group, chatting, waiting for the call, when Olive Thomas, who had been a Follies the preceding year, called us into her dressing room. There was the old hag, dirty and ragged. Years ago she too had been a showgirl, filled with great ambitions for herself. Now she was eking out a living by selling cold cream in the theaters.

"'I was very beautiful, my children,' she said. 'As beautiful as any of you. I was in the Florodora show. That was more than 20 years ago.' We stared at her in horror as she took our nickels. And when she had gone, Olive whispered: 'Isn't that tragic!' Someone said shivering: 'I wonder if that will happen to us.'

"Olive drew herself up proudly and answered: 'Not to me. It can never happen to any of us, if we make up our minds. We all have beauty and talent. Twenty years from now, we will all be famous and successful.' It was then we made our pact" (Madelin Blitzstein, *Every Week Magazine*).

Olive died at age 25 in 1920, just four years after that reunion pact was made. Lilyan Tashman died on March 21, 1934, age 34, after an operation to remove several cancerous tumors that had riddled her young body. Her death was later attributed to her strict diet in order to keep her marvelous figure. She was married to actor Edmund Lowe. Their nine-year marriage was considered one of Hollywood's happiest unions. Martha Mansfield was fatally burned on a film set during the making of *The Warrens of Virginia* (1924). A carelessly tossed match ignited her Civil War costume of billowy hoop skirts and flimsy ruffles and within seconds she was engulfed in flames. Fellow actor, Wilfred Lytell smothered her with his coat and extinguished the flames but it was too late. The following day she died as a result of her severe burns, at age 24.

It is difficult to tell which one of the five women had the saddest death, but certainly Fifi Alsop's was the most sordid. In 1915, before her bout in the 1916 Follies. Fifi married steel billionaire Edward Brown Alsop (she was 17, he was in his seventies). It was far from being a happy union. A few months after the marriage, Fifi was admitted to a sanitarium to recover, as she said, from "too many kisses." Soon the news got out that Alsop had deeded $3,000,000 worth of property to his sons by his former marriage, tying it up in such a way that his wife could not get any part of it either before or after his death. They eventually divorced in 1915.

Fifi went to Europe for a short rest. Then her money gave out completely and she worked for a week or two as a telephone operator in New York. She took a job in the Ziegfeld Follies chorus in 1916. But she could not regain her strength. In 1918 she wrote an article called, "I Am Old at 23," warning young girls never to marry old men merely because of flattery.

Fifi went from bad to worse. The year Alsop died, 1922, Fifi, in a state of poverty, was taken from a cheap, furnished room by police and placed in Bellevue Hospital suffering from alcoholism and veronal poisoning. Time and time again, Fifi was released and sent back. She was still alive a year before the reunion date but, in 1935, she died a miserable death—alone. Her unclaimed corpse remained on a slab in Bellevue hospital for days.

And, lastly, a few years before the reunion, Bessie Chatterton Poole, daughter of a fine New England family, Follies girl, and for long years a member of Broadway's fast set, died under mysterious circumstances after a heated argument in a New York cabaret club. On October 7, 1928, Bessie was a guest at Tommy Guinan's Chez Florence nightclub. All that was ever found out was that during the course of the evening, she was ordered to leave the club and she went back to the rooms which she shared at the Dorset Hotel with Lillian Lorraine.

Soon after Lillian called a doctor because Bessie had fallen very ill, she was taken to a private hospital where she died the next day. She had been drinking very heavily right before her death and the coroner refused to disclose anything other than "her death was related to heart disease." Lillian did say that Bessie had had "a dispute" with two men at a nightclub, but the case was closed.

So there it was, twenty years after six young friends all excitedly agreed to meet again to discuss their lives, all but one were dead. On June 12, 1936, Kathryn Lambert, the last of the six women, kept her promise to her friends and bravely took her place at a table of a busy Broadway restaurant. She ate alone that night. She had no one to tell *her* story to. After leaving the Ziegfeld chorus she had continued to work and struggle, eventually finding a comfortable niche as a producer, a theatrical agent and a writer. Now Kathryn could only reflect on the memories of times past and wonder what cruel twist of fate may soon come to her.

An unidentified newspaper from Olive's hometown of McKees Rocks printed fond memories from a school friend as well as several townspeople who knew her. The article read, in part:

> "Olive Thomas was a lovely and lovable girl and was very popular here," said friends in McKees Rocks yesterday, all of whom expressed grief at the news of her death. "She came quite frequently to her home town after her success on the musical comedy stage and in the motion pictures, and she always came dressed quite simply, and called to visit with her friends of childhood days. She told us of the wonderful times she was having in New York, and that while she would not be contented to live again in McKees Rocks, she liked to come back," they declared.

"The last time Olive was home," said a school friend, "was a little over a year ago at the time of the death of a sister-in-law. I asked her then how she liked married life and she declared she and her husband were very happy together, and remarked what a contrast was her second marriage to her first to Krug Thomas of McKees Rocks, to whom she was married on April 1, 1911, at the age of 16 and from whom she was granted a divorce on February 25, 1915, on the grounds of neglect and desertion."

"Of course, Olive liked to have good times," said another friend, the wife of a local druggist. "She was young and beautiful and full of life and loved beautiful things which she enjoyed, sharing with her mother and step-father. She was always very good to her mother, she declared, to whom she, sometime ago, gave a $100,000 home in Los Angeles. Mr. and Mrs. Thomas of 404 Woodward Avenue, (ex) father- and mother-in-law of the dead actress, also declared they were very fond of her."

The little Pennsylvania town of Charleroi never forgot their Olive. They were aware of Olive Thomas—movie star, but it was Olive Duffy they spoke of, and often. As late as 1976, fifty-six years after Olive's death, Mrs. Edward Sweadner of the Charleroi Historical Society recounted the life story of Olive to a packed audience. An article in *The Valley Independent* (August 25, 1976) recalled the event, saying, in part:

> In June, Mrs. Edward Sweadner recounted the life story of Charleroi's famous early motion picture star, Olive Thomas, wife of Jack Pickford.
>
> Miraculously, many of the audience members remembered Olive Thomas as Olive Duffy, the beautiful young girl who lived on Third Street, attended Charleroi schools and moved to Pittsburgh after the death of her father. Many also remembered seeing her in movies at the Palace, Coyle and Majestic Theaters of Charleroi's early days.

Jane Dixon of the *New York Telegram* (September 12, 1920) summed up Olive's life best, saying:

> Another brilliant butterfly has fluttered across the horizon from whence there is no return.... Overnight are wiped out beauty, youth, fame, fortune in a tragedy that shocks moving picture fans of four continents and carries sorrow to the hearts of hundreds of personal friends and acquaintances who loved and admired the scintillating star.
>
> Physicians and those close to Olive Thomas Pickford are authority for the statement that she visited her bathroom at an early hour of the morning, four o'clock or thereabouts, and under the impression she was taking a sleeping potion, swallowed an alcohol solution of bichloride of mercury.
>
> Despite these official reports the theatrical world, wherein Olive Thomas revolved radiantly, is palpitant with vague rumors. There are those who insist that regardless of all her seeming gaiety and success Olive Thomas was far from happy. Such a tale is difficult to believe. Why should this lucky young woman not be happy?
>
> She possessed beauty in an unusual degree. Kirshner, the artist, pronounced her the most beautiful girl in America. Her dressing room at the Ziegfeld Follies, where she first came full into the spotlight of public approval, overflowed with costly flowers from every clime, tribute to her loveliness.
>
> Her hair was dark and luxuriant. Her eyes were like twin pools, clear and sparkling. Her mouth provocative with upward curls of good humor at the corners. Her profile was perfect as a cameo cut. Her figure was lithe and graceful. She had the gift of wit and the love of laughter.
>
> During "Follies" days Olive Thomas had many suitors. She might have married into the first families of her own land, become a member of that old Knickerbocker set which is the ambition and despair of social climbers from coast to coast. She smiled her rejections and promised to be a sister to more than one millionaire's son who came to the stage door a-wooing.

When certain coroneted gentlemen told her of their patrimonies and castles across the seas she shrugged her dainty soldiers and sighed her regrets. It was inevitable a girl of big heart and vivid imagination like Miss Thomas would marry for love. The pick of the "Follies" beauties ran true to form. She took a "flyer" into the pictures. There she met young Jack Pickford, brother of Mary Pickford. Love rode apace. Friends recall the devotion of Jack Pickford in sweetheart days, how they were totally unable to think or talk about anyone or anything but each other.

Doubters shook their heads. "Olive Thomas will tire of love's young dream before she marries Jack," they said. "Jack will never light in one place long enough to marry," they continued.

But Olive and Jack proved the depth of their affection and the folly of prediction by betaking themselves to the minister and pledging their troth for all time. Those who thought of Olive Thomas pictured her as a favored child of fortune.

Did she not have matchless beauty? Was she not making a fabulous salary in the pictures? Did she not have the public at her feet, fawning in admiration? Was she not possessed of the wardrobe of a princess—soft silks, rare laces, rich velvets and satins, priceless furs and jewels? Did she not go here and there and everywhere, scorning the skyrocketing of the railroad profiteers? Had she not motors and maids and every mundane luxury? And, most of all, had she not her work carried to the heights of achievement? Yes, Olive Thomas Pickford had all of these—and more.

Friends who knew her best say they were not enough. The girl grown woman seemed to have missed the very essence of happiness; the things which bring peace, contentment, living joy. She was just a brilliant butterfly, sipping the sweets from the blooms of life and fluttering restlessly on to the next flower.

Let no girl or woman, secure in the sacred precincts of her happy home, envy the course of the butterfly...

STAGE AND FILM APPEARANCES

As previously mentioned, almost half of Olive's film work is considered "lost." But, thanks to *The AFI Catalog* and vintage publications such as *Wid's* and *Wid's Daily*, in-depth synopses exist on all of her titles, as do several scene stills and lobby cards. These images together with the story outlines help us to understand what each film was about. It's a poor substitute for the film itself but these few rare pieces allow us to preserve and study what's left of Olive's work.

A *lost film* is essentially a film that, for any of several reasons, is no longer in existence. The main reason films are now lost is because the nitrate film used, especially in the silent era, is extremely unstable. Luckily, modern films do not suffer this fate due to the use of acetate-based safety film and the modern-day mindset that a film is a medium to be preserved forever. In the early part of the twentieth century, films were considered a disposable form of entertainment, even to those who made them. There was no market for films after their theatrical run because television, video and DVDs did not yet exist. Prints were often destroyed for the silver content contained in the nitrate and the money would then be used to finance the next project. The film business was exactly that—a *business.*

In order to preserve nitrate films today, they need to be transferred to safety stock or digitized. If not, the decomposition process will destroy them forever. The slogan "Nitrate Can't Wait" is a popular saying in the film preservation world.

Decomposition begins with the film becoming brittle and shrinking. It then discolors and fades until finally secreting a thick brown jelly-like substance. Soon after it will turn into a pile of fine powder. This is known as the cremation process. Nitrate is also highly combustible, making it dangerous to store. Several nitrate fires and explosions occurred in the early part of the 20th century with the most notable nitrate fire (New Jersey, 1937) destroying much of the Fox Film Corporation's silent film collection. MGM held onto more early films than any other company (Disney was a close second) and they were the most thorough of the major studios to transfer everything photographed on nitrate film to safety stock. A long-overdue project began in the late

1960s dedicated to the preservation process. The work eventually covered a twenty-year period, costing over $30,000,000. Everything was converted, no matter how obscure, in this worthy mission. Unfortunately, some time between 1967 and 1972, a major vault fire (Vault #7) in Culver City destroyed many of the films that were awaiting restoration. A staggering 90 percent of silent films are now considered lost.

There have been countless fires at all vaults owned by the major studios, both in the movie industry and in the music industry. Fire sprinklers aren't much help as they ruin the materials. Since the 1960s, many new techniques of storage have been implemented, including gas extinguishers that withdraw the oxygen. However, it became so expensive to keep a vault at just the right temperature and humidity that companies began using salt mines, which contain these elements naturally. If the local environment is not compromised, a fire is unlikely. Fox Studio still owns a salt mine in Kansas where they store over one million films (www.londonfoodfilmfiesta.co.uk).

The films of some of the biggest stars of the silent era have now all but disappeared. Particularly striking is the case of Theda Bara, who was a star on the order of Charlie Chaplin and Mary Pickford during the 1910s. Of the forty films she made, only three and a half survive. Of the fifty-seven films that Clara Bow (the "It" girl) made, twenty are completely lost and five more are incomplete (www.clarabow.net).

The search for lost films and the interest in preserving these gems for future generations has become a booming business for many companies wanting to cash in on the DVD release of what is essentially a new film from another era; a rare Hollywood treasure.

Many important silent-era films, and films which involve important actors, directors, and creative talent exist in single prints in museums, archives, and private collections. These single prints which have not been copied, digitized, or preserved in any way. The possibility of losing these films forever is very real, unless they are preserved—fast!

There are also those films that don't exist in full but for which portions or mere fragments remain. Although not her best work, Olive's *Love's Prisoner* (1919), which is missing the crucial final reel, is the perfect case in point. These examples may be termed partially lost films. Hopefully, one day those lost films will be found and those precious missing reels will be pieced together to form the long-awaited complete picture—literally.

The following filmography is listed alphabetically, by title, in the chronological year of release. An asterisk (*) indicates the film still exists, either in whole or in part.

Stage

* *Ziegfeld Follies* (1915)—"Live Broadway Revue Show"
SUBTITLED: "The Blue Follies"
DIRECTORS: Julian Mitchell and Leon Errol
PRODUCER: Florenz Ziegfeld, Jr.
OPENING NIGHT CAST (alphabetically by surname): Helen Barnes, Lucille Cavanaugh, Ina Claire, Peggy Dana, Ethel Davies, Emil Dwyer, Phil Dwyer, Marcelle Earle, Leon Errol, Gladys Feldman, W.C. Fields, Dorothy Godfrey, Bernard Granville, Flo Hart,

May Hennessy, Justine Johnstone, Evelyn Kerner, Kay Laurell, Gladys Loftus, Muriel Martin, Mae Murray, Oakland Sisters, May Paul, Ann Pennington, Carl Randall, Helen Rook, John Ryan, Dorothy St. Clair, Margaret St. Clair, Melville Stewart, Olive Thomas, Miss Touraine, Lottie Vernon, Nancy Wallace, Dottie Wang, Bunny Wendell, Rose Werts, Will West, George White, Edith Whitney, Bert Williams, Miss Wilson, Ed Wynn.

FEATURED CAST: Ina Claire, Leon Errol, W.C. Fields, Justine Johnstone, Mae Murray, Ann Pennington, Olive Thomas, George White, Bert Williams, Ed Wynn.
SCENIC DESIGN: Joseph Urban
COSTUME DESIGN: Lady Duff-Gordon
PERFORMED AT: New Amsterdam Theater, 214 West 42nd Street, New York, NY
GENRE: Live Broadway revue show
OPENING NIGHT: June 21, 1915
CLOSING NIGHT: September 18, 1915
TOTAL PERFORMANCES: 104
MUSIC BY: Louis A. Hirsch and David Stamper
LYRICS BY: Rennold Wolf, Channing Pollock and Gene Buck
MUSICAL DIRECTOR: Frank Darling
FEATURED SONGS BY: Charles Elbert, Irving Berlin, Seymour Furth and Bert Williams
FEATURED SONGS WITH LYRICS BY: Ward Wesley, Irving Berlin and Will Vodery
SONG LIST IN THIS PRODUCTION:

Act 1: "Under the Sea," "Hold Me in Your Loving Arms," "My Zebra Lady Fair (Zebra Girl)," "I Can't Do Without Girls," "Twenty Years Ago," "The Birth of a Chicken," "My Radium Girl," "Hello Frisco (I Called You Up to Say Hello)," "I'll Build a Home in the U.S.A. (We'll Build a Little Home in the U.S.A.)"

Act 2: "I'll Be a Santa Claus to You," "If the Girlies Could Be Soldiers," "Marie Odile," "Go to Sleep, My Baby," "A Girl for Each Month in the Year," "I'm Neutral," "Indoor Sports," "The Midnight Frolic Glide"

TRIVIA: Due to the brilliant design techniques of Joseph Urban, this 1915 version was the most visually stunning Follies to date. In fact, Urban's unique art deco designs gave the series a visual sense of style no other revues could ever match. The visually stunning opening sequence had showgirls "swimming" in waves of blue light, and massive golden elephants spouting real water through their upturned trunks. W.C. Fields became a star with a hilarious billiards act, and Pennington danced with future Ziegfeld competitor George White.

Built in 1903, the elaborate 1800-seat New Amsterdam Theater introduced art nouveau to Broadway. Showman Florenz Ziegfeld brought his first "Follies" revue to the theater in 1913. By 1937, with the heyday of the revue in the past, it moved with the times and became a movie palace. In 1982, it earned landmark status and was purchased by the Nederlanders, who sold it to the state ten years later. Disney performed extensive renovations and restorations before re-opening the theater in 1997 with a show-stopping Broadway production of *The Lion King*.

In the 1915 Follies, Olive appeared as "Miss January," an aide to the president in the "Nations of the World" skit and one of the "Nightie-night girls." In the more risqué Midnight Frolics show, she appeared as "Miss Central Park" and "Miss Winter New York."

The *New York Clipper* printed a statement by an American in Paris shortly after he heard about Olive's tragic death. He gave a first-hand account of the audience reaction to Olive's appearance on stage as "Miss Winter New York":

I remember so well her first appearance in the "Follies" in that Winter Girl costume. There was a chorus of "oh's" and "ah's" from the biased first nighters and captious critics, who are quite used to beauty. She wore a short white broadcloth costume, with ripples of fur, and her piquant little face, with its framing of brown curls atop of which was the little white fur cap, all made an unforgettable picture. She was a vision of beauty and everyone know that New York would be at her feet in a week—as it was.

Films

★ ***Beatrice Fairfax*—Episode Ten, "Play Ball" (1916)**★

DIRECTORS: Leopold Wharton and Theodore Wharton
CINEMATOGRAPHER: Levi Bacon (Episodes 3, 5, 10 and 15)
RELEASE DATE: August 7, 1916; Silent; 2 reels
RUNNING TIME: 20 minutes
WORKING TITLE: *Letters to Beatrice*
FILMING LOCATIONS: Ithaca, New York (Renwick Park aka Stewart Park)
CAST: Harry Fox (Reporter Jimmy Barton), Grace Darling (Beatrice Fairfax), Olive Thomas (Rita Malone), Nigel Barrie (Donald Jordan/Bert Kerrigan), Bessie Wharton (Mrs. Malone), Bruce McRae (The Bookie).
SUMMARY: Beatrice Fairfax is an investigative reporter and Jimmy is her helper and pal. "Play Ball" centers on gambling and baseball, as well as the usual romance plot. Episode 10 of a series of 15 installments.
EPISODE TITLES:
1. The Missing Watchman
2. Adventures of the Jealous Wife
3. Billie's Romance
4. The Stone God
5. Mimosa San
6. The Forbidden Room
7. A Name for the Baby
8. At the Ainsley Ball
9. Outside the Law
10. Play Ball (starring Olive Thomas)
11. The Wages of Sin
12. Curiosity
13. The Ringer
14. The Hidden Menace
15. Wristwatches

DISTRIBUTION COMPANY: International Film Service, Inc.
PRODUCTION COMPANY: Wharton, Inc.
WRITER: Basil Dickey (Scenario)
TRIVIA: Olive was paid $200 (approximately $3,400 today) for one week's work on the series with an extra $100 (approximately $1,700 today) for the three days over schedule. She also appeared as an uncredited background player in earlier episodes of the series.

★ *Broadway Arizona* (1917)★

DIRECTORS: Lynn F. Reynolds
RELEASE DATE: September 30, 1917; Silent; 5 reels
GENRE: Drama-Comedy
WORKING TITLE: *My Lady Disdain*
CAST: Olive Thomas (Fritzi Carlyle), George Chesebro (John Keyes), George Hernandez (Uncle Isaac Horn), Jack Curtis (Jack Boggs), Dana Ong (Press agent), Thomas S. Guise (Old producer), Leola Mae (Indian squaw), Robert N. Dunbar (Doctor).

SUMMARY: Wealthy rancher John Keyes travels to New York for vacation and falls for a lady of the stage, Fritzi Carlyle. When Keyes proposes, Fritzi takes her press agent's advice for a publicity stunt and accepts the proposal, then denies it next day in all the papers. The downhearted Keyes goes back to his ranch and Fritzi stays in New York, but eventually the stress causes her to break down and leave the stage. Learning of this, Keyes returns to New York and whisks Fritzi back to his ranch, where the bracing Arizona air and the western lifestyle help her to recover. When detectives come looking for the "kidnapped" Fritzi, she dismisses recent events as a publicity stunt and happily announces her engagement to Keyes.

DISTRIBUTION COMPANY: Triangle Distributing Corp.
PRODUCTION COMPANY: Triangle Film Corp.
WRITER: Lynn F. Reynolds (Scenario)
CAMERAMAN: Clyde R. Cook
Variety (September 28, 1917) said:

A combination of Broadway, New York, and the wild and wooly is presented in this Triangle–Kay Bee ... Olive Thomas is the star with a role that required nothing of her than to be just Olive Thomas. The picture is a fair program feature, and can be safely played where the house is running on a "feature a day" schedule.

A western ranch owner and a Broadway star are the hero and heroine. The ranch owner comes to Broadway, sees the actress and falls in love with her. The press agent scents a chance to break a story if she will kid the cowman along and agree to become engaged to him. Result would have gladdened the heart of any press agent, for the story goes over for a double column spread, then the denial is good for another yarn. (Small chance of that happening in New York these days, with the dailies tight as the neck of a two-ounce bottle on space.)

A *Wid's* theater manual (Thursday, October 4, 1917) gave the following evaluation of the feature:

AS A WHOLE: Light comedy with some action, will undoubtedly prove entertaining to most fans.
STORY: Had one or two good twists, considerably good comedy and was helped by titles.
DIRECTION: Kept things moving, gave interesting atmosphere and made action rather convincing.
PHOTOGRAPHY: Generally pleasing, although not exceptional
LIGHTINGS: A few good, but little attempt for effects
CAMERA WORK: Satisfactory
STAR: Quite pleasing; photographed to advantage and was good except when tried to cry.
SUPPORT: Chesebro pleasing, and Hernandez gathered laughs, with others satisfactory.

DETAIL: A few good touches; ambulance kidnapping good idea
TIME: Sixty-one minutes (5 parts)

This light comedy holds the interest all the way and registers a good many laughs mixed in with action that is good without becoming too melodramatic, I believe that most fans will consider the production very good entertainment.

This isn't a film that could be called a sensational success, but it is more than a satisfactory program release figured on the basis of the average program offering.

The plot of this had to do with a chorus girl whose press agent inveigled a Westerner into proposing to her engagement which was to be promptly denied. The Westerner didn't appreciate the situation and became rather peeved when he learned that the girl had played him for a goat. He went back home and stuck around until he learned that the lady of the stage was ailing in health and then he came East and tried to talk her into going to Arizona, his home.

This the lady couldn't see, and so hero and his fat little pal, Uncle Isaac, put over a very neat kidnapping stunt by arriving at the hotel dressed as attendants on an ambulance, carrying the lady out on a stretched after she had been tied and gagged, the waiting ambulance on the outside carrying her to a private car at an outlying station in which was spirited away to Arizona.

As a prisoner on the hero's ranch she rapidly regained her health, but very soon came the avenging "ossifiers." There was a battle in the hills when the detective and the posse tried to capture the hero and Uncle Isaac, who were attempting to make a getaway with the girl, and then, after many honest men and true had almost been shot in the battle, the lady calmly told the sheriff that she had not been kidnapped at all, but that she was out here because she was to marry this guy. It was a twist finish that was in a way anticipated, but by heck!—It seems that she might have told the answer sooner instead of letting 'em shoot at one another so reckless like.

Miss Thomas was very pretty in practically all of her scenes, and, except for one or two occasions when she tried to cry, her work was very satisfactory. As a pleasing little ingénue she should be able to get by nicely, but surely she will never be able to start anything as a dramatic actress.

George Chesebro, as the hero, registered nicely, and George Hernandez, as the fat comedy character, earned many laughs. He was materially assisted by some good titles.

The Box Office Angle

Since this is comedy most of the way, I believe you can consider it a very satisfactory production, based on the quality of the average program release. The atmosphere and action were interesting and a number of laughs were earned.

Although rather a newcomer, Olive Thomas has been photographed to advantage in a couple of Triangle's offerings, so that I have a hunch that she has some friends already. You can safely promise that this is considered her best production, because it really will register as such with most everyone.

If you have been playing Bluebird productions produced by Lynn F. Reynolds, such as *God's Crucible*, which was one of his best efforts, you might refer to the fact that Director Reynolds brought some of his old Bluebird players with him to Triangle. It would depend entirely upon how well Bluebird productions have been going as to whether or not you should make any comment on this, because it so happens that today there are quite a number of Universal directors and players working in the Triangle Studios, this being due to the presence of Mr. H. O. Davis, who was formerly General Manager at Universal City.

In your advertising this you might say: "If you had made up your mind to kidnap a girl who had promised to marry you and then turned you down, how would you go about it? The hero of *Broadway Arizona* did a neat job!"

★ *A Girl Like That* (1917)

DIRECTOR: Del Henderson
RELEASE DATE: January 18, 1917; Silent; 5 reels
GENRE: Crime Drama
CAST: Irene Fenwick (Nell Gordon), Owen Moore (Jim Brooks), Tom O'Keefe (Bill Whipple), Edwin Sturgis (Joe Dunham), Harry Lee (John Gordon), Jack Dillon (Tom Hoadley), Olive Thomas (Fannie Brooks), W.J. Butler (Clergyman).

SUMMARY: Nell Gordon's father was once a burglar, but he has turned over a new leaf. When he falls ill, however, the burglar's old cronies persuade Nell to help them in a bank robbery, supposedly to raise funds for their sick friend. Nell gets a job in the bank and learns how to open the safe, but then she falls in love with Jim Brooks, another bank employee, and decides not to help with the robbery after all. The crooks try to force her father to insist, and when he refuses, they shoot him. Seeing their true colors, Nell forms a plan. She agrees to help with the robbery, but in the middle of the heist she calls the sheriff. Of course the story ends with the crooks in jail and Nell and Jim in love.

DISTRIBUTION COMPANY: Paramount Pictures Corp.
PRODUCTION COMPANY: Famous Players Film Co.
PRODUCER: Daniel Frohman
WRITER: Paul West (Scenario) and Roswell Dague (Scenario)
CAMERAMAN: Lewis W. Physioc

A *Wid's* theater manual (Thursday, January 25, 1917) gave the following evaluation of the feature:

AS A WHOLE: Ancient idea fairly well handled
STORY: "Innocent girl forced to be crook, saved by hero's love" idea; Formula No. 63.
DIRECTION: Gave some human touches, but many scenes missed fire.
PHOTOGRAPHY: Varied
LIGHTINGS: Some good, some poor
CAMERA WORK: Acceptable
STARS: Made characters human
SUPPORT: Some good types
EXTERIORS: Small-town atmosphere, but not artistic
INTERIORS: Good
DETAILS: Several slips
TIME: Fifty-eight minutes

Miss Fenwick and Mr. Moore tried hard to make this human and the characterization given by Mr. Moore helped a lot in keeping some of the wilder melodrama from registering as entirely impossible.

Miss Fenwick ... held the center of most of the action with a characterization which pleased. Certainly her work will do much towards making this acceptable with the average audience, even though they kick pretty hard about the story.

This old formula has seen such service that it seems criminal to try to get back into action as a five-reel feature.

There is nothing that could be called suspense in the development of the situations and any audience will be far ahead of the story all the way. The general atmosphere of the offering was not what could be called artistic; but the small-town stuff was rather well handled.

The safe in the bank, which was the object of attack and consequently very much in evidence during the development of the plot, must have been a very, very old safe, because its face was quite "wrinkled." It seems inexcusable that such a prominent company should permit such an awful prop in a feature production.

The final situation was very badly developed, because there was no logical need for Miss Fenwick to allow the robbery to proceed as it did. The robbers could have been, and should have been, arrested for murder, instead of permitting the robbery to go on.

As pictured, it would seem that Miss Fenwick was as guilty as any of the others. It was also noticed that, despite the fact that he had warning of the intended attempt on the bank, the sheriff didn't arrive until after most of the excitement was over. The two bank robbers fell like dead men when shot, but immediately afterwards they got on their feet and marched away as captives. Truly, "They do it in the movies."

Olive Thomas as Mr. Moore's sister, was rather pretty, and she possibly may be worth watching if given some opportunities. Others in the cast were Tom O'Keefe, Edwin Sturgess, Harry Lee, and Jack Dillon.

The Box Office Angle

Because of the fact that Miss Fenwick and Mr. Moore registered some nice human bits, it may be possible for you to get this by as entertaining.

Miss Fenwick has been starred in a number of productions, but has never appeared to advantage until this picture and her recent Famous Players offering. Mr. Moore is a well-known favorite and their names may be worth more than you think at the box office.

To stir up a bit of interest in this you might use lines along this style: "Sure you would never suspect *A Girl Like That*." Use this line for several days before announcing that this is the name of a picture that you are to show on a certain date.

★ *An Even Break* (1917)★

DIRECTOR: Lambert Hillyer
RELEASE DATE: August 5, 1917; Silent; 5 reels
GENRE: Drama-Comedy
CAST: Olive Thomas (Claire Curtis), Charles Gunn (Jimmie Strang), Margaret Thomson (Mary), Darrel Foss (Ralph Harding), Charles K. French (David Harding), J. Frank Burke (Luther Collins), Louis Durnham (Canning).
SUMMARY: Childhood pals Claire Curtis, Jimmie Strang and Mary grew up together in the country, but as adults, Claire and Jimmie both head to New York—Claire to pursue a stage career, and Jimmie to sell an invention. Reunited in the Big Apple, they soon fall in love. Back home, however, the unscrupulous Harding Brothers, hired to manufacture Jimmie's invention, are plotting to steal his patent. Meanwhile, Mary travels to New York and tells Claire that she, too, is in love with Jimmie. Claire decides to give Mary a chance to win Jimmie's love. But not so fast: Once it seems that Jimmie will lose his fortune, Mary loses interest. Claire and Jimmie then hurry home, stop the Hardings in their nefarious scheme, and save Jimmie's business.
DISTRIBUTION COMPANY: Triangle Distributing Corp.
PRODUCTION COMPANY: Triangle Film Corp.
WRITER: Lambert Hillyer

A *Wid's* theater manual (Thursday, August 9, 1917) gave the following evaluation of the feature:

AS A WHOLE: Started rather well with some good characterizations, but melodrama ruined it.
STORY: Looked promising at first, but soon blew up.
DIRECTION: Had several nice characterization touches and interesting Follies restaurant set, but melodrama ruined general effect.
PHOTOGRAPHY: Artistic on sets, but frequently hard on faces
LIGHTINGS: Some splendid bits, but generally ordinary

CAMERA WORK: Generally good; more close-ups would have helped
STAR: Rather pretty at times, although face a bit hard; expressions seemed to lack sincerity.
SUPPORT: Charles Gunn excellent; others ordinary; some quite actory
EXTERIORS: A few excellent shots; but generally ordinary
INTERIORS: Some very fine; generally quite satisfactory
DETAIL: Excellent cutting for auto accident and nice handling of cabaret set.
TIME: Sixty-one minutes (5 parts).

In the first few reels we got some splendid characterizations in this, with Charles Gunn walking away with the honors because of some very intelligent work registering the effect upon a country boob of getting acquainted with the "white lights."

Miss Thomas was also rather carefully handled in most of these scenes, so that we had several characters nicely developed in some situations which registered very effectively.

There were one or two characters who were quite actory, but all went well until they hit the melodrama in the last two reels, and then the whole works went kaflewy!

They gave us the good old hokum of the striking workmen, the attempt to keep the hero from reaching the mills, the plotting willuns who would kidnap him, the heroine to the rescue with her racing car and an all-night auto chase in which (according to the film) one willun stood up and shot at the rear tires of Miss Thomas' car without success, from sunset until dawn.

Immediately after the title "Dawn" we saw the car bearing the shero and hero rush across in front of a train, with the pursuing car crashing into the engine at the crossing. This bit was very well timed and nicely cut, but unfortunately such things fail to make any impression in this day and age—because they've been done to death in the old feature films and the new Keystone Komedies.

At the end, the militia came from somewhere, and hero and shero drove in just in time to stop the dynamiting of a lot of machines which were needed to save the mills of hero's father. The two villains stood beside the plunger of the charge igniter that was to set off the dynamite, and one wanted to blow 'em up anyway, but the other refused when he saw the shero standing beside the doomed cars. The two willuns then proceeded to fight until the rescue party arrived.

Had this been confined to a characterization study along the line of the work which Charles Gunn put over in the first part of the film, it would undoubtedly have been a very pleasing production. As it runs, you may get by with it as a program release and some of your fans may think this better than the average, but I am afraid that the old hokum meller which comes at the end is going to send them out with a bad impression.

The cast, for the most part, was rather ordinary, but Darrel Foss, playing the part of the son of the willunous factory owner, persisted in acting so much as to mar several scenes.

The Box Office Angle

The name of Olive Thomas probably means nothing to your fans, so if you intend to play this you will have to bill her as the famous beauty from the Ziegfeld Follies. Since she has that sort of a part in this production you might salve it a little heavy on that particular angle. I would also mention the presence of Charles Gunn, since Mr. Gunn is very good in this, and has had several leads in Triangle films, so that many of your fans may remember him.

This is not a big winner, but it will very probably get by for you, and I would say that you can safely put it through as a program release centering the attention upon the fact that it is an interesting study of the career of a country girl who became a cabaret favorite in New York, and the young man who blossomed when he first saw the white lights of Broadway.

★ *Indiscreet Corinne* (1917)★

DIRECTOR: Jack Dillon
RELEASE DATE: November 11, 1917; Silent; 5 reels
GENRE: Drama-Comedy
WORKING TITLE: *Frankly Chaste*
CAST: Olive Thomas (Corinne Chilvers), George Chesebro (Nicholas Fenwick), Joseph Bennett (Rocky Van Sandt), Josie Sedgwick (Pansy Hartley), Annette DeFoe (Florette), Lillian Langdon (Mrs. Chilvers), Thomas H. Guise (Mr. Chilvers), Lou Conley (Aunt Theodora), Thornton Edwards ("Live Wire" Dodge), Edwin J. Brady (P. A. Britton), Harry Rattenberry (Mr. Cotter Brown), Anna Dodge.

SUMMARY: Suffering the ennui of wealth and privilege, Corinne Chilvers is seeking adventure when she responds to a newspaper ad for a woman with a shady past. The job involves persuading a South American millionaire, Nicholas Fenwick, to propose. To draw his eye and his affections, Corinne poses as a masked dancer. Her competition is Pansy Hartley, a woman who actually does have a few skeletons in the closet.

After a series of misadventures, Fenwick falls in love with Corinne, whose parents, scandalized by their daughter's escapades, disown her. Reporting to her employers that Fenwick has proposed to her, Corinne discovers that the young man is not a millionaire, but rather the object of a publicity stunt, which is aborted when Corinne and Fenwick really do get married. Fenwick then approaches Corinne's parents and persuades them to forgive their daughter for her scandalous behavior.

DISTRIBUTION COMPANY: Triangle Distributing Corp.
PRODUCTION COMPANY: Triangle Film Corp.
WRITERS: George Elwood Jenks (Scenario) and H. B. Daniels (Story)
CAMERAMAN: Thomas Buckingham
Variety (November 9, 1917) said:

Supposed to be a press agent's story, and to one in the know of the foxy wiles of some of those "gents," it is a harmlessly wild escapade of two girls, yet not as risky a venture as some P. A. would go to break onto the first page.

To the average spectator of this Triangle, the motive is forgotten, for from an audience standpoint, that doesn't count. *Indiscreet Corinne* is fairly diverting, even though it isn't easy to tell what it is all about at times.

Corinne is a daughter of the rich but craves to create a "past." Pansy seems to have obtained that little thing and is supposed to have a child to prove it, though the kid doesn't figure. Both girls answer the advert of the press agents, who offer a reward to the one succeeding in becoming engaged to a phony South American millionaire. In the person of Nicholas, a youth who doesn't look as though he hailed from the A. B. C. countries. This youth is "in" with the press agents. Rocky, another youth, is a friend of Nicholas. So there is a mixed quartet and it isn't difficult to figure out there will be two weddings in the end, for Rocky takes Pansy unto himself in spite of that past while Nicholas falls for Corinne after seeing her as a masked dancer in a cabaret.

Near the end Corinne tries to pop in on the folks but they turn her cold, having heard of the masked dancing episode. But she loves Nicholas, even though he isn't the wealthy party they said he was. The only ones who get left are the press agents but they are doubtlessly used to that.

A *Wid's* theater manual (Thursday, November 8, 1917) gave the following evaluation of the feature:

STORY: A bored society girl in search of adventure.
DIRECTION: Kept action fast and atmosphere pleasing.
PHOTOGRAPHY: Not exceptional
LIGHTINGS: Some fine
CAMERA WORK: Good
STAR: Very good looking
SUPPORT: Good
EXTERIORS: Satisfactory; not many
INTERIORS: Suited atmosphere
DETAIL: Some groupings not good
TIME: Sixty minutes (5 parts)

A foreword at the beginning of this offering sort of prepared us for what was coming. Olive Thomas was introduced as a society girl bored with her lot, who was in a romantic state of mind and wanted a "past." She started out with her French maid hunting adventure.

They found an ad in the papers calling for two young girls who had had a past, and Miss Thomas interviewed the company and related her "past" to them. It was sure "some" past!

In getting this job Miss Thomas was to work in opposition to Josie Sedgwick trying to get a young South American millionaire in her power. Both girls tried this and the production ended with Miss Thomas marrying the gink.

There were certainly a lot of good lightings in this and the interiors were generally classy, keeping the atmosphere right. The subtitles were well worded and had good comedy touches that will be sure-fire laughs for any audience.

Where Miss Thomas told of her past, this was shown on screen, and it was indeed a most lurid past. She was shown dressed as a Siren, and I must say that it was decidedly alluring.

While on the job Miss Thomas was masked in a cabaret and had a chance to pull a couple of very good dances. After she had made the millionaire curious about her, she got in trouble with the police, and we had what was nearly a Keystone chase of machines. In one place it surely was "Keystoney" because of the mix-ups.

Miss Thomas was very pretty, having plenty of pep and her dancing was certainly "par excellence." Of course, dancing was once her regular job.

George Chesebro, as the South American millionaire, registered a very pleasing personality, and I believe that he will add to his following by his work in this.

The old toothpick millionaire over-reached his points and really was the only jarring note in the production....

The Box Office Angle

This is quite pleasing on the whole. I think you can bank on it as being well worth booking. It isn't big, but it will send them home satisfied.

In advertising this you should lay much stress on the name of Olive Thomas, saying that she does a barefoot dance and an Egyptian dance which are certainly delightful. I would bring to the minds of the patrons the fact that she was formerly of the Ziegfeld Follies and some picker when it comes to good looking girls. I would also mention Mr. Chesebro, because I believe he is winning a following.

In your ads, a line like these might help: "Have you an interesting PAST? ... See Olive Thomas in *Indiscreet Corinne*."

★ *Madcap Madge* (1917)*

DIRECTOR: Raymond B. West
RELEASE DATE: June 24, 1917; Silent; 5 reels
GENRE: Comedy-Romance

CAST: Olive Thomas (Madge Flower), Charles Gunn (Earl Denham), Dorcas Matthews (Julia Flower), Aggie Herring (Mrs. Flower), Jack Livingston (Charles Lunkin), J. Barney Sherry (Earl of Larsdale), J. Frank Burke (Mr. Flower), Gertrude Claire (Letitia Jane Adams).

SUMMARY: Julia Flower seeks marriage, and her financially overextended father and social-climbing mother are perfectly willing to help her land a wealthy husband, preferably an Englishman with a title. The fly in the ointment is little sister Madge, whose high spirits and practical jokes get her expelled from boarding school. While the family winters in Palm Beach, Julia does her best to keep Madge out of the way while she pursues the Earl of Larsdale. Inevitably, the so-called earl elopes not with Julia but with Madge; and although it turns out he is neither English nor an earl, he is the prosperous holder of her father's bank notes, and the family is saved from ruin.

DISTRIBUTION COMPANY: Triangle Distributing Corp.
PRODUCTION COMPANY: New York Motion Picture Corp., Kay Bee
PRODUCER: Thomas H. Ince
WRITER: R. Cecil Smith (Scenario)
CAMERAMAN: Charles Stumar

Variety (June 22, 1917) said:

The first of the Triangle-Ince-Kay Bee features starring Olive Thomas, the former Ziegfeld "Follies" beauty, variously reported as about to marry or married to Jack Pickford.

In making her screen debut Miss Thomas does not display any great promise of ever really hitting the top of the ladder in popular favor. This is just as much due to the story in which she is presented as to her own lack of histrionic ability to create an impression.

[Writer R. Cecil Smith] evidently intended it for a comedy, but it fell short of his intentions, even though they were good. Raymond B. West directed the picture, and with the material he turned out a fairly good film.

A *Wid's* theater manual (Thursday, July 5, 1917) gave the following evaluation of the feature:

AS A WHOLE: Light comedy hokum
STORY: Elementary, ancient, convenient farce situations
DIRECTION: Played for laughs all the way and gathered quite a lot; general atmosphere very good.
PHOTOGRAPHY: Generally good; some excellent bits
LIGHTINGS: Occasionally excellent; generally just good
CAMERA WORK: good
STAR: Pleasing ingénue
SUPPORT: Good; not remarkable
EXTERIORS: Rather good
INTERIORS: Classy atmosphere
DETAIL: Played for laughs
TIME: Sixty-one minutes (5 parts)

...Certainly they should not pin medals on anyone for this [plotline], but the director has simply proceeded to make his picture, playing for laughs all the way, without giving a thought to worrying over the ancient vintage of the situations.

They had all the good old hokum of the pajama party at boarding school, the masquerade dance with several guests in similar costumes, etc., and since Producer West provided rather a pleasing atmosphere so far as sets and locations were concerned, I believe that the average fan will consider this quite satisfactory as light entertainment.

In the pajama party stuff they introduced a young heifer, and here and many other places through the production we had excellent titles. While the heifer was being entertained by the girls in pajamas they cut to a flash of an old cow in the barn, with the title, "Where is my wandering boy tonight?" During the masked ball they shot Miss Thomas into the gathering on roller skates, which provided a lot of Keystone Komedy stuff that got laughs. Since that was what the producer seemed to be after, he must be given credit for having done the only thing possible with the material at hand.

Miss Thomas is rather pretty, looks a bit devilish in a close-up, and registers very satisfactorily as an ingénue in this sort of light-comedy, wild–Indian part.

The Box Office Angle

I believe that comedies are decidedly in demand at the present time, and while the plot of this is very ancient, they got considerable fun out of the old-time situations by handling, and I think the average patron will accept this as worthwhile, even though they don't rave over it afterwards. It should be classed as just a "good" program offering.

The audience who sat in when I saw this got a lot of laughs and a few yells, which is proof of the fact that they got some enjoyment out of it, even though they might afterwards figure that it wasn't of much consequence.

Since Olive Thomas is absolutely unknown so far as your fans are concerned, I would bill her as a famous beauty from the Ziegfeld Follies. That will be an interesting atmosphere to put around her, which should help to get some business.

I would emphasize particularly the fact that this is built for laughs and advertise it as a "light comedy."

★ *Tom Sawyer* (1917)

DIRECTOR: William Desmond Taylor
RELEASE DATE: December 2, 1917 (Premiere: New York City), December 10, 1917 (Nationwide); Silent
GENRE: Adventure-Comedy-Drama
RUNNING TIME: 44 minutes
FILMING LOCATIONS: Hannibal, Missouri.
CAST: Jack Pickford (Tom Sawyer), George Hackathorne (Sid Sawyer), Alice Marvin (Mary Sawyer), Edythe Chapman (Aunt Polly), Robert Gordon (Huck Finn), Antrim Short (Joe Harper), Clara Horton (Becky Thatcher), Helen Gilmore (Widow Douglas), Carl Goetz (Alfred Temple), Olive Thomas (Choir Member).
SUMMARY: Mark Twain's American classic features rowdy, wily Tom Sawyer and his best friend, Huckleberry Finn, the son of the local drunkard. School for Tom is mostly a misery, except for the presence of beautiful Becky Thatcher. Unfortunately he must also cope with the presence, at school and at home, of his goody-goody younger brother, Sid. When Sid commits a misdeed, Tom stands unfairly accused, and so he decides to run away from home. Joining him are Huck Finn and Joe Harper; together they build a raft and sail off on the Mississippi. Back at home, the townsfolk search frantically for the boys and at last decide to hold a funeral. Tom, returning in secret, decides to attend his own service. Discovered in the end, he is forgiven for his mischief.
DISTRIBUTION COMPANY: Paramount Pictures Corp.; Famous Players-Lasky Corp.
PRODUCTION COMPANY: Oliver Morosco Photoplay Co.

PRODUCER: Jesse L. Lasky

WRITER: Mark Twain (novel *The Adventures of Tom Sawyer*), Julia Crawford Ivers (photoplay).

CINEMATOGRAPHER: Homer Scott.

Exhibitor's Reviews for *Tom Sawyer*, as printed in *Motion Picture News* (March 9, 1918):

"Bully picture, had us guessing how to handle the crowds."
"Excellent—pleased greatly."
"The kind we need more of—play it."
"Everybody liked this picture."
"Great—a winner."
"Intend to repeat this one when weather gets warmer, and believe will set record."
"Very fine; this kind of subject will put on top."

TRIVIA: Olive appears as an uncredited choir member in *Tom Sawyer*. In fact, for a short time during the spring of 1919, both Jack and Olive were both working out of the Robert Brunton Studios. As a lark, Olive would drop by the set and appear in a scene or two. This type of behavior caused Mary Pickford to comment, "Jack and Olive play around like a couple of kids." Many of these cameo roles went uncredited, however, *In Wrong* (1919) is another one of Jack's films that Olive is rumored to have appeared in.

Jack Pickford has a star on the Hollywood Walk of Fame at 1523 Vine Street.

★ *Betty Takes a Hand* (1918) ★

DIRECTOR: Jack Dillon
RELEASE DATE: January 6, 1918; Silent; 5 reels
GENRE: Drama-Romance-Comedy
CAST: Olive Thomas (Betty Marshall), Frederick Vroom (Peter Marshall), Bliss Chevalier (Mrs. Hamilton Haines), Mary Warren (Ida Haines), George Hernandez (James Bartlett), Charles Gunn (Tom Bartlett), Margaret Cullington (Miss Catherine), Graham Pette (Gardner), June De Lisle (Maid), Anna Dodge (Gardner's Wife).

SUMMARY: Betty Marshall's father, Peter, has been ruined in business by his partner, Mr. Bartlett. Betty travels to Los Angeles to visit her aunt, Mrs. Hamilton Haines. There she finds that Bartlett's son, Tom, has arranged for Mrs. Haines and her daughter, Ida, to go on a yachting trip. Ida doesn't want her pretty cousin crowding in, so she talks Betty into staying home. On the day of the trip, Tom is on his way to the yacht when he passes the Haines house and sees that Mrs. Haines is advertising a room for rent. Having just quarreled with his father, Tom decides he'll take a room there. He meets Betty, who pretends to be Mrs. Haines' daughter. Tom moves in and is soon in love with Betty. When Tom and Betty marry, the two former business partners discover they are now related by marriage. At first taken aback, eventually they are reconciled.

DISTRIBUTION COMPANY: Triangle Distributing Corp.
PRODUCTION COMPANY: Triangle Film Corp.
WRITER: Jack Cunningham (Scenario) and Katherine Kavanaugh (Story)
CAMERAMAN: Anton Nagy
Variety (January 4, 1918) said:

It is highly improbable and a five-reel tiresome attempt to pad a story that should have been told in two reels. Miss Thomas is a cute heroine and looks rather interesting, but one gets more or less tired of just seeing a star run through scenes that simply mean nothing at all as far as the story is concerned. Charles Gunn is Miss Thomas' leading man, and his personality helped to carry the story, too weak for feature purposes.... Not much of a feature for general consumption.

A *Wid's* theater manual (January 3, 1918) gave the following evaluation of the feature:

> AS A WHOLE: Starts slowly and then loses speed all the way. Very draggy.
> STORY: Highly improbable, does not sustain interest.
> DIRECTION: Good in spots
> PHOTOGRAPHY: Fair
> LIGHTINGS: Just ordinary
> CAMERA WORK: Several good exterior shots
> STAR: Pleasing, but on in almost every scene, until one tires of her
> SUPPORT: Good
> EXTERIORS: Country stuff had atmosphere; several good city scenes.
> INTERIORS: Good
> DETAIL: There are occasional spots where there are lapses.
> TIME: 70 minutes (5 parts).

Just about as slushy and mushy an affair as can be imagined without rhyme or reason, and so frightfully draggy that one loses all interest before the feature is halfway through. Of course there is little Olive Thomas, nice girl and all that, but she has just a couple of little tricks of acting, and when one gets them repeated in about every fifty feet of the feature, then the tricks and she become exceedingly tiresome.

Still, Miss Thomas is about the only thing that there is to the picture. The story is highly improbable and as there is little else to the feature one must naturally condemn that.

Miss Thomas is a little country girl, daughter of an aged prospector who believed that he was fleeced by his brother-in-law (since dead) and his own former partner, in a deal that happened years before. At the time of the opening of the story the former partner as well as the widow of the brother-in-law are living in wealth in Los Angeles, while the poor old miner is struggling along on a farm. But as luck would have it the widow-sister sends an invitation to Betty (Miss Thomas) to spend a long visit in the city. The father, believing that it is a guilty conscience working, urges the little girl to go and have her fling, but first tells her the story of how he was tricked, advising her that James Bartlett was the former partner and to fight shy of him and his kin in Los Angeles.

Now it so happens that the widowed-sister and her daughter are keeping up appearances socially on mighty slim bankroll and angling for Tom Bartlett (son of old Jim, who has millions) as a future husband for the daughter. Things are moving nicely until Betty arrives on the scene. Then as the mother and daughter are invited to a yachting trip on which young Bartlett is also to be present, they leave the house in charge of Betty. She immediately decided that she is going to square accounts for her old dad and figures that by taking boarders while her aunt and cousin are away she will be able to net a tidy sum.

But Tom Bartlett did not go on the yachting trip as was planned. He had a fight with dad and then sold his car and decided to shift for himself and in calling to make his farewells on aunty and cousin, finds them missing and Betty installed. He catches a flash of the sign for boarders and without revealing his identity decides to take a room. Of course there are other boarders and there are jealous moments for Tom, but Betty loves it all and especially loves Tom.

Then to bring about a meeting between the elder Bartlett and Betty, the author arranges an auto accident on a lonely country road. Betty is in her car alone having ridden out to a farm to stock up in eats for the boarders; old man Bartlett is on his way out into the country, the two cars meet on a narrow strip of road and both are forced to take a ditch. Then there is nothing to do for all hands except to spend the night outdoors until help arrives.

Naturally, Betty who has her car stocked with food, proves a good cook at breakfast and wins the old man's heart. She, knowing who he is gives a fictitious name and the old man says that he would give $50,000 to have his son marry a girl like that.

The father has been worried over the boy's disappearance but on his return home after the auto incident gets news that the boy is in town. He hunts him up and arranges for him to come home at a certain hour the next day to meet a girl that has been picked for him to marry. In the meantime he gets into touch with Betty and invites her over. Betty keeps both father and son in the dark regarding her knowledge of the existence of the other and consents to marry Tom before the two go to call on father. Then the "Big expose" and the three-cornered surprise, another crash with the arrival of Betty's father, but his former suspicions are aptly explained away and all ends in a four-cornered clinch.

It would be a better story if some of the slush were cut and a little comedy injected into the titles, for as a comedy it is mighty weak in laughs at present.

The Box Office Angle

Of course you have the fact that Olive Thomas was one of the prize beauties of the Ziegfeld staff to work on, but that won't help a lot in this case. You might make some stock of how to grab off a millionaire husband by running a boarding house, again proving the old adage that the way to a man's heart is through his stomach and point to the fact that it is twice proven in this feature for like father, like son, they both fall for the food stuff. It might be well to work a little on the food problem, especially in these days of high prices, and show how it was solved by this girl who went to the source for her supplies. There isn't much chance with this feature at that and it isn't advisable to plug it too strongly.

Exhibitors Reviews for *Betty Takes a Hand* as printed in *Motion Picture News* (March 9, 1918):

"Very good."
"Not great, but pleasing."
"This star is dependable; fair story."
"Audience liked it."

☆ *Heiress for a Day* (1918)

DIRECTOR: Jack Dillon
RELEASE DATE: March 3, 1918; Silent; 5 reels
GENRE: Drama-Comedy
CAST: Olive Thomas (Helen Thurston), Joe King (Jack Standring), Eugene Burr (Spindrift), Graham Pette (Old Hodges), Lillian Langdon (Mrs. Standring), Mary Warren (Grace Antrim), Anna Dodge (Mrs. Rockland).
SUMMARY: Jack Standring is a rich man, rich enough to get manicures at the Ritz. Naturally, his mother wants him to snag a rich wife. Meanwhile, Jack's manicurist, Helen Thurston, is in love with him. How can this impoverished young woman win the heart of a wealthy man? Then Helen learns that she has come into a fabulous inheritance. Excitedly, she buys clothes and jewelry on credit. She is disappointed when Jack is unimpressed with her new look. Even worse, she learns that her inheritance is only $1,000; the rest has gone to a dissolute cousin. She is pursued by creditors, and while attending a grand ball at the Standring home, she is threatened with

arrest. Jack is moved by her straitened circumstances and proposes elopement. In the end, the cousin violates the conditions of the will, and all of the inheritance passes to Helen.

DISTRIBUTION COMPANY: Triangle Distributing Corp.
PRODUCTION COMPANY: Triangle Film Corp.
WRITER: Robert F. Hill (Scenario) and Henry Albert Phillips (Story)
CAMERAMAN: Steve S. Norton

Variety (March 1, 1918) said:

A most improbable society yarn with a mediocre cast and similar direction, this Triangle. The heroine fails to arouse sympathy, partly because of the scenario, but perhaps, more because she enacts her role without sincerity. It may be logical for a person to acquire snobbishness after suddenly acquiring great wealth but the transition here is too fast.

Helen Thurston, a manicure in a large hotel, falls in love with Jack Standring, whose "grand dame" mother sets her heart on his marrying a debutante of their set. In spite of Helen's position, she attends a dance in the hotel. When Jack's mother finds her son and Helen dancing together, the girl is properly snubbed. Helen's grandfather suddenly dies, and it is noised about Helen had fallen heir to a fabulous sum. Immediately she is taken in the social set and tradesmen vie with each other to sell her costly raiment on credit. It turns out that a cousin, one Spindthrift, is the sole heir under certain conditions.

One is that should Helen live a year within $1,000 bequeathed to her, she is to share in the estate 50–50. Hence Spindthrift aids in her extravagant buying. Then this youth villain, who wasn't content with a paltry ten million, half of the estate, tells Helen the real facts and sicks the tradesmen after her. So Helen hocks her pearls and pays some of them off. Just when she is bemoaning her fate the good old family lawyer arrives to say she wins all the works of deceased grandpop's estate, since the will stipulated that if Spindthrift had encouraged Helen spending more than that $1,000 he was to be disinherited and she to be the sole heir.

There isn't even variety in the names given the cast, either the fault of the author or the scenarioist. The direction was by Jack Dillon, and his results are nil. This feature seems to be a by-product. It wasn't interesting at a private viewing and it probably won't be considered otherwise in the theatre.

A *Wid's* theater manual (February 28, 1918) gave the following evaluation of the feature:

AS A WHOLE: Girl has everything her own way from start to finish so there's neither suspense nor pep; good production will get by as regular program offering.
STORY: Manicurist left thousand by millionaire grandfather pretends she got whole estate to impress rich young man she loves; he shoulders her debts for happy finish.
DIRECTION: Very good
PHOTOGRAPHY: Sharp definition and considerable quality.
LIGHTINGS: Satisfactory
CAMERA WORK: Intelligent
STAR: Sophisticated ingénue
SUPPORT: Generally good
EXTERIORS: Pleasing
INTERIORS: Looked authentic
DETAIL: Interesting
CHARACTER OF STORY: Not very strong on human sympathy; will get by fairly well with mixed audiences.
Time: 55 minutes (5 parts).

There is no getting around it. If you want to have suspense, you've simply got to have something at issue. The minute things go along without opposition, that minute does interest in a play bag. It is because the heroine has little or no opposition in her career that this drama is so weak. She solves all her difficulties off-hand without worrying about them in the least, just by passing the buck to someone else. When she needs money she borrows some from her cousin. When he demands to be paid back, she just pawns the jewels he has given her and the money she gets that way is enough not only to pay him but also to stave off her clamoring creditors. When the other creditors won't wait any longer, she just gets married and lets her husband foot the bills.

The main story is clumsy as the deuce in getting started, jumping around from one group of persons to another in an effort to plant the real opening situation. Considerable footage goes by before these separate facts tie in together and let the story go on without interruption. Nevertheless, the incidents are interesting in themselves, so they get by.

Yet the production itself is well done. The director has squeezed most of the emotional value out of the scenes; his groupings are interesting and effective even if they are somewhat conventional and musical comedy now and then, and photography is splendid. Those things help to cover a multitude of sins.

Broadly speaking, the story of a girl who is reputed to be heiress to millions, taking the lone thousand dollars she gets and posing as an heiress for a day on the strength of that plus her reputation, is amusing; but there is a limit as to how far it may be dragged out; and the continuity goes somewhat over that limit here. It wouldn't be so bad if the issue was more sharply defined; but the interest is scattered over so many diffuse things that in some spots it completely peters out.

...There is an idea lurking in the situation, but its treatment could have been made a lot more dramatic. It is not to the purpose here to point out just how that might have been done, for the play will be released to first-run exhibitors by the time this review is printed and it will be too late then to make alterations.

Joe King is convincing as Standring. His strong resemblance to William Desmond makes one speculate a little about a play in which both might appear, for Desmond is a Triangle player, too. Graham Pette renders an excellent bit as the dying grandfather. Eugene Burr is thoroughly villainous as Spindthrift. Lillian Langdon and Anna Dodge are pleasing as two different kinds of social leaders and Mary Warren as Grace Antrim has some points to her credit.

The Box Office Angle

Spell out the name of the attraction in front of your lobby with stage money. Planting the idea of money in connection with a play always registers the idea of success. The name Olive Thomas should mean something to you provided you have played the other Triangle vehicles in which she has appeared. The line about her being a Broadway beauty from the Ziegfeld Midnight Frolic atop the New Amsterdam Theatre, New York, remains good as something for you to cash in on at your box office, for she has not been in filmdom so many months. The huge dial of a clock with twenty-four hours marked out on it instead of twelve should be a good novelty for the front of the lobby, the advertising matter lettered directly across it, and the hands kept moving.

★ *Limousine Life* (1918)

DIRECTOR: Jack Dillon
RELEASE DATE: February 3, 1918; Silent; 5 reels
GENRE: Comedy
CAST: Olive Thomas (Minnie Wills), Lee Phelps (Moncure Kelts), Joe Bennett (Jed Bronson), Lillian West (Gertrude Muldane), Virginia Foltz (Miss Wilkins), Alberta

Lee (Mrs. Wills), Lottie Du Vaulle (Mrs. Malvin), Lillian Langdon (Mrs. Kelts), Harry Rattenberry (Mr. Wills), Jules Friquet (Jasper Bronson).

SUMMARY: When Chicago calls, country girl Minnie Wills leaves her beau, Jed Bronson, and her small-town life for the big city. As a model in a shop there, she wins the heart of rich ne'er-do-well Moncure Kelts, who is attracted by her innocent charm. Moncure pops the question, but when Minnie says yes, it doesn't take long for Moncure to lose interest. Now eager to get rid of her, Moncure accepts Minnie's counter offer: she'll break the engagement if he will provide her with a limousine, clothes, and a whole lot of money. Having acquired these goodies, Minnie returns to her small town and accepts a proposal from the delighted Jed. Later, Jed and Minnie move to Chicago, where Jed establishes a successful business. One day they run into Moncure on the street, and Minnie generously thanks him for enabling her and Jed to build such a nice life together.

DISTRIBUTION COMPANY: Triangle Distributing Corp.
PRODUCTION COMPANY: Triangle Film Corp.
WRITER: Jack Cunningham (Scenario), Ida M. Evans (Story)

Variety (February 1, 1918) said:

Olive Thomas is starred in this Triangle feature, one of the best she has appeared in to date. She has a few more tricks than in her earlier film productions, and therefore is just about 50 per cent better.

The original story was by Ida M. Adams. Jack Cunningham adapted it for the screen and then while A. Nagy turned the crank, Jack Dillon told the actors what to do. The result is a pleasant feature, one that will pass anywhere....

The production is a fairly good one, cleverly handled, and the case is likewise good. Lee Phelps and Joe Bennett give the star admirable support. The picture is great for a double bill and worth playing as a single attraction.

A *Wid's* theater manual (Thursday, February 7, 1918) gave the following evaluation of the feature:

AS A WHOLE: Clever story, needs lots of speeding up in spots, but generally an interesting feature.
STORY: Small town girl worries her friends sick by wicked associates, but knows how to take care of self and comes through pitfalls safe with money to the good.
DIRECTION: Generally good, but drags at times
PHOTOGRAPHY: First rate
LIGHTINGS: Good
CAMERA WORK: On the job, but just one speed throughout
STAR: Has the right spirit and is well cast
SUPPORT: Generally good
EXTERIORS: Satisfactory
INTERIORS: Well done
DETAIL: O.K.
CHARACTER STORY: Will get by best with a wise crowd; not likely to be understood by most women.
TIME: Fifty-five minutes (4.830 feet, 5 parts)

The secret of putting over subtle observations in the pictures seems to lie in presenting them in very active circumstances. The underlying idea of this is clever, but it's in need of more than the usual treatment to back it up for sure-fire punch. Everything is there in the way of material, but some way the snappy situations do not get over with the pep they should have.

Waving the critical finger over the play to put it on the reason that the play slows down so much in spots, one finds that the fault is a lack of tempo as much as anything—that cutting the important scenes to mere flashes on the screen would speed them up and give the production about fifty per cent more force. Of course, not much cutting could be done because the Triangle program system demands a five-reel feature, but the chopper could be used judiciously and still leave enough film on the spools.

The idea of a little girl whom everybody—relative or friend—is anxious to protect knowing how to take care of herself so well that she is able to go through all kinds of morally dangerous adventures without the slightest harm, is not new, but is new enough to seem original to many persons. It is an idea of the kind that makes you sit up and take notice and it certainly deserves to be handled well.

According to the story, which originally appeared in the *Red Book*, Minnie Wills is the belle of Three Oaks, Iowa, but feels that she wants to visit a regular town, so gets the aid of her hayseed sweetheart, Jed, and goes alone to Chicago. In the big burg she gets a job in a fashionable modiste shop and there she catches the roving eye of Moncure Kelts, millionaire lounge lizard with an eye for fancy poultry. Against the advice of other girls in the shop who once tried to be salamanders and got burnt, she encourages Kelts and he showers all manner of attention upon her, while everybody thinks she sure has gone to the bad.

Instead, Minnie is giving Kelts the dance of his life. Each evening she thanks him for the lobster and goes alone to bed while he looks for fresh rounder wiles to snare ingénue virtue. Even the easy-going landlady is persuaded that Minnie has sold her soul to the devil for her beautiful clothes, when she really got them with money brought by the sale of a necklace Kelts gave her at the beginning.

At last, Kelts, finding that the only way he can catch this wise little squab is to say "I do" under the wedding bells, promises to marry her. So the next time his mother happens into the modiste shop Minnie tells her all about it. The good lady is considerably amazed, to be sure; but when she recovers from her surprise she decides—levelheaded woman that she is—that maybe marriage will settle Moncure down. And she takes Minnie home to live.

Poor Moncure Kelts is all cut up, for he doesn't give a darn about marrying any girl, so after enduring the situation for about a week he puts up to Minnie the proposition that if she will go back to Three Oaks and out of his life he will give her fine clothes, jewelry, his limousine and some more things. Minnie accepts with more ado, because Jed had told her any marriage without love was sinful.

She loses the limousine, however, for in turning a corner she runs down a wagon and is arrested. The license number of the car brings Moncure nto court with his very fishy tale that he gave the valuable machine to this child under sixteen and he is fined $100 while the matron is delegated to ship Minnie back to her home in Three Oaks. There Minnie marries Jed and with the capital she made in Chicago sets him up in successful business.

Perhaps a title not so passive or meaningless to a person who has not yet heard the story—something that would put over the idea of "The-Little-Girl-Who-Knows-How-to-Take-Care-of-Herself"—would put the spectator a little more into the spirit of the thing. Principally, the play needs a keynote to be struck in the beginning to give the spectator the spirit of the story and some idea of what it all is to be about.

But on the whole it's an interesting program feature. Jack Cunningham has written a good continuity, even if it ties events together in narrative style; and Jack Dillon has directed well even if he didn't play up the high spots and slipped on tempo.

Olive Thomas works in the right mood while she lets the fat part carry her through a good part of the time; but she is pleasant and good looking if not inspired and gets over satisfactorily.

Lee Phelps, in the unsympathetic part of Moncure Kelts gives a better performance; Joe Bennett has an interesting bit as Jed and so has Harry Rattenberry as Minnie's father.

The Box Office Angle

This story will be more interesting to men than women. Women are fond of heart interest and elemental emotion stuff and don't care so much for sophisticated plays. The wiser the crowd attending your theatre, the better they will like this production.

But in advertising go after the women strong because they will constitute the patronage most in need of building up. In appealing to them, lay off the wise kid angle and play up the virtue side—the rounder who got all that was coming to him when he ran up against a little girl who knew how to take care of herself.

For lobby decoration and advertising generally, clip pictures of limousines from current magazines and paste them on your signs. If the engagement is extended it may pay you to hire a limousine and run it about the town with signs on it reading, "This is the life!" and giving names of theater, star, attraction and playing date.

Automobile dealers should cooperate with you in advertising and you should get some display in windows of garages. The local taxi service may be willing to carry cards for you on their machines for a slight consideration. A large cut-out of a limousine as near life-size as the space in your lobby will stand, should make a good ground for a sign, with a litho head of Olive Thomas pasted in the window of the car and lettering over the rest.

Exhibitor's Reviews for *Limousine Life,* as printed in *Motion Picture News* (March 9, 1918):

"Olive is always a money-getter."
"Dandy Picture."

★ *The Follies Girl* (1919)★

DIRECTOR: Jack Dillon
RELEASE DATE: April 27, 1919; Silent; 5 reels
GENRE: Comedy
WORKING TITLE: *A Siren in the House* and *Her Downfall*
FILMING LOCATION: Portions were filmed in the Wilshire district of Los Angeles, California.
CAST: Olive Thomas (Doll), Wallace MacDonald (Ned), William V. Mong (Edward Woodruff), Claire McDowell (Nina Lefingwell), J. P. Wild (Swann), Lee Phelps (Basil), Raymond Griffith (Frederic).
SUMMARY: Edward Woodruff is on his deathbed, and his scheming relatives—Nina Leffingwell, her brother Frederic, and her cousin Basil—try to figure out how to get his money. Edward, delusional, keeps calling for a granddaughter who doesn't exist. Nina makes a deal with a Follies girl, Doll, persuading her to pose as the imaginary granddaughter. The plan is that Doll will care for Edward, work her way into his affections, and inherit his money. She will pass the money to the relatives, who will pay her a portion. Surprisingly, however, Doll takes such good care of Edward that he recovers. Nina then sends for Edward's grandson, Ned, who was written out of Edward's will because he married beneath his class. Nina hopes that Ned will send Doll away, but then Ned seems to fall in love with Doll. In the end it develops that Doll and Ned are married and have a baby boy. The delighted Edward forgives Ned.
DISTRIBUTION COMPANY: Triangle Distributing Corp.; S. A. Lynch Enterprises
PRODUCTION COMPANY: Triangle Film Corp.
WRITER: Charles Mortimer Peck (Scenario) and W. Carey Wonderly (Story)
The Nevada State Journal said,

The Follies Girl ... is the second of the new series of Olive Thomas pictures which are to come to the Majestic this year, the first having been *Toton,* played here a little over a month ago.

Like *Toton,* the story of *The Follies Girl* builds around the winsome personality of Olive Thomas, who actually did first dance her way into fame as a member of Ziegfeld's Follies company. While a lighter type of picture than *Toton,* the comedy presented through *The Follies Girl* is said to be not altogether froth, but to have a deeper foundation of genuine interest.

Variety (April 25, 1919) said:

...The whole story could be told in two reels.
An intelligent cast, apparently well drilled in their parts, supports Miss Thomas and the result is a smooth running performance. The whole production is worthy of a theme with more backbone and less frothy. The settings are in keeping with the subject with some interesting and picturesque exteriors.... There is an amusing little love story running through the picture.

An *Exhibitor's Trade Review* synopsis for *Her Downfall,* released as *The Follies Girl*:

Death's hand is drawing near to Edward Woodruff—the sands are running low and all his wealth cannot stay the approaching fate. Lovable, and yet unloved—desiring, yet not desired—he lies on his bed of pain—alone. His wealth has brought luxury and comfort, but no happiness, and yet he would give all to feel the gentle touch of his own dead girl from whom he had become estranged during her life.

And in the background, waiting for the end, are three sinister figures—their hearts hardened to pity and love—filled only with desire. Nina Leffingwell, a distant relative, cold, callous and worldly wise, her brother Frederic, and Basil, her lover, wait for the time when Edward Woodruff shall pass through the shadowy halls of death that they may gain the fortune he must leave.

Their plans are deep laid, for Nina has arranged with Swann, a scheming lawyer, to introduce a girl as Woodruff's granddaughter, hoping that she will inherit the old man's fortune. This accomplished, Nina intends to pay the girl handsomely for her services and thus come into possession of the coveted wealth herself.

With the stage set and the actors waiting, the curtain rises on Nina's plans. The situation is tense and thrilling—it is a drama of life—and death.

Doll, a beautiful girl, fresh from the Follies, comes to the dim and lonely house. She is to be the puppet who shall dance at Nina's command; it is she who is to play the role of Woodruff's granddaughter—it is she who is to deceive a dying old man.

But in the best laid plans there is usually some little flaw which ruins the whole. In selecting a Follies girl, Nina had reckoned on a perfect actress—one whose heart was cold and who would readily act any part for payment.

But the lines Doll was supposed to speak will not rise to her lips; the spangles and greasepaint vanish, revealing a soul as pure and beautiful as the body that holds it. Like Tonio, of "Pagliacci," there is beneath the motley and tinsel a human heart beating with passion.

The floodgates of pity are opened in Doll's heart, and her youth and charm, and tender ministrations, reawaken a desire to live in the old man's heart. Days become weeks, and gradually Woodruff becomes stronger.

Furious at the turn events have taken, Nina sends for Ned, the old man's favorite grandson, disowned because of his marriage beneath his social station. The scheming woman thinks that Ned will oust Doll from Woodruff's heart, but once more her plans are upset, for the happy careless laughter and tenderness which brought back the sunshine to the autumn of Woodruff's life, capture Ned's heart, and he falls deeply in love with the Follies girl.

In a last attempt to obtain the fortune, Nina goes one night to the invalid, telling him that Doll and Ned are together in a lodge on the estate. The old man hurries to the lodge, fear's cold hand clutching at his heart, only to discover that Nina's words are true.

Ned and Doll are together—as man and wife! Doll is the girl whom Ned had married "beneath his social station." A beautiful baby boy is shown to Woodruff, who, clasping the child tightly to him, is eager to forgive and forget, realizing that Ned has found a real woman, whose heart is as golden as the spangles she wears as a "Follies Girl."

An *Exhibitor's Trade* review for *Her Downfall*, released as *The Follies Girl*:

Described as a sparkling comedy cocktail of chorus girls, cash and crooks, it deals with an actress who turns nurse to an old man—not to his pocket book, but to his health!

Apart from the comedy action, there is a strong dramatic vein running through the production, and a heart interest which should appeal to all. The part of Doll, the chorus girl, is particularly suited to Olive Thomas' abilities, especially as it is one which mirrors her real self.

Once more the footlights hold sway over the movie camera, and Miss Thomas is shown as a member of the very Ziegfeld Follies whom she left for the screen, performing in the same show as she previously did in the New Amsterdam Theater on Broadway.

Everyone who delights in good class comedy drama, in which love and suspense are cleverly interwoven, is certainly advised to see *Her Downfall*.

Another *Exhibitor's Trade* review for *Her Downfall*, released as *The Follies Girl*:

The general belief that footlight favorites only exist to help the unwary male to spend his cash is set at naught in *Her Downfall*, a fine Olive Thomas production.

However true or false, this popular idea of stars of the theatrical firmament may be—and the writer has to confess to ignorance on the subject—it certainly would not appear to be the case as far as Doll of the Follies is concerned.

In direct defiance of the supposition, Doll (charmingly played by the late Olive Thomas, who was a theatrical star herself before joining the movies) succeeds in saving the fortune and the life of an old gentleman and gaining not diamonds but love as her payment.

The picture is packed with thrills and emotional interest, and should prove an attractive offering in every sense of the term. Remarkably clear, this splendid photoplay is of all-round excellence, the story and acting being far above the average.

Olive Thomas ... has a part which calls for great versatility, and one in which she makes a decided hit. As the Follies girl she is naturally fitted to the part, though it must be claimed that the tender wistfulness with which she clothes the character of "Doll" is all her own.

Rich in sentimental appeal, and containing a strong plot, much comedy and no few heart-tugs, *Her Downfall* provides splendid all-round entertainment. No matter what your tastes, all are catered [to] in this excellent feature.

TAGLINES:

"Olive Thomas came from The Follies to the pictures, now she returns to the stage in *Her Downfall*, her last and greatest picture."

"The story of a chorus girl who danced her way into the heart of an old man."

"Olive Thomas revives memories of her own past as a dancer in *Her Downfall*."

"Beautiful Olive Thomas in an unusual story of how a chorus girl saved an old man's money instead of spending it!"

"A delightful comedy-drama of footlights, fortunes and felony."

"Olive Thomas, 'the most beautiful girl in the world,' as a stage favorite in *Her Downfall*.

★ *The Glorious Lady* (1919)

DIRECTOR: George Irving
RELEASE DATE: October 19, 1919; Silent; 5 reels
GENRE: Drama
CAST: Olive Thomas (Ivis Benson), Matt Moore (The Duke of Loame), Evelyn Brent (Lady Eileen), Robert Taber (Dr. Neuman), Huntley Gordon (Lord Chettington), Marie Burke (Dowager Duchess), Mrs. Henry Clive (Hilda Neuman), Mona Kingsley (Babette).

SUMMARY: At an annual celebration in which English peasants rub elbows with aristocrats, the Duke of Loame is thrown from his mount in a horse race. At the head of the race is Ivis Benson, a tenant farmer's daughter. She stops to help the duke, and both are hurt. During their recovery, the duke visits Ivis, and soon the two are in love. This is distressing to the duke's mother and to Lady Eileen, who had hoped to be his bride. The duke and Ivis marry, but the duke's mother attempts to drive them apart by having a doctor—who happens to be Lady Eileen's brother—tell the duke that Ivis's injuries will prevent her from bearing a child. Ivis overhears and decides to force her husband to leave her. She pretends to be drunk in public, hoping the duke will feel disgraced and ask for a divorce. Her plan fails, so she leaves the duke outright; but the duke brings her home, and eventually she does, indeed, give birth to an heir.

DISTRIBUTION COMPANY: Selznick Pictures Corp.
PRODUCTION COMPANY: Selznick Pictures Corp.
WRITER: George M. Arthur (Scenario) and Edmund Goulding (Story)
CAMERAMAN: Lewis Physioc
Variety (November 7, 1919) said:

> *The Glorious Lady* ... is a story that will appeal to a certain class of film fans and, while not a whale of a picture, it is to a certain measure entertaining.
>
> ...An excellent cast supports Miss Thomas, including Matt Moore, who is her leading man. The production was made in the East and there are certain touches that indicate a great number of the scenes were shot in the neighborhood of Greenwich, Connecticut.
>
> ...There are a number of really wonderful exterior shots and the interior sets are very effective. The lightings are particularly good and for a story that is all on the surface the direction is all that could be expected.
>
> *The Glorious Lady* isn't a world beater by any means but it is a picture that the general run of fans will like.

A *Wid's Daily* theater manual (Sunday, November 9, 1919) gave the following evaluation of the feature:

> AS A WHOLE: Extremely artistic production built around trite story.
> STORY: Old-fashioned dime novel of the Laura Jean Libby type.
> DIRECTION: Most excellent; artistic with careful attention to atmosphere; did best he could with story material.
> PHOTOGRAPHY: Some of the best that has been shown; beautiful soft and artistic effects.
> LIGHTINGS: Marvelously beautiful
> CAMERAWORK: Excellent throughout
> STAR: Always pleased; beautiful close-ups
> SUPPORT: All that could be desired
> EXTERIORS: Well selected
> INTERIORS: Elaborate, splendid English atmosphere

DETAIL: Production detail good; titles trite
CHARACTER OF STORY: Inoffensive, dealing with intimate family life of English aristocracy.

Length of Production: About 4,539 feet.

Thirty years before moving pictures were ever thought of there was a grade of popular fiction in this country known as the dime novel. It was looked upon as the trashiest kind of trash. This picture has a story of that kind.

It is a shame that such an enormous lot of money and brains, and intelligence, and effort, should have been expanded in the picturization of a story of this kind. For with the exception of the story the picture is beautiful, and possesses every requisite of a big special.

The director and cameraman have done everything in their power to make up for this shortcoming and as a result have evolved a beautiful production. The photography is beautiful, replete with artistic effects. The direction is everything that could be desired; the lightings show great care and skillful technical knowledge; the star is pretty and appealing. Yet with all this the story is so trashy, most of the titles so trite, that there is a feeling of disappointment when it is all over.

The Box Office Angle

"Cheap, Trite Story Mars Otherwise Beautiful Production."

Play up everything in this one except the story and lay off that entirely if possible. The picture has every requisite of a special with the exception of the story. The title has nothing to do with the picture. Your big draw card is Olive Thomas. She is good all the way through and in conjunction with the elaborate production will probably get it over with your fans.

Use the star's name extensively. Also plenty of her pictures. Some of the close-ups of her are of great beauty. Build your advertising around such catch lines as: "Olive Thomas called upon to make momentous decision in *The Glorious Lady*. Was she right?"

If your crowd likes Olive Thomas, ballyhoo it good, otherwise, go easy.

Estimated gross rentals from entire world after January 3, 1920, for *The Glorious Lady*: $154, 504.

★ *Love's Prisoner* (1919)★

DIRECTOR: Jack Dillon
RELEASE DATE: June 8, 1919; Silent; 6 reels
GENRE: Crime-Drama
CAST: Olive Thomas (Nancy "The Bird," later Lady Cleveland), Joe King (Jim Garside), William V. Mong (Jonathan Twist), Harvey Clark (Lord Cleveland), Dolly Dare (Jane, Nancy's sister), Louis Durham (Shorty Dorgan), Ann Forrest (Sadie, Nancy's sister), Walter Perry (Nancy's father), Jean Hersholt (Party guest), Francis McDonald (Party guest).

SUMMARY: Nancy's father is a one-time burglar—and he's innocent of the crime for which he is now serving time. When he dies in jail, Nancy understandably sours on the legal system. Needing money to support her younger sisters, she is helped by an old fence, Jonathan Twist. Then she finds a husband, the elderly Lord Cleveland, but he dies intestate and his nephew inherits the estate. As Nancy struggles to maintain her household, a robber known as "The Bird" begins troubling New York high society with a string of thieveries. While investigating, detective Jim Garside meets and falls in love with Nancy. Then Jonathan Twist is found dead, and Jim suspects Nancy in his death. Poised to arrest her, he discovers that Twist died of a heart attack. Nancy confesses to being "The Bird." Although Jim is reluctant to see her in jail, Nancy wants to pay her debt to society. After she serves her time, she marries Jim.

    DISTRIBUTION COMPANY: Triangle Distributing Corp.
    PRODUCTION COMPANY: Triangle Film Corp.
    WRITER: E. Magnus Ingleton (Scenario and Story)
    An *Exhibitor's Trade Review* synopsis for *Love's Prisoner*:

Poverty, slum life and unhealthy surroundings have hardened the heart of Nancy, a little street waif, against humanity and its ways, but, despite the barren soil of her birth, Nancy has grown into a beautiful flower.

One day, her father, a notorious pickpocket, is arrested and sent to prison for a long term, and bereft of her only comforter, Nancy finds herself alone in a cold and callous world.

Resolved to make her way above her fellows, revenge against society and the law burning in her heart, and faced with the necessity of providing for her two younger sisters, Nancy obtains a post as demonstrator of a new drink. Whilst working in the store that is exploiting the beverage, she meets Lord Cleveland, a wealthy English Peer, who falls head over heels in love with the pretty counter hand.

A whirlwind wooing is followed by a proposal of marriage, and it is not long before Nancy, the crook's daughter, becomes Lady Cleveland!

Shortly afterwards the cruel fate which has pursued the hapless girl again overtakes her. Cleveland dies suddenly, and, by a clause in some legal documents, Nancy is deprived of his English property.

Embittered and despairing, her two little charges left in the care of Jonathan Twist, a jeweler, she determines that the law, her cruel enemy, shall not drive her back to the poverty she once knew.

The law took her father from her, the law, its crafty phrases has taken her inheritance; henceforth she resolves that she will obey no law saves the dictates of her own heart. Taking her place as the brilliant leader of a fast set, Nancy soon dazzles society, and has a meteoric rise to fame.

Meanwhile, however, rich and poor alike have been astounded by a series of daring robberies. A vague shadowy criminal known as "The Bird" gradually creates a reign of terror throughout the countryside. All attempts on the part of the police to snare their elusive quarry end in failure.

"The Bird" is known to be a generous friend of the poor—a modern Robin Hood—who, carrying out these audacious felonies under the very nose of the law, robs the rich to pay their more unfortunate brethren.

At last, in desperation, the Chief of the police places Jim Garside, his cleverest detective and the terror of the evildoer, on the track of the mysterious thief. Weeks of patient waiting and watching bring no clues to Garside, who puts forth every endeavor to trap his quarry.

In the course of his investigations he meets Lady Cleveland, and gradually friendship ripens into love. With dramatic suddenness, Garside stumbles upon his clue. Jonathan Twist, who had acted as "The Bird's" fence, is found murdered.

With breaking heart and torn between love and duty, Garside realizes that the identity of "The Bird" is established—that the girl he loves is the one he must arrest. The famous Lady Cleveland, who entertains society by day, is the mysterious brigand who has robbed them by night!

Suddenly, however, a telegram arrives from the police saying that the real murderer has been captured. Garside is overcome with relief, and it is not long before Nancy's heart is captured by the detective, and she is bound by the chains of Cupid, becoming—*Love's Prisoner*.

    Another *Exhibitor's Trade* review for *Love's Prisoner*:

Olive Thomas, the scintillating star, whose mysterious death in Paris caused such a sensation, is to be seen in a wonderful part in *Love's Prisoner*, a thrilling five-act drama. Packed with tense situations and containing a strong love interest and a baffling mystery, this enthralling film should be missed by none. Miss Thomas, who stars as the mysterious Lady Cleveland, gives a wonderful performance in a difficult role, and is ably supported by William V. Mong and Joe King.

Variety (May 30, 1919) said:

It seems a pity that Triangle could not have found a better vehicle for Olive Thomas than this five-reel feature.

...The story is absurd, unreal and lacks entertaining qualities.... Mechanically the picture is all right, it is clear and sharp. The settings are in keeping and lighting good. But if anything these technical advantages make the shortcomings of the story more pronounced.

A *Wid's Daily* theater manual (May 25, 1919) gave the following evaluation of *Love's Prisoner:*

There are several advertising angles to this offering, but it is doubtful if the picture will hold up to the promises of the advertising. It is certain that it will be a patient audience indeed that sits through its six reels without uncomfortably wriggling. And nobody will tell their friends to be "sure and see that picture!" You might possibly get away with it for one night, but if you depend on word-of-mouth advertising to bring you anything after the first night you'll lose out.

On its merits as a photoplay the offering cannot claim much. It is in six reels, too, and the exhibitor who has to figure time for his show will have little opportunity to bolster up his program with short stuff.

The popularity of Mss Thomas will have to be relied on more than the entertaining value of the production. It does not hold an audience of itself, and while a house catering to transients might possibly get by with it, the showman catering to a regular patronage is advised to go very slowly with it—if at all.

Miss Thomas could be billed as a female Jekyll-Hyde, who to some was the dashing, entertaining Lady Cleveland, while to others she was "The Bird," the cleverest thief the police were ever asked to track down. Catch lines that might be used: "She thought the world owed her a living—and she went out and collected it."... "Olive Thomas in *Love's Prisoner*, a photoplay of conflicting emotions which battle for supremacy."

TAGLINES:

"Thrills and love interest in big Olive Thomas picture."
"Beautiful star makes big hit in *Love's Prisoner.*"
"Who was the illusive criminal known as 'The Bird?'—See *Love's Prisoner* featuring Olive Thomas and Joe King."
"Has the Detective found the right solution? Could the fashionable Lady Cleveland and a notorious thief be one and the same? See *Love's Prisoner*, a five reel drama, starring Olive Thomas."
"A gripping melodrama of thrills and mystery."
"Beautiful Olive Thomas in her last great triumph."

★ *Out Yonder* (1919)★

DIRECTOR: Ralph Ince
RELEASE DATE: December 21, 1919; Silent; 6 reels
GENRE: Drama
WORKING TITLE: *The Girl from Out Yonder*

CAST: Olive Thomas (Flotsam), Huntley Gordon (Edward Elmer), Mary Coverdale (Mrs. Elmer), Louise Prussing (Clarice Stapleton), John Smiley (Amos Bart), Cyril Chadwick (Reggie Hughes), Edward Ellis (Joey Clark).

SUMMARY: Yachting off the New England coast with son Edward and friends, wealthy Mrs. Elmer has a brush with drowning and is rescued by a young woman, Flotsam. Flotsam is the daughter of Amos Bart, the keeper of the lighthouse. Soon Edward falls in love with Flotsam and proposes. Unhappy about the engagement is Amos' helper, Joey Clark. Clark reveals a secret: Amos murdered Edward's father. Amos believes that he did so while drunk. Amos also has other secrets: Flotsam is not his child. Her dying mother gave Flotsam to Amos's wife to raise. Amos tells Flotsam to sail away with the Elmers, but Edward's former girlfriend, hoping to break them up, tells Flotsam about the murder. Then Flotsam and Edward overhear Clark taunting Amos by revealing that he himself committed the murder. Amos and Clark struggle, and the lighthouse's light goes out. Flotsam saves the yacht from hitting the rocky cliffs, and she and Edward then make their marriage plans.

DISTRIBUTION COMPANY: Select Pictures Corp.

PRODUCTION COMPANY: Selznick Pictures Corp.

WRITER: Edward J. Montague (Scenario), Pauline Phelps (play), Marion Short (play)

TRIVIA: Director Ralph Ince was the youngest of three filmmaking brothers, John Ince and Thomas H. Ince. He was also an actor.

An unidentified 1919 newspaper snippet reported on a special effects stunt, saying:

> In a recent scene from *The Girl from Out Yonder*, in which Olive Thomas is starring for Selznick, an airplane was used inside the studio in order to create a windstorm. The noise made by the huge motor was said to be so deafening that it was quite impossible for the director to give any directions whatever, and the workmen, who were obliged to take care of the lights, stuffed their ears with cotton.

Variety (January 16, 1920) said:

> This Ralph Ince production is great stuff. Admirable photography blends the well chosen and impressive settings into a platinum setting which grips a diamond of a story perfectly. Pauline Phelps and Marion Short are responsible for it. The star does her share to make the picture pleasing, and she is well supported against backgrounds supplied by a yacht, the sea, a rocky island and a lighthouse.
>
> [The climactic] scenes are thrilling and impressing. They serve to emphasize Mr. Ince's gift for the picturesque as well as his feeling for a story.

Estimated gross rentals from entire world after January 3, 1920 for *Out Yonder*: $192,890.

★ *Prudence on Broadway* (1919)

DIRECTOR: Frank Borzage
RELEASE DATE: July 6, 1919; Silent; 5 reels
ALTERNATE TITLE: *Prudence Comes to Town*
GENRE: Comedy
CAST: Olive Thomas (Prudence), Francis McDonald (Grayson Mills), Harvey Clark (John Melbourne), John P. Wild (John Ogilvie), Alberta Lee (Mrs. Ogilvie), Lillian West (Mrs. Allen Wentworth), Edward Peil Sr. (Mr. Wentworth), Mary Warren (Kitty), Lillian Langdon (Mrs. Melbourne), Claire McDowell (Miss Grayson).

SUMMARY: Prudence is the daughter of Pennsylvania Quakers who send her off to experience the world in a boarding school. There she indulges her high spirits in practical jokes. Later, on a visit to her aunt in New York, Prudence attracts many swains. Her choice among them is Grayson Mills, but unscrupulous (and married) John Melbourne plots to steal her innocence. He lends her money to pay a gambling debt, then blackmails her into a date by threatening to tell her parents. At dinner, Prudence shows Melbourne an amorous letter that he wrote to an actress. She tells Melbourne that if he doesn't return her to her hotel, the hotel clerk will show Melbourne's wife many other such letters. Melbourne hurriedly complies, then learns that Prudence only had the one letter. Prudence, free of his unwelcome attentions, now becomes engaged to Grayson.

DISTRIBUTION COMPANY: Triangle Distributing Corp.
PRODUCTION COMPANY: Triangle Film Corp.
WRITER: Catherine Carr (Story)
CAMERAMAN: Pliny Horn

An *Exhibitor's Trade Review* synopsis of *Prudence Comes to Town*; eventually released as *Prudence on Broadway*:

Everyone thought that when Prudence came to New York that there would be plenty of fun and novelty, for Prudence was a simple unsophisticated little Quaker Girl, who didn't know the difference between champagne and soda!

There was plenty of fun and novelty all right, but the laugh was on the side of the timid little miss, beneath whose simplicity there lurked a happy, but oh so mischievous heart!

Prudence has been born of strict Quaker parents, but, even in the young ladies' seminary, where she was "finished off," she learnt bridge and other pastimes frowned at by her stern sect. Pure as the driven snow and demure as any daisy, the little Puritan had a heart of gold, which dispensed sunshine wherever she went. Carefree and happy, she went her own way, and in leaving the murky side of life strictly alone, found all its joy and gladness.

Imagine, then, this unenlightened little Quaker, suddenly swept into the whirlpool of a fast society set—a veritable ewe lamb cast into a den of ravening wolves and dashing debutantes!

Society was all-agog for novelty and change at Prudence's expense, and, jaded after the fatigue of a heavy season, anticipated something new in the laughter line. The only member of the set that saw beneath the little dove grey exterior and caught a glimpse of the mischievous little person beneath, was Grayson Mills, the catch of the season, about whose throne fond mothers and hopeful daughters fluttered in thousands.

Grayson Mills was badly smitten—much to the chagrin of Society, and he did not fail to let Prudence know it. That young lady knew quite a lot about the game of courtship, however, and played her cards accordingly.

Meanwhile John Melbourne, a wealthy roué, waited for an opportunity of making love to Prudence. One night the little Quaker lost badly at a poker party, and Melbourne took advantage of the situation and lent her a large sum of money.

Later he threatened to send the cancelled check to Prudence's stern old father in Pennsylvania, unless she promised to meet him at a lonely hotel.

The timid little Puritan went to the hotel, but when Melbourne started to get unpleasant, Prudence produced one of the twenty letters that her companion had written to another girl.

Prudence told Melbourne that the remaining nineteen letters were in town, and would be delivered to his wife unless she were back before 12 o'clock. So Melbourne made a quick return to Broadway, with the little grey dove, getting there fast enough to allow her to see Grayson Mills, who soon put matters right and brought her happiness.

An *Exhibitor's Trade* review of *Prudence Comes to Town*, eventually released as *Prudence on Broadway:*

[Prudence's] trials and conquests are charmingly told, and the fact that she outwits a jaded society scoundrel and captures the catch of the season, make entrancing entertainment.

Poor little Olive Thomas, whose brilliant career was so suddenly stayed by death's cruel hand, fills the role of Prudence with exceptional ability. Carefree and mischievous, she romps through five reels of joyous laughter, which will send picturegoers home the happier for seeing them.

Variety (July 18, 1919) said:

A Triangle feature starring Olive Thomas in the little Quaker story contains nothing that is new or novel in the story and the feature as a whole is rather badly cut.

...The early part of the feature is cut entirely too sharp and the story is exceedingly jumpy as a result of this. The titling is also bad, especially as someone was saving footage and the titles were too short. Later the story is rather badly jazzed up with the end in sight before the picture is run half way through.

Miss Thomas is entirely charming in the role assigned to her and there are moments when she displays a comedy touch that is refreshing. Her support, while not wonderful, is adequate.

In all, *Prudence on Broadway* is a pleasing little picture that will do to fill in on a double feature day, but isn't strong enough to stand alone for any run.

A *Wid's Daily* theater manual (Sunday, September 14, 1919) gave the following evaluation of the feature:

As A Whole: Very light; rather slow; could have been registered satisfactorily in two reels.
Story: One little situation with much too much footage used in building to and registering it.
Direction: Fair mechanical handling of old-time light comedy program quality feature.
Photography: Varied from very good to ordinary.
Lightings: Some very good; some poor
Camera Work: Varied
Star: Cute and Pretty, but plot too light to help her much
Support: Acceptable
Exteriors: Satisfactory
Interiors: Nothing unusual
Detail: Much too much that meant nothing
Character of Story: Nothing to offend; roadhouse bedroom situation turned into a laugh.
Length of Production: About 5,000 feet.

This certainly belongs to the old school lightweight program stuff, which, because of its weakness, forced the new era of fewer and better pictures.

The story has just one little idea, which is the twisting of the well-known roadhouse, meeting into a laugh because of the cleverness of the Quaker shero, but the footage, which slowly played up to this situation, was frequently very tiresome because the story failed to move.

The title suggests the bright lights of the "Gay White Way," but there is not a scene which registers Broadway, with the atmosphere plainly that of California, and the one situation staged in a roadhouse which did not in the least suggest Broadway.

Miss Thomas was presented as a little Quaker maiden who was rather a quick thinker. Although she was Miss Innocence abroad when she hit the large city, she managed to keep her head above water and slip over some very clever twists on the married he-vamp who loaned her money and then forced her to go to a roadhouse with him.

Presented as a two-reeler and played as a light comedy or farce this might have registered satisfactorily, but surely, the story was painfully weak to be presented as a feature film.

Seeing this offering now after the big specials have commenced to come in makes it very easy to realize what the film fans have been suffering and why the big special pictures are going to have such a tremendous success this year, with the lightweight stuff shoved entirely into the discard.

When this was made the producers depended, of course, upon the fact that the star's name would pull, and felt that it was unnecessary to put anything much back of the star, and the fallacy of that theory could be no more cleverly demonstrated than by the fact that this fails utterly to make an impression, and, according to the business the night I saw it, it is also failing to draw the cash customers.

Miss Thomas is certainly a pretty thing, and she has some cute tricks, but her good points cannot offset the weakness of a lightweight plot like this, so that the net result is not anything like good enough to please generally.

The Box Office Angle

"Light Comedy Program Stuff; Not Strong Enough for Feature Billing."

Since there is really only one situation in this, and it is not particularly big, I would say that you should step very softly if for any reason it is necessary that you play this.

Unless you have a contract that calls for this production, or unless you feel that Miss Thomas is sufficiently popular in your community to justify you playing her even in such a lightweight vehicle, I would mark this off the books immediately and forget she ever made it.

Of course, the title, *Prudence on Broadway*, listens rather well, but just the same it has no genuine kick or big pulling power, because we have had plenty of similar titles worked to death in the flood of program features of the past two or three years.

If you have made any fuss whatever about the fact that this year is to bring fewer and better pictures, I certainly would not hand them this one, as they will undoubtedly step on you for it.

You must remember that an educational campaign is underway to inform the public that the exhibitor can pick and choose now, and more than ever before you are going to be severely criticized when you pass the bunk to your cash customers. They will not only tell you about it, but what is even more important, many of them will not tell you but will quietly begin to patronize your opposition.

From no angle can this be considered worthy of more than a filler space in a hole in your bookings that must be plugged, and even from that viewpoint it strikes me that it is not good business to use such a lightweight offering as this as the feature of a bill, because while your fans may get one or two laughs out of it, the production as a whole will send them out with a feeling of having seen a one- or two-reel comedy stretched into five, with rather tiresome results.

★ *The Spite Bride* (1919)*

DIRECTOR: Charles Giblyn
RELEASE DATE: September 21, 1919; Silent; 5 reels
GENRE: Drama
FILMING LOCATIONS: San Francisco, California; Hotel Alexandria, Los Angeles, California; Majestic Theater, Los Angeles, California; Grauman's Chinese Theater, 6925 Hollywood Blvd. Hollywood, Los Angeles, California.

CAST: Olive Thomas (Tessa Doyle), Robert Ellis (Billy Swayne), Jack Mulhall (Rodney Dolson), Claire DuBrey (Trixie Dennis), Irene Rich (Eileen Moore), Dorothy Wallace (Millicent Lee), Lamar Johnston (Arthur Derford), Katherine Griffith (Countess di Raspoli), Molly Malone (Vaudevillian).

SUMMARY: Having left her country home to join a vaudeville act, Tessa Doyle is entangled in a moneymaking scheme developed by her stage partner, Trixie Dennis. It all has to do with a lonely millionaire, Billy Swayne, who has been scorned by his fiancée and is drunkenly determined to marry someone else that very night. Trixie want's Billy's money, which she plans to use to get a divorce. She talks Tessa into marrying Billy, then tries to blackmail Billy. Angrily, Tessa departs the scene, taking no money for herself. Later, she finds a job as a private secretary. As it happens, her employer is Billy's mother. Tessa and Billy are happily reunited.

DISTRIBUTION COMPANY: Selznick Pictures Corp.

PRODUCTION COMPANY: Selznick Pictures Corp.

PRODUCER: Myron Selznick

WRITER: Louise Winter (Novel) and Lillian Ducey (Scenario)

Variety (September 26, 1919) said:

[A] placid feature and only fair as a whole. The story starts out well enough but continues without force and punch. Billy Swayne, scion of a wealthy New York family, becomes piqued when Millicent Lee, a debutante, throws him over for another. To heal the wound, his close friend and adviser proposes a plan whereby Billy would hurt Millicent's pride.

The scheme is for Billy to marry some girl that night, the resultant spread in the newspapers gaining the ends desired. Billy's friend believes a girl in need of money can be easily obtained. By giving such a girl $1,000 and resorting to Reno for a divorce, the trick would be turned. The youths wander abroad on Broadway in quest of a bride.

They in some manner happen into the Alhambra Theatre, where one girl in a sister act seems to fit their idea of the right party. One of the "sisters," Trixie, is whimpering over the fates which do not allow her to gather enough money to win a divorce from a worthless husband. So when the proposition of Billy is made later in a café, Trixie is all for it, but, of course, the bride is her partner, a quiet girl of peach-bloom skin known as Tessie Doyle (Miss Thomas).

The next morning Trixie refuses to accept the thousand, and upon her demand for more, possible later blackmail, the boys kidnap the girls aboard Billy's yacht. That catches fire, but they are rescued, and soon afterwards Trixie is paid her thousand, but Tessie goes her own way, refusing money and just asking to be "let alone."

Sometime later Tessie is found as secretary of a war work committee and at a subsequent bazaar Billy awakens to the fact he loves his hastily wedded bride. He is shot by a jealous man, which brings Tessie into the Swayne household, with the final blessings of Billy's patrician mother to the match.

Miss Thomas is much in the background, far too much. It is her erstwhile vaudeville partner who takes the limelight in nearly all the scenes in which she figures. The slangy speeches of the latter as shown in the titles are amusing and figure prominently in the feature.

With the scenario lacking enough in a feature way and the story no wonder, *The Spite Bride* isn't as attractive as the usual Selznick productions. Miss Thomas needs careful directing, which was not marked here.

Estimated gross rentals from entire world after January 3, 1920 for *The Spite Bride*: $114,709.

★ *Toton* (1919)

DIRECTOR: Frank Borzage
RELEASE DATE: March 30, 1919; Silent
GENRE: Drama
CINEMATOGRAPHER: Jack MacKenzie
ALTERNATE TITLES: *Toton the Apache* and *The Vital Spark*
FILMING LOCATIONS: Exposition Grounds, San Diego, California.
CAST: Olive Thomas (Toton/Yvonne), Norman Kerry (David Lane), Francis McDonald (Pierre), Jack Perrin (Carew).
SUMMARY: David Lane is an American artist in Paris. He is married to his model, Yvonne, and the two are expecting a baby. Just before the birth, however, the death of David's mother forces him to return to America. While he is away, his father, who disapproves of the marriage, sends a lawyer to Yvonne with the phony news that David has abandoned her. In grief, she delivers a daughter and then dies. The child is raised by Yvonne's friend Pierre, who calls her Toton. He dresses her as a boy and teaches her the art of picking pockets. Back home in America, David adopts a boy named Carew. Years later, David and Carew open an art studio in Paris. Pierre comes to rob the studio but recognizes David. Still angry over Yvonne's death, he tells David that Toton hates him. Later, however, Pierre realizes that David was not involved in Yvonne's misfortune, and he tells Toton as much. In the end, Toton and David are reconciled and Toton and Carew are married.
DISTRIBUTION COMPANY: Triangle Distrbuting Corp.; A Triangle Special Presentation
PRODUCTION COMPANY: Triangle Film Corp.
WRITER: Catherine Carr (Story)
TRIVIA: A 1920 *Exhibitor's Trade Review* booklet sent to theaters for promotional purposes advertises *Toton* as *The Vital Spark*. Several photographs of Olive have the captions, "Olive Thomas in *The Vital Spark*," and there are even two one-sheet posters available for the theater owner to order for lobby display with this alternate title. Olive's character name in the film is the only mention of *Toton* within the pages advertising her new release. This promotional booklet is a British publication and sometimes foreign release titles vary. This seems to be the case here.

Within the same trade review booklet, *Prudence on Broadway* is promoted as *Prudence Comes to Town* and *The Follies Girl* is promoted as *Her Downfall*. The lengthy synopsis for *The Vital Spark* (aka *Toton*), currently a lost film, gives a detailed explanation of the story from beginning to end. It reads as follows:

> Deep in the heart of the Paris underworld, in the Quartier Latin, lives Yvonne, a beautiful artist's model. A bohemian, born in bohemian surroundings, she is a member of that happy-go-lucky community, whose life is love and laughter—whose passions are deep, whose whole existence is for Art.
>
> David Lane, a young American artist, meets Yvonne and, inspired by her Madonna-like beauty, implores her to pose for him. The model consents, and in the long days that follow, youth calls to youth and love awakens in Lane's heart. After a brief courtship the two are wed and life is one long spell of happiness, until one day the artist is called to America by the death of his mother.
>
> Lane's hard and stern father, enraged at his son for selecting a wife beneath his social station, takes advantage of the opportunity offered, and secretly secures an annulment of the marriage in Paris.
>
> Lane believes that Yvonne has forgotten him and steels his heart against women through adopting a boy named Carew as a son.

Meanwhile, Yvonne has given birth to a beautiful girl, whom she names Toton, but the strain of the lonely years tells on the frail woman and, her heart yearning for her lover, she passes away.

Toton is left in the care of Pierre, Yvonne's friend—a kind-hearted but passionate Apache. In revenge for the sorrow which Pierre believes the American to have wittingly brought on Yvonne, the motherless little girl is brought up as a boy and trained to become the most skilled pickpocket in Montmartre.

As the years work their magic change, Lane feels a growing desire to return to Paris. Deciding to take his adopted son to the French capital in order to complete his art studies, the American makes his way across the Atlantic.

By a strange coincidence, Toton is given a post as studio boy to Carew. Through her agency, Pierre, the Apache, obtains particulars of the house and attempts to steal some valuable paintings. He is frustrated, however, and recognizing Lane as the American who had broken Yvonne's heart, reveals the identity of Toton. Lane is heartbroken to discover his daughter as a common thief, who has been taught to loathe and despise all things American.

German guns shell Paris and Pierre is mortally wounded. He lives long enough to tell Toton of her father and to see them happily reunited. Toton, who realize the treachery which parted her father and mother, cheers the autumn of Lane's life.

At last, as happiness gains place in her heart, the girl grows to love Carew, who asks her to marry him. Love has conquered the barriers of misunderstanding, and at last Toton finds sanctuary in a strong man's heart.

Photoplay, October 1918, reported that *Toton* is seven reels and that Olive plays a boy in some of it. Commenting on the film, Olive said, "This is the first real thing I've ever done, I think. I hope [audiences] like it. I want them to take my work in it seriously—critically. At least, it gives me a chance to show what I can do; maybe that won't be much, but I can try."

An unidentified 1918 newspaper clipping gave *Toton* the following review:

Staresses must play dual roles these days. *Toton* (Triangle) permits Olive Thomas to depict a girl and a boy—or rather, a near-boy. Olive plays an American artist's model in the Latin Quartier. The painter marries the girl and immediately hurries back to the States to see the usual sick mother. Once away, he forgets and later a family settlement is made with the Parisienne wife. But the ex-model dies after giving birth to a daughter, Toton. The child becomes the ward of an Apache pickpocket and, dressed as a boy, becomes a typical gamin of the streets, stealing whenever the opportunity offers. But the painter-father's adopted son comes to Paris, meets Toton, attempts to reform "him" and of course, upon the girl's sex being revealed, finds that he is in love. Miss Thomas makes quite a little of Toton as a boy, the direction is above the average as to atmosphere, and yet *Toton* as a whole is rather turgid.

Variety (March 21, 1919) said:

Toton is presented as a "special" release by Triangle, working on the idea that the publicity for another series of Olive Thomas pictures may react for them. It is one of the features that was made with her as the star when she was under contract with Triangle about a year ago. The story is rather similar to that which formed the underlying plot for Mizzi Hajos' piece, *Pom Pom*. At least the character assigned to Miss Thomas is a little the same.

As a feature in six reels it seems no longer than the conventional five-reeler.... It is an interesting little story that holds right up to the finish, although the closing scenes are a little wishy-washy.

Exhibitor's Trade review:

Through Five Reels of heart-stirring romance, Olive Thomas, the beautiful film star, whose death in Paris was so greatly deplored, leads us through sunshine and sorrow.

In a wonderful dual role the famous dancer of the Ziegfeld Follies has every opportunity of displaying her remarkable talents, an opportunity she uses to the full.

[It] is a remarkable coincidence that the location of Olive Thomas' unfortunate death should have been selected as the background for one of her last pictures.

The Vital Spark is a truly great picture, and all lovers of the truly artistic are advised to see it.

Exhibitor's Trade suggestions to theater owners for promoting the film:

The obvious angle from which to exploit *The Vital Spark* is that of the district in which this remarkable story is laid. Montmartre, the home of the Bohemian and the artist, always holds out a great attraction for the romance-loving public. Bank strongly on this fact, then, in putting over *The Vital Spark*. Tell your patrons that it is a story of the fierce Passions of the Apache and features beautiful Olive Thomas as an artist's model.

Remember that the story deals with the artistic quarter of Paris. This point immediately suggests many possibilities for advertising. For instance, an excellent lobby attraction could be arranged by getting an artist to paint a large picture of the star. If seated in the lobby during the time your show is open, he would attract the attention of passersby, who are always curious to see an artist at work.

Dress your attendants in the customary costumes worn by the French Bohemian. A purple tam-o'-shanter hat pulled off the forehead, a white smock with flowing black bow at the neck and loose trousers of an olive green shade will give an excellent result.

Send them out during the morning when they are not engaged at the show and let them take throwaways to give out referring to the picture. These should refer to the strange coincidence existing in the film, viz., the fact that Olive Thomas died so mysteriously in the very quarter of Paris in which the plot is laid. As *The Vital Spark* is one of her last pictures it would seem almost a stroke of fate which made it a story of the very city in which the poor little star met her untimely end.

TAGLINES:

"A stirring romance of the Paris underworld."
"'The Most Beautiful Girl in the World,' see Olive Thomas in *The Vital Spark*."
"A gripping drama of love and life in Montmartre."
"Beautiful Olive Thomas is superb in a dual role."
"The love stories of two generations portrayed by Olive Thomas in *The Vital Spark*."

★ *Upstairs and Down* (1919)

DIRECTOR: Charles Giblyn
RELEASE DATE: June 8, 1919; Silent; 5 reels
GENRE: Comedy
RUNNING TIME: 50 minutes
ALTERNATE TITLE: *Up-stairs and Down*
CAST: Olive Thomas (Alice Chesterton), Rosemary Theby (Betty Chesterton), Mary Charleson (Rosalie), David Butler (Tom Carey), Robert Ellis (Terence O'Keefe), Andrew Robson (Sprang)

SUMMARY: What a flirt is Alice Chesterton, the so-called "Baby Vamp" of Long Island society! Her fiance, Tom Carey, is boring, so Alice amuses herself by charming the other male guests at a house party given by Mrs. Ives. Among those she meets is Irish rake Terence O'Keefe, a polo player who has come to New York to buy horses for the British army. She invites Terence to meet her in the Big Apple, where they are spotted carousing together. Distressed by this behavior, Mrs. Ives asks Betty, Alice's sister, to keep an eye on Alice. Instead, Betty falls in love with Terence, and the two make plans to marry. Alice, jealous, cooks up a story to drive Betty away, declaring that Terence "ruined" her. When Betty confronts Terence, he forces Alice to admit she is lying. Meanwhile, scorned fiancé Tom gets advice from Terence on how to regain Alice's love. Using Tom's special "caveman" tactics, he succeeds.

DISTRIBUTION COMPANY: Select Pictures Corp.; A Star Series Attraction
PRODUCTION COMPANY: Selznick Pictures Corp.
PRODUCER: Myron Selznick
WRITER: Lillian Ducey (Scenario), Fanny Hatton & Frederic Hatton (Play)
CAMERAMAN: Lewis W. Physioc
TAGLINE: "Oh U Baby Vamp."

Variety (June 13, 1919) said:

This is a screen version of Frederic and Fanny Hatton's stage comedy by the same name.... At the Strand, June 8, [it] seemed to catch the popular fancy, and the many amusing situations were frequently applauded. It is a laughing, rollicking affair, with Alice Chesterton (Miss Thomas) the chief fun and mischief maker, who delights in getting in and out of scrapes.

Fine photography is the outstanding feature, with unusually picturesque exteriors and country scenes; but there is little or nothing to the story. A real country club atmosphere is maintained throughout, with a fine view of a polo field and the players.

...Miss Thomas makes a jolly-looking "Baby Vamp," as she is termed by her acquaintances of the "country club set." She has a real girlish appearance, and romps through her part, carrying the audience with her. Tom Carey (Davis Butler) and Terence O'Keefe (Robert Ellis) are the two male characters which stand out, and they are both clever in their respective parts, particularly the latter, who is a gay young Irishman and a polo player of note. He looks both. Mr. Ellis shines toward the end, when he uses caveman methods to subdue his sweetheart, who has a preference for this kind of lovemaking. The other members handle their parts intelligently. The titles are clever and up to date.

All through *Upstairs and Down* is an amusing comedy, and should make a good summer program feature.

A *Wid's Daily* theater manual (June 15, 1919) gave the following evaluation of the feature:

AS A WHOLE: Some amusing situations in the presentation of a story supposed to reveal life in the fast set; sympathy is lacking.
STORY: Adaptation of stage play by the Hattons
DIRECTION: Succeeds in giving the settings and characters a certain "smartness."
PHOTOGRAPHY: Very good
LIGHTINGS: A few pretty effects, but more might have been made of the beach scenes at night.
CAMERA WORK: Satisfactory
STAR: Does her best work as the baby vamp in the action toward the close when she is attempting to win Robert Ellis.
SUPPORT: Ellis suits role of the romantic young Irishman, others fill needs of the story.
EXTERIORS: Those representing polo field and grounds surrounding a Long Island estate are first rate.
INTERIORS: Up to the mark.
DETAIL: Titles get as many laughs as the action; many of them were evidently taken from the play; "Midnight Frolic" scenes well-presented.

CHARACTER OF STORY: Concerns the idle rich and their loose morals.
LENGTH OF PRODUCTION: About 4,500 feet.

Considering the material he had to work with, the need for a certain reticence in the treatment of an unwholesome play and the desirability of arousing some semblance of sympathy for a decidedly artificial group of characters, Director Charles Giblyn did a commendable piece of work in *Upstairs and Down*.

Some of his scenes are first rate, although taken all in all they didn't build up much of a story. And here again, there is merely another illustration of the old saying, "You can't make bricks without straw."

Upstairs and Down is rather short on straw of the kind needed by a producer of photoplays. The Hattons wrote a cynical "smart set" comedy that scored big on Broadway largely because it gained a reputation of being risqué. The lines were as broadly suggestive as the playwrights dared to make them and the characters both upstairs and down, meaning in the drawing room and the kitchen, were a pretty worthless lot.

The picture, in tone at least, is an improvement on its stage parent. You don't need to be afraid of it on that score, although it isn't going to increase the respect with which simple-minded folk regard the idle rich. Probably it will give almost everybody a few laughs and then they will forget about it, for this isn't the sort of a film that strikes deep.

"Baby Vamp" has becomes a household word. No community is complete without one or two innocent eyed, wiser-than-their-years young women who steal the men from their mature sisters. The baby vamp received her name and her first boost to fame in *Upstairs and Down*. This is the part filled by Olive Thomas in the picture, and she makes full use of "the baby stare," kittenish mannerisms and the plea, after she has been caught in some bit of trickery, "But you know, I'm only a child."

Miss Thomas is entertaining even if she isn't appealing, the part forbids that, and the plot is so arranged that she is kept in the foreground most of the time. Incidentally, it may be remarked that the "downstairs" element in the play is touched on only casually with the occasional introduction of a disapproving butler and a valet who forces his attentions on the maid....

The Box Office Angle

"Most Likely to Get Across in Big City Theaters."

The location of your theater and the kind of a crowd you are trying to reach must be considered in estimating the box office value of *Upstairs and Down*. It strikes me as being essentially a city show, or at any rate one best adapted to please a moderately sophisticated audience. There is not much than can be called heart interest and the worldly-wise attitude of the characters may not exactly fit in with the ideas of a family group.

For the benefit of the fans that keep track of the movements of their favorites and are interested in the producing organization with which they are allied, it might be well to make some fuss about this being the first of Olive Thomas' pictures under the Selznick management. The young star has received enough publicity in the past to assure some interest in her present activities.

Although the play *Upstairs and Down* probably is much better known in New York than elsewhere, the title is worth something. Refer to the picture as an adaptation of Frederick and Fannie Hatton's sensational Broadway stage success dealing with the life of the millionaire smart set. Bring in some mention of the baby vamp in all of your exploitation, for she is made the central character of the story.

CATCHLINES: "Did you ever meet a real baby vamp? Olive Thomas will introduce you to the model for all vamps in *Upstairs and Down* at the Blank Theater." Or: "How does a baby vamp work? Olive Thomas will show you in *Upstairs and Down*." Another one: "Don't miss Olive Thomas as the baby vamp in the smart set comedy *Upstairs and Down*."

Estimated gross rentals from entire world after January 3, 1920 for *Upstairs and Down*: $74,093.

TRIVIA: An unidentified Seattle newspaper dated February 16, 1919, printed an interesting snippet in relation to Olive's on-set antics whilst filming *Upstairs and Down*. It read:

> Olive Thomas' company was at work up to a late hour at the Los Angeles studios making scenes for *Upstairs and Down*. There were a dozen extras on the set at 11 o'clock, it was cold and everybody was beginning to be hungry. A part of *Upstairs and Down*, as will be remembered, is laid in the kitchen, and for this portion of the picture a truly wonderful kitchen set has been erected. Miss Thomas herself began to feel the pangs of hunger; she looked at the suffering extras, then she looked at that beautiful practicable kitchen and she at once made up her mind. During a lull in work, she turned on the gas, sent for a coffee pot, coffee and cups, butter and ham and bread from the cafeteria on the lot, and soon had everybody happy and comfortable.

An unidentified New York newspaper clipping dated February 22, 1919, claimed that director Mickey Neilan was almost nabbed to play opposite Olive in *Upstairs and Down*. Robert Ellis stepped into the role at the last minute. Myron Selznick cornered Neilan at the Los Angeles Athletic Club and in desperation asked him to step in and play the part. Neilan promised Myron that if he was still without a leading man when it came time to shoot, he would do it. At the last minute, however, Gasnier, of Pathe, loaned Robert Ellis, another director who was in charge of the Ruth Roland productions, and Neilan was able to get his release. Ellis played the same part in the movie version of *Upstairs and Down* as he did on the stage.

Ellis was thrown from his pony and had two ribs broken during the filming of polo scenes in the film.

A *Boston Massachusetts Record* (January 22, 1919) ran a report stating that Olive was to star in *Upstairs and Down*, but the second film mentioned remains a mystery. The article read:

> Myron Selznick, who has just signed up Olive Thomas to appear in a series of photoplays under his direction, plans to introduce the famous Folly beauty in *Upstairs and Down*. When this is completed, Miss Thomas will begin work on a screen version of *Mary's Ankle*. This played here two seasons ago and Bert Lytell and Irene Fenwick were the featured players. Now it is to be recorded for the screen.

Another unidentified newspaper snippet dated February 1, 1920, said, "Myron Selznick has purchased the film rights to *Mary's Ankle* for $10,000, which he will use as a vehicle for Olive Thomas."

Mary's Ankle was indeed recorded for the screen but it wasn't a Selznick Production and it didn't star Olive Thomas. According to *The AFI Catalog*, *Mary's Ankle* was a Thomas Ince Production, released by Famous Players Lasky. Directed by Lloyd Ingraham and released on February 15, 1920, the cast included Douglas MacLean, Doris May, Victor Potel, Neal Burns, James Gordon, Lizette Thorne and Ida Lewis.

★ *Darling Mine* (1920)

DIRECTOR: Laurence Trimble
RELEASE DATE: August 16, 1920; Silent; 5 reels
GENRE: Drama
CAST: Olive Thomas (Kitty McCarthy), Walter McGrail (Roger Davis), Walt Whitman (James McCarthy), Barney Sherry (Gordon Davis), Margaret McWade (Agnes McCarthy), Betty Schade (Vera Maxwell), Richard Tucker (Jay Savoy), Colin Kenny, Andrew Arbuckle, Mrs. George Hernandez.

SUMMARY: Irish colleen Kitty McCarthy accepts an invitation to visit her Aunt Agnes in New York City. Lost on the streets of the city, she seeks directions from a passing gentleman, playwright Gordon Davis. Following his directions to her aunt's East Side address, Kitty discovers Aunt Agnes living in a tenement, struggling with alcohol addiction. Kitty cares for her aunt and helps her to recover from her alcoholism. One day Gordon Davis reappears with an intriguing offer: He wants Kitty to take a part in one of his plays. She joins the cast and strikes up a friendship with actress Vera Maxwell. Vera is pining for a former love, Oscar Savoy. Kitty manages to reunite the two lovers. At the same time, she is unlucky in her own romance, for she suffers from unrequited love for Davis's nephew, Roger. Finally, Davis brings them together.

DISTRIBUTION COMPANY: Select Pictures Corp.
PRODUCTION COMPANY: Selznick Pictures Corp.
PRODUCER: Lewis J. Selznick
WRITER: John Lynch (Scenario) and Laurence Trimble (Scenario)
Review: *The Lima News* ran the headline, "*Darling Mine* Is Notable Play—It's Only Because 'Twas Last Work of Olive Thomas."

It went on to say:

Darling Mine is notable only because it is one of the last works of little Olive Thomas. And we are a morbid nation, at that. Large crowds, all eager to see the dainty little star who was no more, witnessed the first appearance of the film at the Lyric.

The picture has to do with a happy little Irish girl, Kitty McCarthy, whose wholesome Irish philosophy has kept her always smiling, though she and her grandfather are very poor. When the old gentleman dies, little Kitty embarks on the great ocean to find her Aunt Agnes, who in her last letter said, "I am groping in darkness." Little Kitty means to find out all about it.

Arrived at the wharf with her pet goat, she claims the attention of a theatrical magnate, who decides she is just the type for his new play. And she succeeds in finding her Aunt Agnes, a perfect wreck, who speedily rises out of the depths for the sake of little Kitty, to whom everyone is good, no matter how bad.

You can imagine the rest of the picture. She is a hit in the show and also with the magnate's nephew, and after misunderstandings galore, we find them perched up a tree, giving everyone the impression that they will soon be married and live happily ever after.

Walter McGrail as the object of little Kitty's affections is splendid and Miss Thomas, though she has done better work than in this production, is delightful. There's a beautiful dog and a frisky little goat which furnish some amusement and the picture as a whole should please the majority.

A Selznick Pictures house telegram, dated April 21, 1920, sent by Olive to Myron shortly before production began on *Darling Mine*, read:

MR. MYRON SELZNICK:
EVERYTHING FINE MET TRIMBLE THINK I AM GOING TO LIKE HIM LOTS HE SAYS WE HAVE GOOD STORY GOING OVER IT TODAY START WORK THIS WEEK JACK GOT ME BEAUTIFUL CAR VERY HAPPY BEST LOVE TO DADDY DAVID MOTHER AND YOURSELF OLLIE.

"Trimble" is Laurence Trimble, the director. "Daddy" is L.J. Selznick and "Mother" is Mrs. Selznick. Interestingly she relays the fact that Jack bought her a new car and that she's "very happy." This telegram was sent just a few months before her trip to Paris. No signs of marital troubles here.

★ *Everybody's Sweetheart* (1920)★

DIRECTORS: Laurence Trimble and Alan Crosland
RELEASE DATE: October 4, 1920; Silent; 5 reels (released posthumously)
GENRE: Drama
CAST: Olive Thomas (Mary), William Collier Jr. (John), Joseph Dowling (General Phillip Bingham), Aileen Manning (Mrs. Willing), Martha Mattox (Miss Blodgett), Hal Wilson (Corporal), Bob Hick (Mr. Willing).

SUMMARY: Orphans John and Mary live at the county poor farm, which is run by a sweet headmistress. One day, however, a terrible harridan replaces the beloved headmistress, and soon John and Mary flee. Traveling with them is an old soldier once employed by the farm. On their journey he falls ill, and John and Mary seek shelter in the home of an old southern gentleman, Phillip Bingham. The old soldier dies and Bingham pledges to support John and Mary. He gives John a post as gardener and makes Mary his special charge. The attention given to John and Mary is displeasing to two other household residents, Willing and his wife Jessica, who have been planning to inherit Bingham's money. One day Bingham notices that John resembles his deceased son. Indeed, John is the grandson of Phillip Bingham. John and Mary are married, much to Bingham's pleasure.

DISTRIBUTION COMPANY: Select Pictures Corp.
PRODUCTION COMPANY: Selznick Pictures Corp.
PRODUCER: Lewis J. Selznick
WRITER: John Lynch (Scenario and Story)
CAMERAMAN: Robert Newhardt

TRIVIA: Director Alan Crosland started his career as an actor and stage manager. He joined the Edison company in 1912 and performed a variety of duties with them. In 1914, he became a director of shorts and directed his first feature in 1917; by 1925 he was hired by Warner Bros.

Married to actresses Natalie Moorhead and Elaine Hammerstein (granddaughter of Oscar Hammerstein), his son Alan Crosland, Jr., also acted in and directed films. Crosland died as a result of an auto accident when his vehicle skidded on a sharp curve on Sunset Boulevard and rolled over twice through a construction zone. He was 41 years of age.

Movie ads advertising *Everybody's Sweetheart* as "the last picture of Olive Thomas" saturated newspapers across the country. One ad for the Lyric Theater stated:

> This, the last and by far the greatest production of the famous star, brings to the American people a photodrama of tremendous appeal. It is indeed, her masterpiece—a production with which no comparison can be made. Her acting in the play discloses undreamed of artistry and marks a new standard, even for her. It is truly a rare treat.
>
> A story that flows from the great human heart of humanity. A soul stirring, intensely human story of love, pathos and delicious comedy that will long live in your memory. It's an answer to the world old yearning for sunshine and laughter, wonderfully enacted by an artist, at whose bidding, the eyes of the multitude dim with the mists of life's shadows.

TAG LINE: "The Last Opportunity You'll Ever Have To See America's Prettiest Screen Star."

An unidentified newspaper review said:

This picture is the last work of little Olive Thomas and as such is attracting much attention. We've seen Miss Thomas as a baby vamp, a bride, an Irish colleen and even a "follies" girl—now we see her as a poor little nobody on the country farm—no matter what she is she's always delightful.

...Miss Thomas, always a delightful little personality, did not have the opportunity to do her best work in *Everybody's Sweetheart*. And it certainly is hard to picture the ragged and happy little Mary as the beautiful and reckless Paris suicide.

William Collier Jr. plays the opposite role and does splendid work. Joseph Dowling as the general is wonderful. Some good photography and direction make *Everybody's Sweetheart* a most credible and entertaining film.

Moving Picture World (October 23, 1920), reported the following:

The interest shown by exhibitors and their patrons in the subjects starring the late Selznick star, Olive Thomas, is considered one of the most timely and fitting tributes yet displayed in her memory. From all over the country requests have come into the Selznick offices for productions in which Miss Thomas has the star part; a nationwide tribute to her memory.

The sweet nature displayed by the character in *Everybody's Sweetheart*, Miss Thomas' late picture, is bound to live as an example of the star's actual personality. This role shows Miss Thomas as she lived, an adorable and sweet character, whose main object in life is to make those around her happy.

Variety (October 8, 1920) said:

It is fitting that the last picture that the late Olive Thomas appeared in should contain a consistent note of sadness....

The first part of the picture is very drab, the scenes for the first three-reels being laid in and around the poor house. The last two reels are devoted to showing the children in the rich environment of the grandfather's home.

Miss Thomas played the role of the little girl, and endowed it with a certain sweetness and charm. The little boy is William Collier Jr., who also offers a simple direct characterization. Joseph Dowling as the grandfather is legitimate in method, and Martha Mattox as the matron of the poor house also plays humanly. Unusual character work is contributed by Hal Wilson as the Civil War veteran. Aileen Manning, who is the second matron to take charge of the poor house makes the character necessarily disagreeable, but true to life. Bob Hick does a bit satisfactorily.

Everybody's Sweetheart under ordinary circumstances would be a commonplace program feature. As to its box office powers throughout the country, that depends on just how curious the picture public will be to see a favorite who has passed away.

The director did as well as anyone might be expected to do with the story in hand. The title incidentally has nothing whatever to do with the story and seems to have been tacked on for commercial purposes.

One thing this posthumous film of Olive Thomas does show, that had Miss Thomas lived she would have developed into the leading screen ingénue. While the story, as stated at the beginning, is sad, it isn't tragic, and although very light, holds a fair measure of entertainment.

Exhibitor's Herald (October 9, 1920) said:

In response to queries relative to the distribution of the last Selznick production starring Olive Thomas, *Everybody's Sweetheart*, which was completed just prior to the star's sailing for Europe, it was definitely announced this week by Selznick Enterprises that the picture will be published according to schedule.... [I]t is stated that with the release of this production the thousands of her admirers after viewing *Everybody's Sweetheart* will feel more keenly the passing of one of the screen's celebrities.

Exhibitor's Herald (October 30, 1920) said:

A picture as sweet and simple as the star herself, weighed with sad interest in the fact that it was the last picture to be made by the late Olive Thomas, comes to the screen with abundant pathos and humor happily balanced.

That patronage to which the humanitarian tendencies of people poor of purse but rich of heart appeal will be completely pleased by this portrayal of the happiness-spreading nature of the little girl, Mary, who gives so much to life and gets so little from it. The part, characteristically an Olive Thomas role, could offer no better one with which to leave her memory. All the tribute to her beauty of spirit that was paid by her associates at the time of her death seems manifested in the way in which she mothers the old soldier, Joe, at the county poor farm, where she makes her home, and with which she so solicitously sees that her pal, John (William Collier Jr.), gets as square a deal as possible.

Two Civil War veterans residing at the farm bring highlights in characterization to the feature, but the old Corporal and John and Mary produce the bulk of excellence in dramatic skill.

The atmosphere of the county farm is excellently effected and scenes in the home of the General are attractive. The pets with which Olive Thomas characteristically surrounds herself are there, particularly a pet hen, one "Miss Blodgett," over whose remains an interesting funeral is held with "military honors." Military terms permeate many of the titles with good effect.

Children at the State-Lake Theatre, Chicago, at the time this picture was being reviewed, appeared to enjoy it immensely, and grown-ups will be certain to like it for it carries the irresistible essence of youth and optimism.

There are suggestions galore for exploitation to the ingenious exhibitor who can enlist a Civil War veteran in uniform. The reminder that this is Miss Thomas' last picture should be stressed in advertising, but in a dignified way, to keep its appeal one of respectful interest rather than sensational curiosity.

A *Wid's Daily* theater manual (Sunday, October 24, 1920) gave the following evaluation of the feature:

AS A WHOLE: Fairly good comedy and human interest picture
STORY: Very slow at start; story's one twist results from very bald coincidence; touches register.
DIRECTION: Satisfactory
PHOTOGRAPHY: Good
LIGHTINGS: Average
CAMERA WORK: Average
STAR: Whatever work she does the thought of her tragic death remains uppermost.
SUPPORT: Headed by Willie Collier, Jr., with Joseph Dowling and Walt Whitman in character roles.
EXTERIORS: Satisfactory
INTERIORS: Adequate
DETAIL: Satisfactory
CHARACTER OF STORY: Romance of two poor farm kids.
LENGTH OF PRODUCTION: 5,050 feet

Disregarding outside influences, *Everybody's Sweetheart* is a fairly good comedy and human interest picture, its entertaining value springing solely from touches injected by author, director, star and supporting cast. The plot is a thing null and void, inasmuch as it contains no dramatic situations, while its one twist is accomplished by means of a terribly obvious case of coincidence.

[There are] more cute little touches in the scenes taking place in the general's home and the juvenile romance between John and Mary is handled adeptly. The scenes between the corporal, played by Walt Whitman, and the general, played by Joseph Dowling, are very well done and the death scene of the former is likely to produce a tear or two. Both the star and her young leading man appeared to attractive advantage.

The Box Office Angle

"Will Star's Death Have Any Effect on This?"

Like many of the recent pictures made by Olive Thomas, this is light in theme and may get over fairly well with audiences that like this type of entertainment. There is, however, the question of whether or not audiences will care to be reminded of little Olive Thomas, whose recent tragic death in Paris may be remembered by many of them. It is a serious question whether audiences really do go in for this sort of recollection, although it can hardly be doubted that the better-posted fans do.

All of the young girls who "loved" Olive Thomas will undeniably recall her tragic death. Whether they will make up a sufficient percentage of your audience to be reckoned with will be up to you to determine. On the other hand there may be a sentimental value attached to this inasmuch as it is her last picture and they may want to see it particularly because of this.

It is a question whether much of this so-called audience opposition to a dead star isn't bunk. Just remember that practically none of your audience has even seen any of the stars they like, and figure for a moment from that angle.

INTERESTING TRIVIA: The initial release of *Everybody's Sweetheart* was made the week of October 4 at the Broadway Theater in New York. Here it was seen by thousands who looked upon the occasion as an opportunity to show their admiration and respect for the departed star. Following the Broadway presentation, the production is being distributed for release throughout the country.

★ *The Flapper* (1920)★

DIRECTOR: Alan Crosland
RELEASE DATE: May 10, 1920; Silent; 6 reels
RUNNING TIME: 88 minutes
GENRE: Comedy
WORKING TITLE: *Dangerous Paradise*
CAST: Olive Thomas (Ginger King), Warren Cook (Senator King), Theodore Westman Jr. (Bill Forbes), Katherine Johnston (Hortense), Arthur Houseman (Tom Morgan), Louise Lindroth (Elmina Buttons), Charles Craig (Rev. Cushil), William P. Carlton (Richard Chenning), Marcia Harris (Mrs. Paddles), Bobby Connelly (King Jr.), Norma Shearer, Athole Shearer, Dorothy Kent, Russell Hewitt, Aleene Bergman, Maurice Stewart Jr., Mildred Cheshire, Barbara Butler.

SUMMARY: Ginger King has come from a small town to attend an Eastern boarding school, and she has a boyfriend, Bill Forbes, in military school. It's not a bad life, but she dreams of more excitement and glamour. She sees her opportunity for adventure when she strikes up an acquaintance with an older man, Richard Channing, who escorts her to a dance. Having had a taste of a new world, Ginger soon is an easy mark for two crooks who ask her to safeguard some jewels they have stolen. Ginger decks herself in the finery and shows up at home looking like a floozy. But the crooks return, and Ginger realizes she has had a brush with danger. She gives up her pursuit of excitement and returns to trustworthy Bill.

DISTRIBUTION COMPANY: Select Pictures Corp.
PRODUCTION COMPANY: Selznick Pictures Corp.
PRODUCER: Myron Selznick

WRITER: Frances Marion (Scenario and Story)
CINEMATOGRAPHY: Jack Brown
TRIVIA: Frances Marion wrote both scenario and story for *The Flapper*; in fact, she was eventually credited for writing 325 scripts throughout her career. Her writing caught the attention of Mary Pickford and the pair became fast friends. Frances was soon employed as the "exclusive" screenwriter for "America's Sweetheart."

She also directed and produced half a dozen films; was the first Allied woman to cross the Rhine in World War I; and served as the vice president and only woman on the first board of directors of the Screen Writers Guild. She painted, sculpted, spoke several languages fluently, and played "concert caliber" piano. As if that wasn't enough, she was as pretty, if not prettier than the movie stars she wrote for.

She was also close friends with Olive. Frances sent Olive two postcards from Madrid, Spain, one on April 7, 1920, the other on April 8. In the first she mentions working out a story, with a foreign sequence, that she hopes she and Myron will like. Obviously, this proposed film for Olive was never made, since Olive would live only five more months after these postcards were written. The first one read:

> Ollie dearest—
>
> I hope everything is going well with you. So disappointed not to see you before I left. Am working out a story I am sure you and Myron will like, and taking loads of pictures so the foreign sequence will be well interpreted. They talk about their beautiful French and Spanish girls—they ought to see our American Ollie.
>
> Love to Myron, Frances.

The second postcard, dated the very next day, read:

> Just passed a theatre where your picture was playing. A crowd was waiting to get in. It made me suddenly homesick. They call you the little gazelle here, and are crazy about you because you resemble so many paintings of the Madonna. Now Ollie, what have you been keeping from me!

After four husbands and dozens of lovers, the vivacious Frances would tell her closest friends she spent much of her life "searching for a man to look up to without lying down." She credited the two sons she raised on her own as "my proudest accomplishment"—they came first and then "it's a photo finish between your work and your friends."

Marion was the first woman writer to win an Oscar (1930, for her original story, *The Big House*). Since 1917, she was the highest paid (and most prolific) screenwriter in Hollywood, male or female. She has long been hailed as "the all-time best script and story writer the motion picture world has ever produced." She died May 12, 1973, aged 84.

Variety (May 21, 1920) said of *The Flapper*:

> This is the fluffiest sort of fluff, but good summer booking just the same, though any but the best type of houses may find it lacking in dramatic meat. This is due to the delicacy with which Alan Crosland has directed Olive Thomas, who here continues her trip toward film fame. Photographic and laboratory work were of the high class Selznick has led us to expect in his pictures.
>
> The story, moreover, is better than this firm's usual run. Frances Marion wrote it, and it concerns the escapades of a schoolgirl. Too strictly brought up, she gets into all sorts of innocent trouble when the chance comes. Some of the titles are humorous in the best sense. All were well thought out and phrased.

More interesting than any of the commercial phrases of the picture is Miss Thomas herself. Her appeal is the sex appeal. Very sensibly her director has assented to the fact. Miss Thomas has too heavy a makeup in the first reel and her dresses should not fit so tightly.

This light, whimsical story remains, nevertheless, excellent market stuff for the more appreciative audiences.

A *Wid's Daily* theater manual (May 23, 1920) gave the following evaluation of the feature:

AS A WHOLE: Has the makings of a delightful light comedy but is handicapped by superfluous footage.

STORY: Just the thing for this star; cleverly written with many amusing situations, but latter reels should be compressed.

DIRECTION: Good for the most part but takes story too seriously toward close.

PHOTOGRAPHY: Very good

LIGHTINGS: Good

CAMERA WORK: Very good

STAR: Appears to excellent advantage as young boarding school flapper.

SUPPORT: Theodore Westman Jr., fine boy performer

EXTERIORS: Some pretty snow stuff and contrasting southern scenes

INTERIORS: Fitting

DETAIL: All right

CHARACTER OF STORY: Adventures of young boarding school girl who wanted to be thought wicked.

LENGTH OF PRODUCTION: About 5,000 feet

Here is a delightful and real little light comedy idea that is handicapped at the end by a lot of superfluous footage. At the start and up to a point at which the average length feature would conclude, the action is rarely amusing, but there is too much detail employed in straightening out the tangle at the end and the action becomes wearisome. Some careful cutting would result in a mighty fine picture, especially if the editor removed some of the scenes in which the director has taken the story altogether too seriously.

Frances Marion's plot and the wealth of amusing situations she has provided center around the life of a young boarding school girl who, realistically, wants to be thought older than she is and who, in the bargain, would like to be looked upon as sophistication itself. It is a role ideally suited to Olive Thomas, one which she handles extraordinarily well. Furthermore, the director has for the greater part of the picture kept in a light mood, only at the end falling into a serious vein that makes his work remarkably dull.

Miss Thomas appears as Genevieve King, a southern youngster who is sent to a northern boarding school by a more or less harassed father. At the military academy across the way is Bill, Genevieve's childhood playmate. This part is excellently taken by a boy actor, Theodore Westman Jr., and Bill's scenes of calf-like romance with Genevieve and his showing off before the smaller boys at the academy all strike a very real and amusing note.

The situation confronting Genevieve when the head of the school goes to drag her away from a country club dance whither she has gone with Richard Channing, a handsome stranger idolized from afar by all the girls, is real in its comedy and excellently played.

They work in a very amusing farcical sequence when Genevieve returns to her home dressed in the latest vamp outfit from New York. She shocks all the natives by feigning a "double life." It is in straightening out this tangle in which two crooks are introduced, that the director has run into a totally out of place serious mood and burdened the action with tiresome detail.

On the whole, however, *The Flapper* can be considered a very amusing comedy. It is splendidly subtitled and there is a wealth of pretty snow scenes as backgrounds.

The Box Office Angle

"Has Big Appeal for the Feminine in Your Audiences."

If [they had better edited] the latter reels you would be sure of a pretty nearly perfect light comedy. It deals with a younger girl in as real a fashion as the Booth Tarkington stories do with young boys. And that's saying a lot. But whether the film is edited or not you can run it and be pretty sure that it will more than satisfy. The majority of it is so good that they'll be quite liable to overlook the bad spots in the last two reels.

Make your appeal to the girls and the feminine sex in general in your advertising. A line such as: "The adventures of a real girl who went to boarding school and wanted to be thought 'wicked'; full of humor; one big laugh" might be used. If your crowd likes Olive Thomas, play her up well as she does fine work here. Also mention Frances Marion's name. She is one of the few very well known screen authors. Cash in on the publicity and popularity that are hers.

Estimated gross rentals from entire world after January 3, 1920 for *The Flapper*: $200,000.

★ *Footlights and Shadows* (1920)

DIRECTOR: John W. Noble
RELEASE DATE: February, 1920; Silent; 5 reels
GENRE: Drama
WORKING TITLE: *Out of the Night*
CAST: Olive Thomas (Gloria Dawn), Alex Onslow (Jerry O'Farrell), Ivo Dawson (Peter Shaw), Mr. Farrell (Doctor), May Hicks (Colored mammy), E. Van Beusen (Mr. Johnson/Frank Reynolds), Mr. Busby (Detective), Robert Keeling (Manager).
SUMMARY: Gloria Dawn is a star in the Follies. She is engaged to a wealthy man, Peter Shaw, and her fortune seems secure. However, one night a young man with amnesia arrives at her door. A doctor says the sick man must not be moved, and Gloria dedicates herself to his recovery. He does well physically, but his past remains a mystery to him. Gloria loses her heart to this troubled young man. One day, she discovers that he is a millionaire named Jerry O'Farrell. She rushes home to tell him, but he has vanished. He continues to wander, and soon he forgets all about Gloria. One night, however, he is in the audience at the Follies when a fire breaks out. Gloria sees him, recognizes him, and hurries to his rescue. But Peter Shaw is also present, and, having learned of her affections for Jerry, he threatens her. Jerry, his memory recovered, steps between them and saves Gloria, and their love can now be openly declared.
DISTRIBUTION COMPANY: Select Pictures Corp.
PRODUCTION COMPANY: Selznick Pictures Corp.
WRITER: R. Cecil Smith (Scenario) and Bradley King (Story)
CAMERAMAN: Jack Brown

Variety (February 13, 1920) said:

Olive Thomas has at last reached the point where repayment on the investment should begin coming in wholesale. This is evident from the latest Selznick release *Footlights and Shadows*.

It is a second-rate direction by John W. Noble. Mr. Noble is a good director, but the cutting room takes too many liberties with him. This they dare not do with Ralph Ince. As for the star, she makes love and kisses wonderfully. So do most women as pretty as she is; only they don't do it before a camera and they like a chance to study the work of a professional. As for the men, properly played this picture should pull them in evenings for any exhibitor.

Another thing helping to prove the reality of Miss Thomas' arrival as a picture star is the weakness of her support and the relative failure of her scenario writer in this picture. The lead was played by a man who fell short as a lover. The heavy was well done, but the story and inserts were not handled by any master. Why these picture companies don't go out and buy first-class ability is a mystery they'd better clear up before someone does it for them.

The scenarist explains [the storyline] clumsily, but the director gives a chance to glimpse Miss Thomas' lingerie and her figure seen through the shower bath curtains helps fascinate.

A *Wid's Daily* theater manual (February 15, 1920) gave the following evaluation of the feature:

> AS A WHOLE: Generally interesting romance of Broadway dancer; shows as the best produced picture Selznick has turned out.
> STORY: Not strong by any means but maintains steady interest throughout.
> DIRECTION: Average
> PHOTOGRAPHY: Average
> LIGHTINGS: Meet requirements without showing anything extraordinary
> CAMERA WORK: Good
> STAR: Gives satisfactory performance while her prettiness will certainly attract.
> SUPPORT: Average
> EXTERIORS: Plain City Shots
> INTERIORS: Good, including big roof garden scene
> DETAIL: All right except for useless silhouette of star undressing
> CHARACTER OF STORY: Plain romance in a Broadway setting
> LENGTH OF PRODUCTION: About 5,000 feet
>
> *Footlights and Shadows* is the best-done Selznick picture that has been released and while it contains no strong dramatic moments in the romance of Broadway that it presents, it is generally interesting throughout, well put together and attractive by reason of the star who shows to her best advantage.
>
> ...Not substantial stuff by any means but it is treated in good taste with but few exceptions, the scenario runs smoothly and the action is illuminated occasionally by interesting scenes on the roof garden showing Gloria rendering her dance specialties. The fire scenes are handled pretty well although the devices employed in bids for thrills are rather obvious.
>
> Olive Thomas registers satisfactorily in the stellar role and her beauty is sure to attract. Ivo Watson as Shaw is acceptable with the supporting cast, never prominent save in the case of the hero, is competent.
>
> *The Box Office Angle*
>
> "Get Your People In: They'll Hardly Be Disappointed."
> It's merely a case of how much you care to promote just a satisfactory production along exploitation lines that confronts you in *Footlights and Shadows*. The picture is worth advertising, for it's worth in showing, and as a consequence the only problem is how far you want to go and along what lines.
>
> The picture offers good advertising possibilities. Mention of the star and the fact that she appears in the role of a dancer on Broadway are advertising assets, particularly the latter, inasmuch as your people will realize that Miss Thomas is appearing in element.
>
> Catch lines and readers written around the trick by which heroine and hero become acquainted prove attractive. Something on this order is suggested: "How had he come into possession of a key to her apartment? Why had he come tumbling in while all the

city slept? Was this the beginning of the romance that her old Mammy had predicted? See *Footlights and Shadows*."

Estimated gross rentals from entire world after January 3, 1920 for *Footlights and Shadows*: $200,000.

★ *Youthful Folly* (1920)

DIRECTOR: Alan Crosland
RELEASE DATE: March 8, 1920; Silent; 5 reels
GENRE: Drama
ALTERNATE TITLE: *Glorious Youth*
CAST: Olive Thomas (Nancy Sherwin), Crauford Kent (David Montgomery), Helen Gill (Lola Ainsley), Hugh Huntley (Jimsy Blake), Charles Craig (Reverend Bluebottle), Harry Truesdale (Jonathan Ainsley), Florida Kingsley (Aunt Martha), Eugenia Woodward (Aunt Jenny), Pauline Dempsey (Mammy).

SUMMARY: How dull life is on the Southern plantation where Nancy Sherwood whiles away the days with her three maiden aunts. Things seem to brighten, however, with the arrival of Nancy's lively New York cousin Lola. Although she is married to Jonathan Ainsley, Lola is in love with David Montgomery. She decides to keep David handy by engineering his marriage to her cousin. After the wedding, Nancy is unhappy with David's coolness, and she grows close to his ward, Jimsy Blake. But David, contrary to Lola's plan, eventually comes to love his wife, and Lola grows jealous. Lola reveals to Nancy that the whole wedding was a scheme to keep David near, and Nancy is devastated. Then she sees Jonathan approaching with a gun, bent on killing David. She saves David's life and takes the bullet herself when she jumps in front of the gun. David is grief-stricken, confessing his love for Nancy.

DISTRIBUTION COMPANY: Select Pictures Corp.
PRODUCTION COMPANY: Selznick Pictures Corp.
PRODUCER: Lewis J. Selznick
WRITER: John Lynch (Scenario) and Olive Thomas (Story)
CAMERAMAN: Jules Cronjager

A September 18, 1920 edition of *Picture Show* magazine printed a story written by British actor Crauford Kent. Entitled, "Screen Stars I Have Wooed—and Won!" Kent writes about his co-starring role with Olive in *Youthful Folly*:

> Olive Thomas, if she will pardon my saying (and I know she will), is more fun than a barrel of monkeys! She is just a regular tomboy, although a very beautiful one. She is very easy to make love to, and yet at the same time difficult, for just in the middle of a romantic scene she will whisper some funny remark in one's ear, thereby upsetting one's equilibrium considerably.
>
> We had a very adventurous time during the making of her picture, *Youthful Folly*, for it occurred at the time of the great floods in America, which did ten million dollars worth of damage.
>
> We left New York on the Monday night, bound for New Orleans, where we were to take exteriors. We should have arrived at our destination Wednesday morning, but as a matter of fact we did not put in an appearance till late on Friday evening, as you shall hear.
>
> Everything went well till we reached Atlanta, Georgia, where we got in at 10.30 P.M., only to learn that we should probably be stranded there for three days, owing to the floods having washed away the bridges and lines! On the other hand, we were advised to keep in the train, as help might come sooner than expected. Miss Thomas and myself, however, together with two other members of the cast, resolved to "take a chance" and go into town for a little recreation—a dance, maybe.

Unfortunately, the amusement halls were just closing, so instead we made merry at a funny little refreshment stall outside the station, where we had hot drinks and Frankfurters or "hot dogs" as they are called, and where also we were able to purchase some comical masks, which appealed, somehow, to our Bohemian spirits.

Upon our return to the station we found the train still in, so we promptly boarded it, and after sitting up till two o'clock in the morning, laughing and talking, settled down for a much needed rest. Slumber, however, was not for me, for I had no sooner settled in my berth than I was afflicted with heartburn. "Bi-carbonate of soda for me!" I said, and went in search of the porters.

Variety (April 2, 1920) said:

Olive Thomas continues success in this latest release by Selznick starring her.... Crauford Kent played the lead. The rest of her support were adequate to throwing her undoubted beauty and her growing charm as a screen actress into pleasant and stimulating relief. The result is an excellent market product, but to those who have been watching her grow there is a peculiar interest in studying the story which is perfectly adapted to her style.

She appears first as a young girl of sixteen that two old ladies are rearing. Right under their noses she raises the dickens, and everything amusing happens except a spanking. A distant cousin, who lives in New Orleans, has gotten into a scandal. To save her face she rushes to the country and marries off the man in the case to the girl impersonated by Miss Thomas. The rest of the story deals in a swift and interestingly melodramatic manner with the way this husband comes to fall in love with his own wife, who continues to be a cut-up and a kid. Once when he is entertaining some older men and she is flirting with his boy ward she hangs out of the window and appears to the astonished men below with her skirts every which way. A less amusing touch is where she rushes between an avenging shot and her husband. This finally brings them together.

Miss Thomas knows how to be charming. She photographs beautifully. If well trained by one of the best directors she will certainly develop as an actress and should have a great future.

A *Wid's Daily* theater manual (Sunday, April 4, 1920) gave the following evaluation of the feature:

AS A WHOLE: Despite bad start this develops into very pleasing comedy-drama.
STORY: Concocted from vintage material but some good comedy sequences and well done climax register it satisfactorily.
DIRECTION: Has fallen down in some sequences particularly at first but has put important ones over.
PHOTOGRAPHY: Good; very pretty in southern exterior shots.
LIGHTINGS: Very nice
CAMERA WORK: Commendable
STAR: Registers a lot of comedy and appeal in this one.
SUPPORT: Generally very good
EXTERIORS: Very pleasing southern shots
INTERIORS: Very good
DETAIL: Some small comedy touches don't show skill but the important stuff gets over well.
CHARACTER OF STORY: Husband learns to love young wife whom he married for "convenience."
LENGTH OF PRODUCTION: About 5,167 feet.

Youthful Folly credited to the authorship of Olive Thomas proves to be a very pleasing and at times hilarious comedy drama, despite its bad start, which is quite actionless and which is burdened by subtitles of excess verbiage. Once the main line of action is penetrated and they move Nancy from the country estate in Virginia to New Orleans as the wife of David Montgomery the interest picks up wonderfully and the comedy and human interest touches are plentiful.

David had married Nancy for convenience, merely to stop gossip from connecting his name with Lola's, Lola being a distant married cousin. He pays small attention to Nancy after the marriage. They then get in a hilarious comedy sequence [in which] Jimsey, David's ward, pursues Nancy demanding a kiss. He breaks into her room, bowls over the Negro mammy and then chases her out the window.

Nancy descends via the edges on the side of the house to the room on the next floor where her husband is attending a directors' meeting. The directors get a little relief from business when they see Nancy's nether extremes protruding in the window. This sequence is played fast and registers as sure comedy.

Of course David ultimately discovers that he loves Nancy. A well-sustained climax sequence is introduced when Lola's husband, jealous with rage, comes to David's house and fires a pistol at him. Nancy intercepts the bullet and for a time her life hangs in the balance. When she recovers they work in some very entertaining romantic scenes between Nancy and David which are unusually well played.

Much of the comedy touches striven for in the early part of the picture fail to register. While they don't evince much skill it is probable that they would have gotten over if the plot had made its appearance first. Among these "attempted" touches can be enumerated the exceedingly old stuff with the burlesqued minister as the central character and the inevitable parlor "Bolshevists." Sometimes it looks as if they had tried everything to see what would register. For instance, the racetrack scene, though well enough done, has nothing to do with the story. It's merely a decoration.

Olive Thomas plays very well in the role of Nancy, getting over some good ingénue comedy and playing her dramatic and romantic sequences with a convincing show of feeling. Crauford Kent is good as David and Hugh Huntley and Howard Truesdell give skilled performances. Helen Gill as Lola, an old-fashioned "villainess," is unable to make the role's extreme demands convincing.

The Box Office Angle

"Good Publicity Angles to Arouse Fan Curiosity."

This is cut out of vintage material all right but at the same time they've put a lot of good stuff over, enough in fact, to overshadow its faults and make of it a very pleasing comedy-drama. Advertise as a light subject and hint at the plot which, though old, is attractive. Olive Thomas does her best work in this and should attract generally. Her last picture *Footlights and Shadows* was also a pleasing one and this might be mentioned in the advertising.

You can develop a good publicity angle in the fact that Olive Thomas is credited with having written the story of this. Fans will want to see what sort of a vehicle a star writes for herself. Also mention the fact that Crauford Kent is her leading man. Kent has played leads a long time and has been featured in other pictures. Folks ought to know him as a very good actor by this time and be attracted by his name.

Estimated gross rentals from entire world after January 3, 1920 for *Youthful Folly*: $200,000.

BIBLIOGRAPHY

Books

Ardmore, Jane, with Mae Murray. *The Self-Enchanted: Mae Murray; Image of an Era.* New York: McGraw-Hill, 1959.

Balio, Tino. *The American Film Industry.* Madison: University of Wisconsin Press, 1976.

Baral, Robert. *Revue: A Nostalgic Reprise of the Great Broadway Period.* New York: Fleet Publishing Co., 1962.

Basinger, Jeanine. *Silent Stars.* Wesleyan University Press, 2000.

Beauchamp, Cari. *Without Lying Down: Frances Marion and the Powerful Women of Early Hollywood.* Berkeley: University of California Press, 1997.

Bellamy, Madge. *A Darling of the Twenties.* Vestal Press, 1989.

Bitzer, G. W. *Billy Bitzer: His Story.* New York: Farrar, Straus and Giroux, 1973.

Bodeen, DeWitt. *13 Castle Walk.* Pyramid Books, 1975.

Bordman, Gerald. *Jerome Kern: His Life and Music.* New York: Oxford University Press, 1980.

Brown, Gene. *Movie Time: A Chronology of Hollywood and the Movie Industry from Its Beginnings to the Present.* New York: Macmillan, 1995.

Brown, Karl. *Adventures with D.W. Griffith.* New York: Farrar, Strauss and Giroux, 1973.

Brownlow, Kevin. *The Parade's Gone By....* Berkeley: University of California Press, 1976.

Burke, Billie. *With a Feather on My Nose.* New York: Appleton Century Crofts, 1948.

Carter, Randolph. *The World of Flo Ziegfeld.* New York: Praeger Publishers, 1974.

Coffee, Lenore. *Confessions of a Hollywood Screenwriter.* New York: Cassell, 1973.

Davis, Lee. *Scandals and Follies: The Rise and Fall of the Great Broadway Revue.* New York: Limelight Editions, 2000.

Earle, Marcelle, and Arthur Homme, Jr. *Midnight Frolic: A Ziegfeld Girl's True Story.* Twin Oaks, 1999.

Everson, William K. *American Silent Film.* New York: Oxford University Press, 1978.

Farnsworth, Marjorie. *The Ziegfeld Follies.* New York: Putnam, 1956.

Fox, Donald Charles, and Milton L. Silver, eds. *Who's Who on the Screen.* Ross Publishing Co., 1920.

Fussell, Betty Harper. *Mabel.* New Haven: Ticknor and Fields, 1982.

Golden, Eve. *Anna Held and the Birth of Ziegfeld's Broadway.* Louisville: University Press of Kentucky, 2000.

Harris, Warren, G. *The Other Marilyn: A Biography of Marilyn Miller.* New York: Arbor House, 1985.

Herndon, Booten. *Mary Pickford and Douglas Fairbanks.* New York: W.W. Norton, 1977.

Higham, Charles. *Ziegfeld.* Chicago: Henry Regnery, 1972.

Kennedy, Rod, Jr., and Elizabeth Ellis. *Hollywood in Vintage Postcards.* Utah: Gibbs Smith, 2003.

Lockwood, Charles. *Dream Palaces: Hollywood at Home.* New York: Viking, 1981.

Mizejewski, Linda. *Ziegfeld Girl: Image and Icon in Culture and Cinema.* Durham: Duke University Press, 1999.

Moore, Colleen. *Silent Star.* Garden City, NY: Doubleday, 1968.

Robinson, David. *Hollywood in the Twenties.* New York: A. S. Barnes, 1968.

Thomas, Bob. *Selznick.* Garden City, NY: Doubleday, 1970.

Thompson, David. *Showman: The Life of David O. Selznick*. New York: Knopf, 1992.
Whitfield, Eileen. *Pickford: The Woman Who Made Hollywood*. Louisville: University Press of Kentucky, 1997.
Windeler, Robert. *Sweetheart: The Story of Mary Pickford*. New York: Praeger, 1974.
Yallop, David. *The Day the Laughter Stopped: The True Story of Fatty Arbuckle*. New York: St. Martin's, 1976.
Ziegfeld, Patricia. *The Ziegfeld's Girl Confessions of an Abnormally Happy Childhood*. Boston: Little, Brown, 1963.
Ziegfeld, Richard, and Paulette. *The Ziegfeld Touch: The Life and Times of Florenz Ziegfeld, Jr.* New York: Harry N. Abrams, 1993.

Magazine Articles

"The Actress on the Cover." *Moving Picture Stories*, March 15, 1918.
Blitzstein, Madelin. "One Kept the Tryst That Six Had Made—Death Claimed the Rest." *Every Week Magazine*, 1936.
Carr, Harry. "The Tragic Life Story of Mabel Normand." *Screen Secrets*, October-November, 1929.
_____. "Untold Tales of Hollywood." *Smart Set*, December 1929–February 1930.
"A Domestic Olive." *Motion Picture Magazine*, June 1920, Volume XIX.
Dramatic Mirror. April 3, 1920.
Evans, Delight. *Photoplay*. October, 1918.
_____. *Photoplay*, April, 1920.
"Film Gives Public Chance to Pay Tribute to Olive Thomas." *The Moving Picture World*, October 23, 1920.
"Follies Girl With Ince." *Motography*, April 14, 1917.
Goldbleck, Willis. *Motion Picture Magazine*, September, 1921.
Howe, Herbert. "Can a Beauty Have Brains?" *Motion Picture Classic*, February, 1918.
"In Memory of Olive Thomas." *Variety*, September 17, 1920.
Kent, Crauford. "Screen Stars I Have Wooed—And Won!" *Picture Show*, September 18, 1920.
"The Latest Studio Capture from Broadway." *Motion Picture Classic*, July, 1917.
Lloyd, Jack. "A Broadway Queen Gone West." *Photoplay*, December, 1917.
Motion Picture Classic. March 20, 1920.
Motion Picture Magazine. June, 1919.
Motion Picture News. March 9, 1918.
Motography. July 1, 1916.
Movie Weekly. April 1, 1922.
"Obituary." *Variety*, September 17, 1920.
Oderman, Stuart. "Jack Pickford and Olive Thomas." *Films in Review*, November-December, 1995.
"Olive Thomas' Death Was Accidental: Lewis J. Selznick Pays Her Tribute." *The Moving Picture World*, 1920.
"Olive Thomas Has Big Ambition." *The Moving Picture World*, October 14, 1916.
"Olive Thomas Left No Will." *The Moving Picture World*, October 16, 1920.
"Olive Thomas: She Sometimes Sighs to Be a Little Sales Lady in a Shop Again." *The Moving Picture World*, n.d.
"Olive Thomas with Triangle." *The Moving Picture World*, April 21, 1917.
Peltret, Elizabeth. *Motion Picture*, June, 1919.
Photoplay. December, 1917.
_____. March, 1918.
_____. May, 1918.
_____. July, 1918.
_____. January, 1919.
_____. May, 1919.
_____. October, 1919.
_____. May, 1920.
_____. June, 1920.
_____. July, 1920.
_____. January, 1925.
Picture Show. August 2, 1919.
Picture World. September 25, 1920.
Price, Guy. *Variety*, March 21, 1919.
Roberts, Sue. "An Olive in Sunny California." *Motion Picture Classic*, April, 1919.
Rockwell, Helen. *Exhibitor's Trade Review*. January 6, 1920.
"Selznick Pictures a Family Affair." *The Moving Picture World*, March 15, 1919.
"Selznick Starts a Big Campaign." *Motion Picture News*, March 8, 1919.
Star. August 15, 2005.
"Stars' Cars Hit Boys." *The Moving Picture World*, March 22, 1919.
Sumner, Smith. "Olive Thomas Estate Reported at $37,094." *The Moving Picture World*, July 29, 1922.
Sutherland, Sidney. "Madcap Mabel: The True Story of a Great Comedienne." *Liberty*, September 6, 1930.
Variety. September, 1916.
_____. March 9, 1917.
_____. June 22, 1917.
_____. September 21, 1917.
_____. September 26, 1917.
_____. September 28, 1917.
_____. November 9, 1917.
_____. January 4, 1918.
_____. February 1, 1918.
_____. March 1, 1918.
_____. March 28, 1919.
_____. April 25, 1919.
_____. May 30, 1919.
_____. June 13, 1919.
_____. July 18, 1919.

_____. November 7, 1919.
_____. January 16, 1920.
_____. February 13, 1920.
_____. April 2, 1920.
_____. May 21, 1920.
_____. October 8, 1920.
_____. May 6, 1921.
Weitzel, Edward. "Olive Thomas Has Narrow Escape from an Embarrassment of Actors." *The Moving Picture World*, March 6, 1920.
"Women and Girls Storm Church to Attend Funeral of Olive Thomas: Many Tears in the Vast Audience." *The Moving Picture World*, October 9, 1920.
"Yup! They're Engaged!" *Photoplay*, September, 1917.

Newspaper Articles

"American Makes Hit in Paris." *The Olean Evening Times*, November 2, 1920.
Bertelli, C. F. *Los Angeles Examiner*, September 12, 1920.
_____. September 19, 1920.
"Broadway Throngs Gaze at Flashing Sign: Olive Thomas." *Indiana Evening Gazette*, September 20, 1920.
"Charleroi Area Historians Have an Active Summer." *The Valley Independent*, August 25, 1976.
"Charleroi Girl Now Performing in Movies." *The Charleroi Mail*, September 28, 1916.
Cronyn. Thoreau. "The Truth About Hollywood." *New York Herald*, March 19–April 2, 1922.
"*Darling Mine* Is Notable Play." *The Lima News and Times*, November 19, 1920.
"Drive Garbage Element from Movies." *Omaha Bee*, February 26, 2006.
"Evil Hollywood." *Detroit Free Press*, February 9, 1922.
Exhibitors Herald. October 9, 1920.
_____. October 30, 1920.
Fairburn, W. Forbes. *Los Angeles Examiner*. September 11, 1920.
_____. September 13, 1920.
"Four Girls in a Room." *The Mansfield News-Journal*, March 24, 1934.
"Friends All Quit Dead Movie Star." *The Bridgeport Telegram*, September 15, 1920.
Frohman, Ray W. "Interview in Jazz with Fun Girl of Films." *Los Angeles Herald*, November 18, 1919.
"Funeral Services for Mrs. McCormick." *The Charleroi Mail*, March 3, 1924.
Golden, Eve. "Olive Thomas: The Midnight Frolics Girl." *Classic Images* (No. 238), April 1995.
Harpman, Julia. "Mabel Normand: Victim of an Unkind Fate." *Sunday News*, New York City, June 29, 1924.
"Hollywood Must Be Purified by U.S. Government." *Gary-Post Tribune*, February 10, 1922.

"I Alone Survive!" *The Port Arthur News*, July 5, 1936.
"Interview with Bernard Krug Thomas." *The Pittsburgh Press*, May 4, 1931.
Los Angeles Herald. September 5, 1918.
_____. January 11, 1919.
_____. September 10, 1920.
Los Angeles Times. August 8, 1918.
_____. September 5, 1918.
"Lure of Night Life of Paris Is Held Responsible for Olive Thomas' Death: Stories Vary." *The Daily Northwestern*, September 11, 1920.
"Movie Actress Is Near Death by Poison Dose." *New York Herald* (Paris Edition), September 9, 1920.
"Myron Selznick Starts Film Co. of His Own." *The Morning Telegraph*, November 30, 1918.
New York Clipper. September 15, 1920.
New York Herald (Paris Edition). September 6, 1920.
_____. September 11, 1920.
_____. September 13, 1920.
_____. September 14, 1920.
New York Telegraph. June 30, 1918.
_____. August 18, 1918.
_____. July 9, 1920.
New York Times. September 10, 1920.
"Obituary for Olive Thomas." *The Oakland Tribune*, September 10, 1920.
"The Officials Order Autopsy." *The Mansfield News*, September 11, 1920.
"Olive Thomas Is Dead of Poisoning." *The Decatur Daily Review*, September 10, 1920.
"Olive Thomas Mourning Loss of $5,000 Bracelet." *New York Telegraph*, January 3, 1920.
"Olive Thomas, Movie Actress, Dies Suddenly." *Indiana Evening Gazette*, September 10, 1920.
"Olive Thomas, Screen Star Is Near Death in French Hospital." *The Bridgeport Telegram*, Friday, September 10, 1920.
"Olive Thomas: Selznick Star." *New York Telegraph*, December 18, 1918.
"Olive Thomas Today's Feature at Majestic." *Nevada State Journal*, July 20, 1919.
"Olive's Death Due to Poison." *The Mansfield News*, September 13, 1920.
"Paris Death of Charleroi Movie Queen Is Recalled." *The Valley Independent*, September 13, 1960.
Parsons, Louella. "Just a Little Irish Girl." *New York Telegraph*, May 11, 1919.
"Personal Items About the Movie Stars." *The Middletown Times-Press*, March 21, 1918.
"Poisonous Drugs: Doctor Says They Should Be Sold Only on Prescription." *New York Times*, June 16, 1913.
Rice, Mark. "Silent Film Industry Blossoms in Ithaca." *The Cornell Daily Sun*, February 9, 2005.
Sprague, Chandler. "Mabel Normand's Own Life Story!" *Los Angeles Examiner*, February 17, 1924.

"The Sweetheart of the Movies." *The Decatur Daily Review*, July 12, 1914.

Thayer, John E. "Silent Heartbreaks." *Classic Film Collector*, undated.

"Thoughts on Hollywood." *New York Times*, February 26, 1922.

"The True Tragedy of Olive Thomas." *Syracuse Herald*, October 3, 1920.

"Wharton Brothers to Use Natural Beauties of Ithaca for Scenes of Picture Plays." *The Cornell Daily Sun*, March 18, 1914.

"Wharton Motion Picture Co. to Start Work Soon." *The Cornell Daily Sun*, May 12, 1914.

"Whartons Send Car Over High Cliff." *The Cornell Daily Sun*, July 17, 1915.

"What Olive Thomas Saw in Gay Paris Before She Killed Herself: How the Tragic Death of the American Actress in Paris Has Given Impetus to a Movement to Wipe Out the 'Palaces of Shame.'" *The Syracuse Herald*, October 31, 1920.

Wid's. January 25, 1917.

_____. July 5, 1917.

_____. August 9, 1917.

_____. October 4, 1917.

_____. November 18, 1917.

_____. January 3, 1918.

_____. February 7, 1918.

_____. February 28, 1918.

Wid's Daily. May 25, 1919.

_____. June 15, 1919.

_____. September 14, 1919.

_____. November 9, 1919.

_____. February 15, 1920.

_____. April 4, 1920.

_____. May 23, 1920.

_____. October 24, 1920.

"Women Faint at Olive Thomas Rite." *New York Times*, September 29, 1920.

Websites

www.afi.com
http://www.angelfire.com/az/Taylorology/
www.assumption.edu/ahc/1920s
http://www.brightlightsfilm.com/50/olive.html —*Beautiful Dead Girl.*
http://cayugawaterfronttrail.com
www.clarabow.net
www.cornellsun125.com
http://eh.net/hmitppowerusd—*How much is that worth today?*
www.findarticles.com—*Lost Films from the Silent Era*
www.flapperjane.com
www.foxnews.com
www.francesfarmersrevenge.com
http://geocities.com/Hollywood/Hills/2440/thomas.html
http://hometown.aol.com/yposada/olliestardom.html—*Olive Thomas: Hollywood's Lost Star.*
www.ibdb.com—*Olive Thomas Filmography*
www.imdb.com—*Olive Thomas Filmography*
www.jimsdeli.com—*New Amsterdam Theater*
www.londonfoodfilmfiesta.co.uk
www.marypickford.com
http://mic.imtc.gatech.edu
www.musicals101.com
www.nyc-architecture.com
www.nytimes.com—*Archives 1851–1980*
www.parlorsongs.com
http://www.pittsburghlive.com/x/valleyindependent/artsmag/s_269410.html—*Everybody's Tragic Sweetheart.*
www.playbill.com—*The Ghosts of Broadway*
www.prairieghosts.com
www.sfae.com
http://silentladies.com/PThomas.html
www.silentsaregolden.com—*The Mysterious Death of Olive Thomas* by Tim Lussier.
http://www.suite101.com—*Live and On-Stage—Olive Thomas (1894–1920) The Marilyn Monroe of the Early Twentieth Century* by Joyce E. Eberly.
http://www.things-and-other-stuff.com/movies/profiles/olive-thomas.htm
http://web.bvu.edu—*New Amsterdam Theater*

Periodicals

Many of the articles relating to Olive Thomas are now touching 90 years of age. The Selznick Files at the Harry Ransom Center at the University of Texas was most helpful in understanding the financial side of Olive's contract and relationship with the Selznicks. Certain clippings and snippets have lost their exact dates of publication due to three things: Time, mishandling and moths! The fact that some of the original articles have survived at all is quite miraculous. With that said, the following publications were partly identified and used in various stages of this book:

American Classic Screen, American Movie Classics, The Encyclopædia Britannica (1911), *Films in Review, Good Old Days, The Hollywood Reporter, Hollywood: Then & Now, Modern Screen, Motion Picture, Movie Show, Movie Stars Parade, Parade, Photoplay, Screen Facts, Screen Stars, Screen Stories, Screenland, Silver Screen, Wid's* and *Wid's Daily.*

INDEX

Academy Awards 23, 188
addictions: Follies showgirls 142; Hollywood folklore 77–78; Normand, Mabel 9; Pickford, Jack 36, 38, 42, 77, 92, 115–116, 119, 123, 125; Pickford, Mary 89–90; Pickford family 89–90; Reid, Wallace 12; Selznick, Myron 74
Aitken brothers 51
Almey, Fred 76, 106
Alsop, Edward Brown 142
Alsop, Fifi 142
Amendola, Dana 133–134
American Church in Paris 95
American Hospital, Paris, France: death of Jack Pickford 125, 127; death of O.T. 80, 82, 91–92, 118
Anger, Kenneth 78
Arbuckle, Roscoe "Fatty" 8–9, 11, 51, 79, 118
Astaire, Fred 23
automobile crashes 13, 24–25, 38–39, 45, 76, 121, 184

Baker, Sarah 70
Ball, Lucille 23, 135
Bara, Theda 146
Barrie, Nigel 27, 148
baseball 25–26
Beatrice Fairfax series 24–27, 65, 148
Beauchamp, Cari 49
Beekman, Rev. Dr. 95–96
Bellamy, Madge 14
Bennett, Joe 162, 163, 164
Berlin, Irving 107, 147
Bertelli, C.F. 80–81

Betty Takes a Hand 66, 158–160
Billy Bitzer: His Story (Bitzer) 45
Bitzer, Billy 45–46
Blanche (servant) 44–45
Bodeen, DeWitt 77
Bolger, Ray 21
Bonaparte, Mrs. Jerome 109
Bow, Clara 146
Brice, Fanny 21, 23, 141
Broadway Arizona 66, 149–150
Brunton Studios 38, 50, 59, 158
Buck, Gene 106, 147
Burke, Billie 2, 18, 21, 23, 122
Burr, Eugene 160, 162
Butler, David 179, 180

California: Forest Lawn Memorial Park 114; home of Jack Pickford and O.T. 73; location shooting 29–30, 31–32, 165, 175, 177; Pickfair 89, 90, 123
Cantor, Eddie 21
Carrington, Harry 106
Carter, Frank 120–123, 126
Carter, Randolph 18
Catrou, Police Commissionaire 93
Chaney, Lon 140
Chaplin, Charles 12
Charisse, Cyd 23
Charleroi, Pennsylvania 1, 143
Chesebro, George 149–150, 155
Choate, Dr. Joseph 82, 86–87
Christy, Howard Chandler 14
churches: American Church (Paris) 95; Church of the Holy Trinity (Paris) 93; St. Bartholomew's (New York) 126; St. Thomas Episcopal (New York) 105–108
Ciarlo, Penny 23
Claire, Ina 17, 141, 147
Cody, Lew 9
Coffee, Lenore 15
Coffin, William Haskell 15, 130
Collier, William, Jr. 107, 184, 185, 186
comedians 17, 21, 147
contracts: honoring 108; "morality clause" 6; Selznick Pictures 42, 43, 49–51, 56, 58–59; Triangle Pictures 12, 27, 49, 51, 178
Cosmopolitan Pictures 51
costumes: films 66–67, 69, 70, 157; Ziegfeld Follies 20, 134, 147
Creighton, Cleva 140
Crisp, Donald 125
Crosland, Alan 69, 184, 187, 188
Cunningham, Jack 163, 164

dancing 33, 35, 128, 155
Darling, Grace 27, 148
Darling Mine 70, 130, 182–183
A Darling of the Twenties (Bellamy) 14
Darlington, Bishop James Henry 106
Davies, Marion 12, 21
Davis, H.O. 150
Dawson, Ivo 190, 191
death of Olive Thomas: blaming Paris 1, 102; burial 110–114; conflicting

199

accounts 103–105; disposal of the estate 109; first Hollywood scandal 1, 7–8; funeral service 22, 105–108; increase in ticket sales 70–71, 187; Jack Pickford's account 78, 81–83, 89, 91–94, 116; media coverage 1, 7–8, 103, 140; murder theories 102–103; official reports 91–94, 140; reactions 7–8, 37, 73, 79–80, 86, 115, 142–143; sable cape story 78; suicide theories 46, 62, 73, 77–78, 80, 86, 89, 102–103, 123, 139
deaths: Arbuckle, Roscoe "Fatty" 11; Carter, Frank 120–123; Duffy, James (O.T.'s father) 13; Fairbanks, Douglas 90; Harron, Bobby 116–117; Marion, Frances 188; McCormick, Oliveretta 136; Miller, Marilyn 125–126; Pickford, Jack 125, 127; Pickfords 90; by poisoning 84–85, 84–86, 88, 142; Rappe, Virginia 8, 11, 79; Reid, Wallace 12; Rogers, Will 23; Selznick, Myron 74; Taylor, William Desmond 8–10, 9–10, 12, 77; Thomas, Bernard Krug 128; Ziegfeld, Florenz 21–23; Ziegfeld Follies showgirls 125–126, 141–142; *see also* death of Olive Thomas
Delmar, Ethel 141
Delmont, Maude 11
Dillon, Jack 38, 151, 152, 160, 161, 163–165, 169
Disney *see* Walt Disney Company
divorce: Bernard Krug Thomas and O.T. 17, 46, 130, 143; Fifi Alsop and Edward Brown Alsop 142; Jack Pickford and Marilyn Miller 124; Jack Pickford and Mary Mulhern 125; Marilyn Miller and Chet O'Brien 126; Owen Moore and Mary Pickford 89, 117
Dodge, Anna 160, 162
dogs 14, 31–32, 40, 125
Dolly Sisters 80, 87, 117
Dove, Billie 21
Dowling, Joseph 184, 185, 186, 187
Dream Palaces: Hollywood at Home (Lockwood) 77, 89
drug use: in Hollywood 5; Olive Thomas 77, 92; in Paris 1, 77, 79, 88, 92, 95–96, 100–102; *see also* addictions
Duffy, James (O.T.'s brother) 13, 15–16, 86, 106
Duffy, James (O.T.'s father) 13
Duffy, Oliveretta Elaine *see* Thomas, Olive
Duffy, Rena *see* Van Kirk, Lorena
Duffy, William 13, 15–16, 41, 44–45, 86, 106
Dunne, Irene 21
Durfee, Minta 118–119
Durling, E.V. 52
Dwan, Allan 105

electric signs 63, 71–72
Ellis, Robert 179, 180, 182
Errol, Leon 17, 21, 147
An Even Break 65, 152–153
Everybody's Sweetheart 66, 70–71, 184–187

Fairbairn, Forbes W. 81–82
Fairbanks, Douglas 51, 61, 89, 90, 117
fans of O.T.: appreciation of 33, 45, 53, 66–67; generosity of 18, 45; reactions to her death 7–8, 105–108
Farnsworth, Marjorie 16, 121, 125
Faye, Alice 21
Fenwick, Irene 151, 152
Fields, W.C. 17, 21, 141, 147
film preservation 70, 145–146
film studios: criticism of 6, 12, 190; distribution systems 164, 175; injuries to actors 12, 182; "morality clause" 6; preservation of nitrate films 145–146; production facilities 30, 32, 57, 59; *see also* Hollywood; individual companies
Fish, Mrs. Stuyvesant 109
Fisher, Harrison 15, 16, 55, 81, 106
The Flapper 130; author 187–188; filming 75; O.T. on 57–58, 66–67; publicity campaign 187–190; reviews 69–70, 188–189; showings 72–73
flu *see* Spanish flu
The Follies Girl 64, 165–167, 177
Footlights and Shadows 66, 130, 190–192
Forest Lawn Memorial Park 114
Fort Lee, New Jersey film studios 57, 59

Foss, Darrell 152, 153
Fox, Harry 27, 148
Fox Film Corporation 145–146
funerals: Florenz Ziegfeld 22; Frank Carter 121–122; Olive Thomas 71, 105–108, 110, 113; O.T.'s grandmother 136

Garland, Judy 23, 127
Garrison's Finish 115
ghost lights 132–133
ghost stories 132–137
Giblyn, Charles 62–63, 64, 175, 179, 181
gifts 38–40, 47, 120, 121, 130
Gill, Helen 192, 194
A Girl Like That 27, 151–152
Gish, Dorothy 8, 67, 69, 86, 116, 117
Gish, Lillian 51
The Glorious Lady 64, 168–169
Goddard, Paulette 21
Graham, Wilfred 76
graves: Carter, Frank 122–123, 126; Miller, Marilyn 126; Pickford, Jack 114, 134; Pickford family 114; Thomas, Olive 107, 110–114, 122–123, 131, 134
Gray, Cyril 76
The Great Ziegfeld 23
Griffith, D.W. 51, 116
Gunn, Charles 152, 153, 158, 159

Hamilton, Cosmo 55, 61
Hannibal, Missouri, location shooting 157
Hardy, Sam 141
Harris, Warren G. 121
Harron, Bobby 116–117
Hatton, Fanny 180, 181
Hatton, Frederick 180, 181
Haver, June 127
Hearst, William Randolph 12, 24, 51
Heiress for a Day 27–29, 160–162
Held, Anna 23
Her Downfall see The Follies Girl
Hernandez, George 149–150
Hick, Bob 185
Hicks, Andi 70
The Hill Billy 115
Hollywood: folklore 43, 78, 89; pioneers 51; self-preservation 7–8, 12; temptations of 5–6; *see also* addictions; contracts; film studios; scandals
Hollywood 115

Hollywood Babylon (Anger) 78
Hollywood folklore: Pickford family 36, 90
Hollywood Haunted (Jacobson) 135
Hollywood scandals *see* scandals
Hollywood studios *see* film studios
Hollywood Walk of Fame 158
homes: California home of Jack Pickford and O.T. 73; New York apartment 46–47; Pickfair 89, 90, 123
hospitalizations: Miller, Marilyn 126; Pickford, Jack 125; Reid, Wallace 12; Thomas, Olive 41–42, 47, 80, 82–83; Van Kirk, Lorena 40, 47
Hotel Ritz 75–76
Huntley, Hugh 192, 194

In Wrong 158
Ince, Ralph 171, 172, 190
Ince, Thomas 12, 18, 27, 51, 79, 156, 182
Indiscreet Corinne 66, 154–155
influenza *see* Spanish flu
injuries to actors 12, 182
insurance *see* life insurance
interviews: about O.T. 87, 118–119, 128–131, 141, 142–143; about the Pickfords 118–119; with Jack Pickford 81–83; *see also* Thomas, Olive, interviews with
Ithaca, New York, location shooting 24–25, 148

Jack Pickford Productions 59
Jacobson, Laurie 135
Jennie 59
jewels 18, 39–40, 42, 109
Johnstone, Justine 17, 147
Jolie, Angelina 139

Kay Bee Pictures 149, 156
Kelly, Gene 23
Kent, Crauford 192–193, 194
Kern, Jerome 127
Keystone Komedies 153, 155, 157
King, Allyn 141
King, Joe 29, 160, 162, 169, 171

Lahr, Bert 21
Lake Placid, New York, location shooting 75
Lamarr, Hedy 21
Lambert, Kathryn 141, 142
Langdon, Lillian 160, 162
Lee, Harry 151, 152

life insurance on Olive Thomas 42, 62, 86, 102, 103, 109
Limousine Life 29, 162–165
The Lion King 147
Little Lord Fauntleroy 115
location shooting: California 29–30, 31–32, 165, 175, 177; Hannibal, Missouri 157; Ithaca, New York 24–25, 148; Lake Placid, New York 75; New Orleans 75, 192
Lockwood, Charles 77, 89
Look for the Silver Lining 127
Lorraine, Lillian 142
lost films 65–66, 145–146
Love's Prisoner 64–65, 146, 169–171
Lowe, Edmund 141
Loy, Myrna, as Billie Burke 23
Lytell, Wilfred 141

Madcap Madge 27, 30, 66, 155–157
Malone, Dudley Field 107
Manning, Aileen 185
Mansfield, Martha 141
Marion, Frances 188–189, 190
marriage of Jack Pickford and O.T.: divorce rumors 46, 80, 86; gift giving 35, 38, 39–40, 42, 47; homes 46–47, 73; Mary Pickford's opinions 119, 158; Paris trip 59–62, 75; Pickford family reactions 1, 35–38, 43, 59, 119, 130; secrecy 35, 43, 119; separations 38, 40, 43, 59, 75, 76, 114
marriages: Bernard Krug Thomas and O.T. 14, 17, 128–131, 143; Fifi Alsop and Edward Brown Alsop 142; Florenz Ziegfeld and Billie Burke 2, 18, 21, 23, 35, 122; Jack Pickford and Marilyn Miller 120, 122–124; Jack Pickford and Mary Mulhern 125; Lilyan Tashman and Edmund Lowe 141; Marilyn Miller and Chet O'Brien 124, 126; Marilyn Miller and Frank Carter 120–121; Mary Pickford and Douglas Fairbanks 61, 117; Owen Moore and Mary Pickford 119
Marx, Samuel 109
Mary's Ankle 182
Mattox, Martha 185
McAvoy, May 89
McCormick, Oliveretta H. 136–137

McGrail, Walter 182, 183
McKee's Rocks, Pennsylvania 128–129; *see also* Pittsburgh, Pennsylvania
McPhail, Addie 11
Meighan, Thomas 35, 36, 43, 106
"Memories of Olive" (painting) 1–3
mercury bichloride: accidental poisonings 84–86, 88, 103; antidotes 105, 118; effects 83–84, 92, 139–140; uses 83, 88–89, 103–105, 140
Meredith, Lois 77
MGM Studios 145
Milestone Films 70
Miller, Marilyn 115, 120–124, 125–127
Minter, Mary Miles 9–10
Modeling 13–16
Mong, William V. 40, 169, 171
Moore, Matt 168
Moore, Owen 76, 117; acting roles, 151, 152; death of O.T. 83, 87, 89; funeral of O.T. 106; and Jack Pickford 81–82; and Mary Pickford 89, 119
Morgan, Frank 23
Mulhern, Mary 125
Murray, Mae 17, 21, 87, 92, 147

Neilan, Mickey 182
Nelson, Fred 76
New Amsterdam Theater: ghost sightings 132–137; reconstruction 132–136, 147; rooftop theater 18–20, 136; *see also* Ziegfeld Follies
New Orleans, location shooting 75, 192
New York City: electric signs 63, 71–72; O.T.'s first impression 13; *see also* New Amsterdam Theater
New York Motion Picture Corporation 156
nitrate film 145–146
Noble, John W. 190
Normand, Mable 9, 10, 79, 109

O'Brien, Chet 124, 126
O'Brien, Dennis 110–111, 113, 114
O'Connor, Johnny 80–81
O'Keefe, Tom 151, 152
Olive Thomas: Everybody's Sweetheart 50
O'Meara, John 107

One Hundred Years of Hollywood (Time-Life Books) 79
The Other Marilyn (Harris) 121
Out Yonder 64, 65–66, 75, 171–172

Paramount Pictures 12, 27, 157
Paris, France: blamed for O.T.'s death 1; "Dead Rat" nightclub 87–88, 96, 103; depicted in films 177–179; drug use in 1, 77, 79, 88, 92, 95–96, 100–102; entertainment 19, 98–101; Hotel Crillion 78; Hotel Ritz 75–76; O.T.'s last trip 59–62, 75–76, 81–82; reputation for depravity 71, 79, 80, 92–102; *see also* death of Olive Thomas; Pickford, Jack, death of
Parsons, Louella 43–45, 48–49
penicillin 88
Pennington, Ann 17, 141, 147
Perry, Kathryn 141
pets 14, 31–32, 40, 125, 186
Pette, Graham 160, 162
Phelps, Lee 29, 162, 163, 164
photographers 15, 18
Pickfair 89, 90, 123
Pickford, Charlotte 35–36, 43, 90, 114, 119, 130
Pickford, Jack: addictions 36, 38, 77, 92, 115–116, 123, 125; bisexual rumors 77; death of 125, 127; dependence on family 36, 40–41, 59, 105, 115–116, 118–119, 127; grave 114; marriage to Marilyn Miller 120, 122–124; marriage to Mary Mulhern 125; military service 40–41, 47, 123; movie career 36, 41, 59, 67, 157–158; syphilis 36, 83, 88–89, 103, 123, 125; thoughts of suicide 105; *see also* marriage of Jack Pickford and O.T.
Pickford, Lottie *see* Rupp, Lottie Pickford
Pickford, Mary: alcoholism 89–90; conflict with O.T. 37–38, 61; death 90; grave 114; marriage to Douglas Fairbanks 61, 117; marriage to Owen Moore 89, 119; movie career 51, 67, 188; opposition to Jack and Olive's marriage 36–38, 114, 158; reminiscences 36–37, 115–118, 119, 120

Pickford family: alcoholism 89–90; graves of 114; reactions to Jack's marriage to O.T. 1, 35–38, 43, 59, 119, 130
Pittsburgh, Pennsylvania: early life 13; escape from 14; visits to 17, 27, 40, 42, 47, 143
plane crashes 12, 23
Play Ball 24, 25–27, 65, 148
poisonings 140; *see also* death of Olive Thomas; deaths, by poisoning
Poole, Bessie Chatterton 142
portraits of O.T.: by Alberto Vargas 1–3; by Harrison Fisher 81; at New Amsterdam Theater 134
Powell, William 23
Prohibition 19
Prudence on Broadway 64, 172–175, 177
publicity: death angle 70–71, 70–72, 94, 187; electric signs 52; eulogies 108–109, 139, 143–144; Hearst style 12, 122; Mary Pickford style 37, 41, 90, 105, 109, 114, 116, 123; media campaigns 43, 52, 63–64, 178, 190, 194; modeling prize 14–15; special release 178; stunts 44; wedding of Jack and Marilyn 123; *see also* death of Olive Thomas, media coverage

Rainer, Luise 23
Rappe, Virginia 8, 79
Rattenberry, Harry 163, 164
Ray, Charles 67
Ray, G.A. 76
Reid, Wallace 12, 79
reviews of O.T.'s work: Betty Takes a Hand 159, 160; Darling Mine 183; Everybody's Sweetheart 184–186; The Flapper 69–70, 188–189; The Follies Girl 166, 167; Footlights and Shadows 190–191; The Glorious Lady 168; Heiress for a Day 161; Indiscreet Corinne 155; Limousine Life 163, 164, 165; Love's Prisoner 64–65, 171; Madcap Madge 156; Out Yonder 172; Prudence on Broadway 174, 175; The Spite Bride 176; Toton 178–179; Upstairs and Down 64, 180, 181; Youthful Folly 193
Reynolds, Lynn F. 149, 150

Ritz Hotel 93
Robert Brunton Studios 38, 50, 59, 158
Roberts, Sue 42, 61–62
Rogers, Will 21, 22–23
Rubens, Alma 51
Rupp, Lottie Pickford 36–37, 43, 90, 114, 119
Rupp, Mary 38, 43–44

scandals 5; Arbuckle trial 8, 9, 11; backlash 6–8; damage control 79, 80–81, 89; drug use 5, 12; Hollywood folklore 77–78; Ince shooting 12; Madame Black scams 11; Taylor murder 8–10, 12, 77, 79; *see also* death of Olive Thomas; Paris, France; Ziegfeld, Florenz, romances
Sedgwick, Josie 154, 155
The Self Enchanted (Ardmore and Murray) 87
Selznick, Daniel 48, 50–51, 73
Selznick, David O. 50, 52, 55–56, 61, 74, 139
Selznick, Florence 49, 52, 183
Selznick, Howard 52
Selznick, Lewis (L.J.) 48–52, 55–56, 71, 106, 109, 183
Selznick, Myron: alcoholism 74; death of 74; at O.T.'s funeral 71, 106; relationship with O.T. 55–56, 59, 61–62, 73, 188; role at Selznick Pictures 48–52, 62–63, 66, 130, 182, 183; talent agency career 49, 74
Selznick Files (Harry Ransom Center, University of Texas) 56
Selznick Pictures: contract with O.T. 42, 43, 49–51, 56, 58–59; demise 57, 74; financial problems 58–62; financing 48–49; formation 47–50, 52, 62–63; insurance on O.T. 42, 62, 109; media campaigns 52, 63; production studios 50, 56–57, 59; stars 50, 58; suspension of Olive Thomas 61; *see also* films starring Olive Thomas
Sennett, Mack 9, 10, 12, 51
Shearer, Norma 21
Shelby, Charlotte 9–10
shooting locations *see* location shooting
Showman (Thomson) 50
Skelton, Red 23
Skelton, William 106

Spalding, Captain (drug dealer) 92
Spanish flu 40, 41–43, 45, 47, 48
special effects 172
The Spite Bride 55, 64, 66, 175–176
Stanlaws, Penryhn 15
Stanwyck, Barbara 21
Stires, Rev. Ernest M. 106
Storyline: Recollections of a Hollywood Screenwriter (Coffee) 15
studios *see* film studios
stunts 24–25, 29
Sturgess, Edwin 151, 152
suicides 101, 116–117
Sunshine and Shadow (Pickford) 37
Sutherland, Eddie 89
Sweadner, Mrs. Edward 143
syphilis 36, 77, 83, 88–89, 103, 123, 125, 126

Talmadge, Constance 58, 63, 67, 69
Talmadge, Norma 49, 58, 63, 67, 69
Tashman, Lilyan 141
Taylor, William Desmond 8–10, 12, 77, 79
Thirteen Castle Walk (Bodeen) 77
Thomas, Bernard "Krug" 14, 17, 46, 128–131, 143
Thomas, Olive [*and see* death of Olive Thomas]: acting ability 27–29, 37, 130; ambition 32–35, 39, 143, 194; attitude toward beauty 24, 53, 130, 141; charm 30–34, 45, 61–62, 66–69, 108, 119, 142–143, 192–193; dancing 33, 35, 128–129, 155; descriptions of 1–2, 14–15, 16, 18, 29, 37, 44, 48, 143, 148; early life 13–16, 17, 128, 143; earnings 1, 17, 49, 50–51, 56, 58–59, 62; generosity 16, 17, 40, 45, 108, 130; hard work 24, 27, 32, 73, 108; hospitalizations 41–42, 47, 80, 82–83; independence 13–14, 16, 35–36, 46, 129–130; inquisitiveness 30–34; intelligence 30–34, 53, 67, 119; nicknames 2, 13, 15, 30, 32, 37; portraits 1–3, 81; publicity campaigns 52, 63, 177–179, 190, 191, 194; sense of humor 29–32, 45, 46, 53, 62, 66–67; singing talent 20; syphilis 36, 102, 103, 123; writing ability 39, 194; Ziegfeld Follies 16–17, 20, 53, 130, 141, 146–148; *see also* reviews of O.T.'s work; Selznick Pictures, contract with O.T.; Triangle Pictures, contract with O.T.
Thomas, Olive, family: Duffy, James (brother) 13, 15–16, 86, 106; Duffy, James (father) 13; Duffy, William (brother) 13, 15–16, 41, 44–45, 86, 106; McCormick, Oliveretta H. (grandmother) 136; Rupp, Mary (niece) 38, 43–44; Van Kirk, Harriet (sister) 13, 43; Van Kirk, Harry M. (stepfather) 13, 106; Van Kirk, Lorena (mother) 13, 42, 86, 106
Thomas, Olive, interviews with: E.V. Durling 52–55; Helen Rockwell 66–69; Louella Parsons 43–45; *Motion Picture* 45, 140; *Motion Picture Classic* 46–47, 61–62; Sue Roberts 42, 61–62
Thomson, David 50
Through the Back Door 115
Till the Clouds Roll By 127
Tom Sawyer 157–158
Toton 64–65, 177–179
Triangle Pictures: contract with O.T. 12, 27, 49, 178; demise 51, 64; distribution system 164, 175; formation 51; key players 51, 150, 153, 155, 162, 171; studio discipline 32–33
Trimble, Laurence 182, 183
Truesdell, Howard 192, 194

Upstairs and Down 43, 55, 62–64, 130, 179–182
Urban, Joseph 16, 20, 147
urban legends *see* ghosts

The Valley of the Giants 12
Van Kirk, Harriet 13, 43
Van Kirk, Harry M. 13, 106
Van Kirk, Lorena 13, 42, 86, 106
Vargas, Alberto 1–3, 15
The Vital Spark see Toton

Walk of Fame 158
Walsh, Raoul 79
Walt Disney Company 132, 133, 145, 147
Warner Brothers 11
Warren, Mary 160, 162
West, Raymond B. 156–157
Westman, Theodore, Jr. 187, 189
Wharton, Dr. 82
Wharton Brothers Studios 24–25, 148
White, George 17, 147
Whitfield, Eileen 125
Whitman, Walt 186, 187
Williams, Bert 17, 147
Williams, Esther 23
Wilson, Hal 185
Winter, Louise 55, 176
Wise, Helene 128
With a Feather on My Nose (Burke) 2, 21
Without Lying Down: Frances Marion and the Powerful Women of Early Hollywood (Beauchamp) 49
The Woman Who Made Hollywood (Whitfield) 125
Woodlawn Cemetery 107, 110–114, 122–123, 126–127, 131, 134
The World of Ziegfeld (Carter) 18
Wulfelt, Florence 76
Wynn, Ed 17, 147

Youthful Folly 66, 130, 192–194

Ziegfeld, Florenz: death of 21–23; fear of death 21–23; films about 23; financial problems 20–21, 23; and Jack Pickford 35, 123; marriage to Billie Burke 2, 18, 21, 23, 35, 122; romances 2, 18, 35, 55, 120, 122–124; showmanship 16–17, 18–21
Ziegfeld, Patricia 23
Ziegfeld Follies 16–17, 23; costumes 20, 134, 147; depicted in films 23, 165–167, 190–191; description 146–148; history 19–21, 23, 147; Midnight Frolic 18–21, 130, 147; Prohibition 19; reunions 141, 142; set designs 16, 20–21, 147; showgirls 18, 20–21, 23, 125–126, 134, 140–142, 146–147; *see also* Miller, Marilyn
The Ziegfeld Follies (Farnsworth) 16, 121, 125
Ziegfeld Girl 23
Ziegfeld: The Man and His Women 23
Ziegfeld Midnight Frolic 23

www.ingramcontent.com/pod-product-compliance
Ingram Content Group UK Ltd.
Pitfield, Milton Keynes, MK11 3LW, UK
UKHW050526150426
5217IPUK00026B/1816